A TALE OF SURVIVAL

A TALE OF SURVIVAL

(MEMOIR OF AN HISPANIC WOMAN)

Grace Flores-Hughes

authorHOUSE®

AuthorHouse™
1663 Liberty Drive
Bloomington, IN 47403
www.authorhouse.com
Phone: 1-800-839-8640

First published by AuthorHouse   11/15/2011

ISBN: 978-1-4634-4108-1 (sc)
ISBN: 978-1-4634-4107-4 (hc)
ISBN: 978-1-4634-4109-8 (ebk)

Library of Congress Control Number: 2011913189

Printed in the United States of America

Any people depicted in stock imagery provided by Thinkstock are models, and such images are being used for illustrative purposes only.
Certain stock imagery © Thinkstock.

This book is printed on acid-free paper.

INVICTUS

William Ernest Henley, 1849-1903
Modern British Poet

Out of the night that covers me,
Black, as the Pit from pole to pole,
I thank whatever gods may be
For my unconquerable soul.

In the fell clutch of circumstance
I have not winced or cried aloud.
Under the bludgeoning of chance
My head is bloody, but unbowed.

Beyond this place of wrath and tears
Looms but the Horror of the shade,
And yet the menace of the years
Finds, and shall find, me unafraid.

It matters not how strait the gate,
How charged with punishments the scroll,
I am the master of my fate:
I am the captain of my soul.

CONTENTS

For Harley

For Elsa and Christian

For the Taft, Texas, Taft High School Class of 1965

And in memory of: my mother, Catalina San Miguel
Plata, my maternal grandparents, Lazarita and Catarino
San Miguel, my in-laws, Bernita and Arnold Hughes
And the little angel, my sister, Refugia "Cukita" Trevino

From the Author

These pages are not meant to be a rigourous documentation of my life or the events in the lives of those who were there with me. Rather I wanted to show how the Hispanic culture framed our experiences, plus how thoroughly our survival depended on the depth (or lack thereof) of Anglo prejudice. If any of my friends and family who were in Taft, Texas during the 1950's and 60's write their own tale, it could very well be an entirely different read than mine. But this one is born of my memories and attempts to reconstruct them with as much accuracy as possible, while also trying not to cause those I've writen about any pain or embarrassment. There are a few characaters mentioned in the book by other than their true names. In the final analysis, this is the life that I lived.

Acknowledgements

When you write a book for as long as I have—10 years on and off—there is going to be a list of people to thank that is longer than the Rio Grande. My first inclination is to summarize that list to the best of my ability; otherwise, you'll read this section more than the actual story itself. I begin by thanking my grandparents, Lazara Esquivel San Miguel and Catarino Sanchez San Miguel who without their coming together and moving from Mexico to south Texas in 1920 this book couldn't have been written. Even though they've both been gone for almost half a century there isn't many a day that goes by that I don't think about either one of them. They inspired me, loved me and most importantly protected me in a time when I needed protecting.

It was one hell of an effort trying to unhinge valuable but personal family history from family members since in our culture that kind of information is best kept under the rug, yet much of this history could be deliberately sprinkled throughout the family circle. But in the end, cooperative some of them became. I thank my mother, Catalina S. Plata who surprised me with her candid portrayal of family lore. She not only provided anecdotes of family life but did it with such emotion and clarity that convinced me this book had to be written. My brother Enrique and sisters, Susie and María also helped beyond the call of duty. My cousins on my mother's side, Mike Villarreal, Jr., Milli Zukowsky and Max Villarreal, thank you for being there for me. And not to be ignored, on my father's side, cousins Ricardo F. Alvarado, Pauline Gonzalez, Cipriano "Polon" Alvarado and Tío Chico Flores were most helpful and supportive. My grand nieces Belinda Acosta and Brittany Campbell and my nephew Chris Acosta helped by reading some of the manuscript and helping with some of the research. They are the next generation of family members to tackle life's challenges and I expect much from them.

Thank you to the following folks who without their eagerness to help and encourage me to stay on track and finish the book I may be still fiddling. Early on I had the support and professional advice of; Jeff Shear, David Kosar, Henry J. Ramos, Don Fruehling, Linda Wolfe Keister, Rachel Howard and Kerry Hannon. I want to thank my editors, Jill Hacker and B.J. Snow for their critical improvements to my manuscript. They are both women of extraordinary talent and a delight to work with on this book project. A special acknowledgement and praise goes to Juliann Tigert who believed in my story.

There were many current and former Taft residents that lent a helping hand. Among them were; Eliseo "Cheo" Torres, Manuel Hinojosa, Ginger W. Cartwright, Maureen Britton, Roy Johnson, Yolanda "La Quatita" Salazar, Richard Rojas, Gloria Zapata, Yvonne, "La Bonnie" DeLeon. Your help in remembering facts and events was of absolute importance and invaluable. Others that lent a necessary and warm hand consist of; Melinda S. Gonzalez, Col. George R. Dixon, USAF (Ret), Richard Blaylock, Ben Montanez, Martha Bodenheim, Laura Boston, Thomas Hughes, Gunnery Sgt, USMC (Iraq & Afghanistan), Dr. Harry Pachon, Felix Sanchez, Dr. Fernando Torres-Gil, Alana Chavez-Langdon, and Anthony Chavez.

Special mention goes to those dear friends that helped review some of the manuscript and provided exceptionally useful comments. John Trevino, Alex Trevino, the Embry sisters, Lydia and Janet, Eula Thomas, Leonard Spearman, Jr., Phyllis Belford, Jeff and Nazli Weiss, Col. Minnie Anaya St. John, USAF (Ret), Erica Moorhead, Serena Carroll and Caitlin Carroll.

I especially want to thank my long time and dear friends, Alfredo J. Estrada, Kamala Lopez, Rudy Beserra, Rowland Perkins and Dr. Jerry Haar for their endorsements of this book. Their willingness to support this project early on gave me the confidence I needed to continue and finish this project.

In 2011 I had the honor of teaching Honors American History at Bishop Ireton High School in Alexandria, Va. The three classes of juniors that I taught enriched my life beyond imagination. The students are too numerous to mention but they know who they are and how much I care for each and every one of them. May God bless the Bishop Ireton Class of 2012.

Since it took me awhile to write and finish this book there were those who helped me early on but who unfortunately didn't get to read the final product. In memoriam of my very special and dear friends who answered quickly when I called for their advice and thoughts. They include my dear friend and the maid of honor at my wedding, Bea Gonzalez, Dr. Guillermo Rojas, Oscar N. Diaz, Bobby Caceres, my beloved nephew Zeke Perez who taught our family tolerance and who made our family proud by winning so many awards for his teaching ability, and the one and only Anglo I truly could call my friend at Taft schools, Lowry Lee Pressley.

In my research I received exceptional assistance from the staff of the San Patricio County Court Records, the San Patricio Publishing Company, the Taft Library and the Blackland Museum. I relied on numerous books, magazine articles, and the internet throughout the writing process among them: "The Taft Ranch" by A. Ray Stephens, "History of San Patricio County" by Keith Guthrie, "Villa and Zapata," by Frank McLynn, and "Empire of the Summer Moon," by S.C. Gwynne.

Finally, I cannot thank enough my best friend and husband, Harley for his support from day one. When I came to him of my wish to write about growing up in south Texas, his remark was, "start writing." I'd stay up at all hours of the night until I'd hear, "Sugar, it's time to go to bed." He repeated this many times over the course of the ten or so years it took me to have the courage to tell the story the way I wanted to tell it. There was many a night that he'd serve me dinner while I anxiously pressed at the computer keys. And every time I'd finish a chapter he'd serve me a glass of wine. What a guy! Not too bad for an Okie!

Preface

"Life is a gamble at terrible odds—if it was a bet, you wouldn't take it."
Tom Stoppard, 1937
British Playwright

It was Grandma Moses that said, "Life is what you make it, always has been, always will be." True enough. There are those who possess the ability and the resources to make life what they want from day one, regardless of the circumstances under which they were born. Poverty doesn't have to be a part of determining how successful a person will be if that person has the desire to self-empower (through ability or luck or both); with or without family support and resources that person can make his or her life turn pretty much the way they want, barring an act of God. Conversely, a person born wealthy into a loving family and unlimited resources may have a leg up over a poorer counterpart, but if that person doesn't possess the desire to manage the path they've been issued at birth, it won't turn out the way they want.

But life isn't just about wanting to self-empower and having the resources to make of ourselves all that we could hope for. It's much more than that. Consider those who truly want to be successful but cannot, because they are impossibly challenged from the day they're born—some even while still in the womb. Their chances of beating the odds can be slim to none and slim left town.

To complicate matters further the direction of one's life can be changed by events that are out of our control. Are our lives preordained or dictated by divine intervention or are our lives based on a roll the dice? Are our lives already set from the day we're born? If so, do we take a backseat and allow ourselves to be taken where we may, given that it's destined anyway, or do we tempt fate and try to create our own path? While this book may not answer every aspect of these questions it is an illustration of coping and taking control at the most propitious point in life.

My journey began with two young people who met in a small south Texas town named "Taft," which was founded by the Sinton and Taft families of Cincinnati, Ohio more than 60 years ago. The Cincinnati families were the type of people my family had nothing in common with—at least not in the beginning—more about that later. It seems that many of America's rich and famous came from Ohio. Somehow that doesn't seem fair. You'd figure every rich and famous person should have been born in my razzle-dazzle home state of Texas. But it didn't happen that way. But then why should it? After all, Ohio and the Ohio River served as a major gateway for western expansion of the United States of America and the development and fueling of the industrial revolution. So Ohio, a small, industrial, Midwestern state, outlined by the Ohio River and bordered by Lake Erie, bears claim for many famous and wealthy people. The Sintons and Tafts were among them, and they started, my hometown of Taft, Texas, which set off the chain of events that led to what Taft became and what I became in turn.

Ulysses S. Grant was born in Ohio. He was the highly decorated Union Army general that defeated the Confederacy and won the Civil War. Shortly thereafter, General Grant went on to become president of the United States not once but twice. But, like many of the famous, Grant didn't return to his roots. He ended up in New York City and is buried there.

Still, there are others. The infamous Joe Eszterhas and Harvey Pekar were born in Ohio. I am not sure I should put these two in the same category. After all, Eszterhas was known for his screenplays and Pekar for writing comic books. Pekar never left Ohio, and Eszterhas couldn't stay away. He left the glamour of Hollywood to return to his Cleveland roots. One of the world's best golfers, Jack Nicklaus, was born in Ohio, as was the comedian Red Skelton. And not to forget women, there is Gloria Steinem, the woman who coined the term, "Ms."

So something must be said about Ohio. It must have been an opportune place for the Irish, English, Hungarians, Jews, Italians, freed slaves and others to begin realizing their impossible dreams.

But there is one family from Ohio that most fascinates me and who are the root of the beginning of my story: the Tafts of Ohio. The Tafts have held just about every major elected office in America. They've been president of the United States, Supreme Court Justice, Congressman, Senator and Governor. This particular family, more than the Kennedys or the Bushes, has managed to work itself into the political mainstream of American politics for more than one hundred years. My years of public service may not match those of the Tafts, but my career, much like theirs, has been on a continual and constant road.

You've heard that Jim Bowie came to Texas via Kentucky and Davy Crockett, who many thought was a Texan, was actually born in Tennessee. And then there was Sam Houston the first President of the Republic of Texas who came to Texas for the sole purpose of helping Texans fight the Mexicans—was actually a Virginian. But you've probably not heard that Charles Phelps Taft, a half brother of President William Howard Taft, came to south Texas in the late 1800s as a majority holder of the Coleman-Fulton (CF) Pasture Company and of the Taft Ranch which later became my hometown of Taft, Texas.

The Taft Ranch became one of the largest ranches in south Texas during the late 1800s. And the Green Hotel and *La Quinta* were built to house the many local and foreign guests that visited the Taft Ranch. Among those visitors was William Howard Taft, the twenty-seventh president of the United States. It turned out that Charles, who was the publisher of the *Cincinnati Times-Star,* worked very hard on William Howard Taft's 1908 presidential campaign. After that, it seemed only fair that the newly elected president visit the Taft Ranch for a week. Although his wife Nellie, a woman of independent nature did not accompany her husband, President Taft, it seemed, was overjoyed with his trip to south Texas. Taft was overheard telling his half brother, "Charley, old boy, you said, 'Let's go to Texas and rough it.' I don't call this roughing it."

During the early 1900s, David Sinton who was one of the wealthiest men in America, having made his money from manufacturing pig-iron became ill, turning over the majority of the C-F Pasture companies' assets to his daughter, Anna and her husband Charles P. Taft. Shortly after Sinton died on August 31, 1900, Anna and her husband began selling the Taft Ranch and its major land holdings for tax purposes. But Charles P. Taft, like Joe Eszterhas, missed his roots and returned to Ohio, where he died in 1929.

The Taft Ranch became an incorporated town in the early 1900s and all of the land on the North Side of town was sold to White Europeans, or as we Mexicans call them, Anglos. In fact, we Mexicans from Taft call any person with a white complexion Anglo—Jews, Italians, Hungarians, Czechs—it doesn't matter; they are all Anglos to us. The new landowners came mostly from places such as Ireland, Germany, and England. In 1941, my maternal grandfather bought a very tiny parcel of land on the South Side of town from what was left of the CF-Pasture Company, which had once served as a subsidiary of the Taft Ranch.

Mine is a story of a modern woman whose ride was bumpy from the beginning. It was up to me and me alone to absorb the bumps and find a smoother path. How to do both and become somewhat successful was my challenge; an understatement if there ever was one. Having to cope with a cranky, elderly grandmother, a henpecked grandfather, a single, independent-minded, preoccupied mother, a half-brother with a death wish (mine, that is), and a gob of half-sisters with as many self serving agendas as stars in a south Texas sky is only a part of my story.

This book is not intended for one group of people or one particular type of person; it is for anyone that wants to take a moment to reminisce about the lives they left behind while at the same time it is meant to inspire. "Hold the Salsa" is not my style. This is a brutally honest and provocative portrayal of this girl's journey. In the end, I believe that Tom Stoppard was only half right.

I invite you to help me relive what has been an exciting and interesting journey!

Chapter 1

In the beginning . . . . Blackland

*"My advice to those who are about to begin, in earnest,
the journey of life, is to take their heart in one hand
and a club in the other."*
Josh Billings, 1818-1885
American Humorist

From the beginning I thought my first name was *bastarda*. That name seemed to carry a negative connotation but to me it was my name. Later on when I entered school on the North Side of town my name changed to wetback. And when my teachers tried calling me by my given name Graciela they mispronounced it so badly that my classmates giggled and pointed for most of my early school years. It's possible that this burden and the first inklings of the rabid abuse within *el barrio* of Mexican-on-Mexican inside the family as well as outside begin the germination of the idea that I would leave Taft. I, in an effort to make my life easier in America, changed my name to Grace. Those early beginnings are likely what made me such a keen observer of the, so called, human nature. So that's how it all started for me, an endless search of who I was and why I was here and how I would make life for myself different from that available in *el Barrio*.

In 1946, the year I was born, Taft, Texas, was bursting at the seams economically. It had been that way for my hometown since the days it had been known as the Taft Ranch, which was established in 1879. During the summer months, the rich, black soil of Taft produced some of the largest cotton crops in Texas, boosting profits for the Anglos who owned the land and even in the poorer South Side where the residents were of Mexican heritage. At harvest time, out-of-towners came, nearly doubling Taft's population, to help pick the cotton that would ship nationally and internationally, becoming the town's biggest cash crop of the 1940s and 1950s. The cotton crop of Taft dressed many a man, woman, and child from Texas to Italy. A handful of second and third generation Europeans also held stakes in the gas and oil trades, which contributed to the overall well-being of the local economy. Even during America's Great Depression, Taft's farming community might have suffered some low commodity prices, but there weren't any soup lines crawling down Green Avenue, nor were any of Taft's business owners jumping out of their office windows. No sireee Bob, the black land of Taft made it possible for every resident, black, brown or white, to be a part of the town's economic boom.

But it wasn't just the town bursting at the seams; so were the wives of the soldiers that returned a year earlier when World War II ended. The sex-starved soldiers were welcomed by equally sex-starved wives with open arms, and a year later the population boom hit Taft like so many other towns throughout America, with an explosion. In my case, I was probably in that handful of babies born in 1946 whose fathers hadn't served in the military during the war. But never mind that, the Census Bureau, when it came collecting information on the American population, didn't ferret out those children whose fathers served, so I, deservingly or not, became a member of the baby boom generation.

But before I tell about my journey through the black land, allow me to take you back to the early days when the land of my birthplace supposedly sat at the bottom of what is now known as the Gulf of Mexico.

During my early childhood I spent many an evening listening to Buelito's *cuentos*. Buelito was the primary source of the knowledge I acquired early on, so when I heard that Taft had once sat at the bottom of the Gulf of Mexico, he was the first person I approached for the answer.

"*Buelito es verdad que* Taft *estuvo cubierto por agua*?" I asked perplexed.

"*Si, es possible*," Buelito answered matter-of-factly.

His casual response left me even more confused. How could it be that the property our house sat on actually had been nothing but sand and water at one time?

The story was as strange as the Spanglish exchanges I observed between Amá and her best friend, Roque.

"*Cata, vamos a tomarnos unas* beers with our *hombres*?" It was interesting to hear Spanish and English intermixed so fluidly in conversation, but it was in this way that I, and most Mexicans in Taft, learned to speak; the mixture of Spanish and English—Spanglish, represents the necessity to learn the English language, and the reliance on our native Spanish to help us through that transition.

As history played out, the flat mesquite-and chaparral-filled land of my birthplace had sat lonely for centuries. During the mid 1500s, when the Spanish conquistadores found their way from Mexico into south Texas, they found a land flatter than a Spanish omelet and so filled with mesquite trees that they took to calling the land of my future hometown *Mesquital*, Spanish for mesquite. But there were at least two known bands of Indians already living in *Mesquital*, the Coahuiltecans and the Karankawas.

The Coahuiltecans were said to originate from the Mexican state of Coahulia and could be found roaming anywhere from San Antonio to northern Mexico. History tells us that the Coahuiltecans were living in Mexico and Texas as far back as the 16th century, but of course they could have lived there much earlier. It's been said that they might have been related to the Paleoindian peoples who came from perhaps the Pyrenees to the area of northern Mexico more than 13,000 years earlier. Interestingly, not much of the Coahuiltecan culture was left after they ceased to exist in the late mid 1800's but one item of their culture remains. The word *mitote*, which they called their religious ceremonies is a word loosely used in south Texas today to refer to either a festival or some kind of an uproar.

The Karankawas were a band of unusually tall, semi-naked Indians who are believed to have come from the Caribbean around the 1200's. They mostly roamed the south Texas gulf coast and were known as "Karankawas," but later as things commonly went in my culture on the South Side of Taft, they were given a nickname, the "Kronks." There was one tale after another about the Kronks' cannibalistic ways. It's been reported by historians and archaeologists alike, that the Kronks ate the flesh of those enemy warriors they captured. They didn't eat the flesh as part of their dietary needs but rather to get the magic power of the dead. However, there is one particularly gruesome story told by A.J. Sowell an early south Texas settler that leaves one to suspect the Kronks were more than just casual tasters of human flesh. Sowell told about a Karankawa raid on an Anglo settlement near the Brazos River where they killed the entire family and took off with the youngest child.

"After going some distance, they camped, killed the child and proceeded to eat her, first splitting open the body, then quartering it, and placing the parts on sharp sticks and cooking them."

While they feasted on the youngster, a band of white settlers surprised the Kronks, and killed them all. Buelito and his friends incorporated talk during evening sessions about *los indios* that lived in south Texas *muchos años pasados*. They laughingly reasoned the Indians were the reason so many potential settlers had stayed away from south Texas for so long.

During the western expansion of America in the 1800s, the Kronks were eliminated by the force of mostly Irish and German settlers along with help from two unsuspecting but determined Indian bands, the Comanches who came from Wyoming and the Lipan Apaches who came from western Canada. For a very long time south Texas belonged to these Indian bands. They attacked the Irish, Germans, and other European settlers during their early attempt to settle in south Texas. The Comanches were especially brutal and vicious—scalping and skinning their white enemy at will. They kidnapped many a white settler including their famous captive Cynthia Ann Parker who became the mother of the last Comanche Chief, Quanah Parker. The Mexicans and Texans didn't fare any better. They fought at times as much with each other as with the Comanches and Lipan Apaches during Texas's struggle for independence from Mexico in the early 1800s. It was only after Texas became a state on December 29, 1845, that the settlers along with the Mexicans, in a unified effort, began to eliminate the Indian threat. By 1850, the Comanche world barely existed.

But back to the rich black land of Taft that initially belonged to Youngs Coleman, Thomas M. Coleman, John M. Mathis, Thomas Henry Mathis, and George W. Fulton. In the early 1800s those five men formed a partnership known as the Coleman-Fulton (C-F) Pasture Company to raise and sell cattle. During the era of the "Big Drive," where cattle were driven from Mexico and the lower Rio Grande Valley to the slaughter houses in the Midwestern part of the United States, south Texas begged for a cattle crossing station. The CF-Pasture Company established such a crossing while at the same time building one of the largest cattle ranches in Texas, which became known as the Taft Ranch.

By 1885, the vast majority of the ranch land in south Texas was owned by a handful of second generation Europeans. Among those ranches were; the Taft Ranch which owned 32,000 head of cattle on 170,000 acres, and the nearby King Ranch which owned 40,000 head of cattle on 640,000 acres. The Taft Ranch land was mostly acquired by the purchase of adjoining property from original land grantees and through awards of Headright, Bounty, Donation, and Script certificates from the Republic of Texas.

The King Ranch was founded by Captain Richard King a poor Irishman from New York. Captain King worked on steamboats during the Mexican War, then came to south Texas in the mid-1800s and bought many Spanish land grants. Captain King's ranch spanned most of the land in south Texas, making his the largest privately owned ranch in the world. King's initial land holdings (15,500 acres) were acquired through the purchase of grants from the family of Juan Mendiola of Camargo. He went on to purchase more land from willing grant owners who either didn't care much for the desolate area or simply needed the money at the time. It is well documented that King went to great lengths to insure his land acquisition was legal and above board. To be fair, another view is held by many that the massive ranch lands in south Texas were gained through force and intimidation.

The Taft Ranch sat on some of the richest and fertile soil in America, which allowed it to expand its business beyond cattle. The Taft ranch owners were luckier than the devil. They benefited from the crossroads that General Zachary Taylor and his troops built in the County of San Patricio, where the CF-Pasture Company had most of its roots. San Patricio County was established on April 18, 1846, and named by its predominantly Irish settlers for Ireland's patron saint. It came into existence with the accidental help of General Taylor who was sent by President Polk to keep order in case trouble broke out between Mexico and Texas over Texas' decision to annex from Mexico. A year before, General Taylor had been looking for a direct route to move his troops from Corpus Christi, where they were camped, to his headquarters in San Antonio. The area he chose is now part of the Artesian Park in Corpus Christi. By establishing the much-needed crossroads, General Taylor transformed San Patricio into a busy traveling artery, which in turn helped the Taft Ranch several years later, become a major agricultural business operation in the United States.

Settlers from Europe but mostly from Ireland began their long journey across the Atlantic Ocean to be a part of the ranch. The famous phrase G.T.T., "gone to Texas," was heard from Dublin, Ireland, to the Taft Ranch.

It wasn't long after the rush of European settlers began to arrive in south Texas that Anna and Charles P. Taft of Cincinnati began selling the Taft Ranch in the early 1900s. The larger parcels of land were bought up primarily by Irish and German settlers, while the smaller plots went to mostly Mexican-Americans and newly arrived immigrants from Mexico. The land that was left of the Taft Ranch led to the establishment of the town of Taft in 1920, the year my Amá and her family came to America. Its rich black soil earned Taft the nickname "Blackland" throughout Texas. In later years Taft, with its continuous enormous cotton crop, became known as the "friendliest cotton-picking town in Texas."

From all that I can remember, nothing about Taft particularly captivated me. If I had had any say, it would not have been my first, second, or even third choice of places in which to spend the first eighteen years of my life, never mind the rest of my life. However, as Taft is where my journey began, it was from there that I navigated and set off on the path before me.

Taft is located just 18 miles north of Corpus Christi and the gulf coast, and as a result it suffered from year-round strong gulf winds that nearly blew the roof off of our house. There seemed to be dust devils swirling all the time on our street that we blamed on the strong winds from Corpus. My friend María, whom we called *la Bolilla* because of her fair skin and yellow hair, always warned, "*Chela, ahi viene el Diablo!*" Her warning had me racing down West Pecan Street for my very soul, convinced that if the twirling cyclone caught me, I would be swirled away down to hell in a cloud of dust and gravel.

The hot, sticky weather suffocated Taft most of the year except during the welcoming cooler months of January and February. During the summer the heat was so intense that when the sun's rays kissed my olive skin it was instantly baked to a dark bronze color. I should have been happy with a year-round suntan, but my glowing dark skin only served to have the Anglos call me a "dirty meskin" and to have my brother Enrique call me, *la Negra fea*.

Hot, humid south Texas was a prime breeding ground for revolting insects of all shapes and sizes. At any given time, we could find ourselves nourishing pesky mosquitoes, or swatting at black flies the size of my thumb; it was not uncommon for my Amagrande to rescue these giant, tropical nuisances from the large aluminum pot filled with *caldo de res* with a huge wooden ladle. But no insect was more encroaching than the illustrious cockroach; no matter how many times we had our tiny house exterminated, those dark, nasty critters crept into the most concealed of crevices, and multiplied and mutated into larger and more disgusting pests. Soon there were thousands of them; evidenced by the endless trail of droppings left upon our dinnerware, framed photos, clothing, and whatever else they could find their way into. The more we tried to kill them, the more food they seemed to find, and so the more they grew, and the harder they became to kill. The entire process seemed a bit like a dog chasing its own tail.

In 1952, Taft was prosperous—with a population less than 2,000, the town had two banks and a street full of busy stores selling everything from automobiles to toy telephones. I remember the first day I went to *el pueblo* with Amá, The hot burning sun beat over us like an inferno and walking made it even worse. The trip from the South Side to the North Side of town seemed to take forever and I could only wish we had owned a car. As we walked across the railroad tracks, and onto Green Avenue, I anxiously reached for my Amá's hand. I was afraid of the unknown more than I was of *los*

Americanos or *los Bolillos,* as we Mexicans called the Anglos, who, Amá warned, didn't like Mexicans.

Amá said the street we walked on was named for a very important man. That man was none other than Taft Ranch Superintendent Joseph F. Green, who had incorporated the town. I was overwhelmed and a bit frightened at the sight of the simple, square, brick buildings lined up in rows on either side of the avenue; they seemed gigantic and new to me, though they were only one and two stories high, and had been built during the 1900s.

I became overjoyed to see so many people of all ages and all sizes scurrying up and down the avenue and in and out of the stores with their big and little shopping bags. It was a time of prosperity throughout America, and the cash registers rang up and down the main streets of Taft, as well. The town parking lot was filled with the newest models of popular cars. But it was the lumberyard, bustling with activity that captured my eye. The lumberyard occupied a large section of land off of Green Avenue, and the line of *Bolillos* waiting to purchase lumber stretched all the way to the street, while other men hurriedly loaded their materials into pickups and sped away toward Highway 181. I wondered what the men planned to build with all the lumber they were hauling away—maybe a house or a *tiendita.*

As we walked further down the avenue, we saw the showroom of a car dealership filled with people admiring the newest car models. Amá pointed to one of the cars inside the showroom. "*Me voy a comprar ese carro el primer día que tenga dinero,*" she said convincingly, though I was more focused on the hustle and bustle of the town than on Amá's chatter. I could never picture Amá behind the wheel of a car, and didn't want to, after she had insisted on trying to drive a friend's manual transmission, and nearly killed everyone in the car in the process. She struggled to shift gears and steer the car at the same time, but didn't do a very good job of either, driving the car into a wide and empty ditch with everyone in the car screaming bloody murder. It was a good thing for us in that poor little stick shift car that someone had the good sense to build the ditch years earlier. Aside from not having faith that my Amá would learn to drive, I didn't think that she'd ever have enough money to buy herself a new car. The only people I saw driving new cars were *Bolillos* and our Catholic priest, Father Joe. A very small handful of Mexican women knew how to drive, and even fewer could find themselves in a position to buy a new car; I couldn't see how Amá was going to be any different.

As we passed the dealer's showroom and Amá's fantasies of driving dissipated, she led me inside the drugstore, where our downtown adventure continued.

"*Vamos a comer algo!*" Amá proclaimed excitedly.

She walked briskly through the aisles to the center of the store and I trailed behind her sheepishly, uncertain of our destination. At last, we came to a long counter lined with people perched on rotating stools. One small, redheaded boy laughed joyfully as he spun himself round and round on his seat. I almost slipped on the shiny floor, and as I grabbed Amá's hand to steady myself, I caught my own reflection looking back at me from below my feet. As Amá and I took our seats at the soda fountain, I was startled to find us surrounded by people whose skin was pale as the moon; their glistening, yellow hair and deep, blue eyes took me by surprise. The only person I'd ever seen who looked like them was my friend *la Bolilla* but not even her hair was so yellow, nor her skin as white. The pale-skinned diners paused from their meal long enough to dance the mambo with their eyeballs, bouncing back and forth from their food to us two, then back and again twice as much. The young looking *Bolilla* taking food orders took a long time with her other customers before coming to take our order.

"Tu greel shes sanwitches," Amá said, in broken English. "Tu cokes," she added

The grilled cheese sandwich turned out to be the best food I'd ever tasted. While we ate, I felt the stares from the wrinkled, old Anglos trailing the line at the medicine counter, all the way to the store's entrance. I whispered to Amá to look at how the Anglos stared but she ordered me to keep eating.

"*No están impuestos a ver Mexicanos comiendo aquí,*" she said coldly.

I didn't understand her comment and she didn't bother to explain further. But there would be many more occasions when Amá and I went into town together, and with each trip I became more and more accustomed to the exciting but unusual way of downtown life on Green Avenue.

On one trip into town, Amagrande came along with us, embarrassing sight as she was. She complained all the way up Davis Road and onto Green Avenue about the boiling heat, about her black, leather, clunky shoes that were too tight, and about the deep pain in her knees. Amá bent down and whispered to me that part of her reason for wanting to buy a car was so that she could drive Amagrande into town.

Amagrande wore *luto* since the day in 1948 when her youngest son, Victor, was struck and killed by a train, while serving in the U.S. Army in Japan. Her dress was black from head to toe, including the black hosiery shifting about her skinny legs, coming loose and sagging after no particular amount of walking. During our trip, Amagrande stopped a number of times to bend and retie the hosiery knots slipping apart at her ankles. She wore her long, salt-and-pepper hair in big, waist-length braids, which she concealed beneath a dark, heavy scarf. The tips of her braids spilled out of her scarf, swaying and wiggling like two stowed-away squirrels' tails as she walked. Without the scarf to wrap them in, Amagrande let her braids rest upon her large, saggy breasts, making her look a bit like the Indian on the five-cent coin. She looked as if she was from some far-off, ancient civilization, rather than the small town founded by the Tafts of Cincinnati. I was thankful she had brought along her scarf, but Amagrande's braids were the least of my worries.

Amagrande, who had a habit of breaking wind at the most inopportune time, was letting it rip on Green Avenue. The smells coming from behind her could have choked a moose; passersby frantically waved their hands back and forth to fan away the odor and find fresh air to breathe. I pointed out to her that she was farting, and that it smelled awful. She laughed.

"No me importa. Que se vayan al demonio," she answered matter-of-factly.

Amá walked ahead of us and asked that I hold Amagrande's hand and make sure she didn't lose her balance, as she was prone to doing. I figured that Amá wanted to walk ahead so that the mostly *Bolillo* shoppers, staring up and down at us, wouldn't mistake her for the one making those nasty farts. Badly as I wanted to run up the street and join Amá, the more I tried to wrestle my hand away, the tighter Amagrande clung to it. The further we walked into the downtown district the more *los Bolillos* stared at us. It was interesting to watch the shoppers try to guess whether the curly mop-headed little girl or the old woman in the Halloween-looking costume was the culprit polluting the air. All afternoon, I wished to be a tiny ball, rolling down Green Avenue and as far from Amagrande as possible.

If I could have changed one thing about myself early on, it would have been my bouncy, black, curly hair. I would much rather have had people take notice of my cute dimples, or the two beauty marks on the right side of my cheek; but strangers of all shapes, sizes, and colors would come up and marvel at my hair. It wasn't enough for them to touch it—they had to be convinced that it was real, so they'd slip their greasy palms all over my scalp, rustling my mane as if they were dusting out a mop. Curly hair was a rarity on the South Side, as it seemed most local Mexicans' hair was as straight as the yellow line dividing the road.

Every morning on my way to school, I stopped at the Johnsons' café, where Amá worked as the short order cook. Amá would save me a glazed doughnut from the stack that she baked. One morning I was late, so she handed me a white paper bag containing my morning treat all wrapped up inside. As I started to walk out the back door, Mrs. Johnson, the café owner's wife stopped me and excitedly gushed, "Oh my! Let me touch those curls." Mrs. Johnson reminded me of a Hollywood movie star. Her milky white skin was flawless and her sparkling eyes seemed to dance as she ran her long, bony fingers through my hair, tugging in supposed admiration. She slipped her fingers again and again through my hair, and then ordered, "Come, follow me." She was not a tall woman by any means, but she was imposing, and at my small stature, her height meant authority. She led me to the restaurant's main dining room, where the town's ranchers and farmers sat eating heaping platefuls of biscuits and eggs.

"Looky what I've got me here! Catalina's daughter—ain't her hair the most unusual ya'll have ever seen!" she exclaimed. The roomful of men all clad in western style, turned to me and laughed heartily as the woman continued tugging playfully at my curls.

"Look how her curls spring back to their original place," she exclaimed again. The ranchers looked up again and laughed, and some even got up to take a closer look at my curly hair. I felt like some sort of circus freak.

The downtown trip with Amagrande seemed endless. The air began to clear, and as the bank came into sight Amagrande began to ramble on as if nothing had happened.

"*No señor, yo no tengo fé que los americanos cuiden mi dinero,*" she declared.

"*En donde guarda su dinero Amagrande?*" I asked.

"*Todavía no he olvidado en donde he escondido mi dinero,*" she answered defiantly.

Amá stopped and pointed excitedly when we came across one of the Cage brothers; J.B. and Leland Cage owned the majority of the businesses in Taft, and were highly respected throughout the town.

"*Ese señor es uno de los Cages,*" she gleefully announced.

"*Quién son los Cages?*" I cautiously asked.

"*Eres un tonta! Ellos son los más ricos del pueblo y vale más que los respetes,*" Amá ordered sternly. "*Además, tu Tía Lina trabaja en la casa de uno de los Cages y dice ella que el Cage y su esposa la tratan muy bien, no como otros Americanos,*" she added humbly.

One of the few businesses not owned by the Cages was Herman's clothing store, owned by Mr. Herman Leibowitz. Mr. Leibowitz was short and stocky, with skin the color of mayonnaise, and on most days he could be found in front of his store, hands clutched behind his back, pacing back and forth. His earth-tone business suits stood apart from all the denim, Stetson hats, and leather cowboy boots the Anglos typically favored. His belt cinched awkwardly around his waist, just below his breastbone, leaving his pant legs to rise and dangle several inches above his shoes. While Mr. Leibowitz was not much of a talker, he was pleasant to Amá and me when we shopped in his store.

I liked going to Herman's to sift through the racks of pretty clothes and try one pair of shoes after another, but it was a special treat for me to be waited on by the pretty Mexican girl behind the cash register. It felt good to see a Mexican working side-by-side with the store owner instead of cleaning the store windows or mowing the lawn, as so many other Mexicans did for businessmen on the North Side. The pretty girl wore her light brown hair to her shoulders, and it would bounce up and down against her back as she walked around the store. I remember her voice, sweet as a honey drop. She was my first inspiration; I looked forward to the day I would be old enough to work the cash register at Herman's.

One warm, spring day, as I walked home from school with some of my third grade classmates, something happened that made me afraid to go back into Herman's ever again. As we approached the clothing store and I saw Mr. Leibowitz in his usual place at the storefront, I ran up to greet him.

"Hello Sir," I said cheerfully. Mr. Leibowitz looked down at me softly and opened his mouth to speak, when suddenly my classmates' shrieks drowned out his words.

"Graciela! Graciela! Run! Run! **Run!**" they screamed at the top of their lungs.

I locked eyes with Mr. Leibowitz, whose smile spread wide across his face.

"Run, Graciela," they screamed again.

I didn't know whether to run toward my screaming classmates or stay with the smiling Mr. Leibowitz

"He killed Jesús, and he'll kill you too!" my classmates hollered all at once.

Mr. Leibowitz's smile quickly fell from his face, and his pale complexion turned suddenly a bright red. I stood frozen in front of Mr. Leibowitz, mouth agape in disbelief. As I began to back away gently from the man, I could not believe I was face-to-face with the person who had killed Jesús Christ, my savior! In all of Father Joe's talk of the crucifixion of Jesús, never once had he mentioned that the killer was living in our town of Taft! I ran, screaming and running like a bat out of hell, bumping into shoppers along Green Avenue with the rest of my hysterical classmates.

I couldn't wait to get home to tell Amá what I had learned about Mr. Leibowitz. I could think of nothing or no one but him the entire way home. When I got home I found Amá sitting in her new two-toned brown Nash, with her friend Roque in the passenger seat. Amá had bought a new car, after all, and as was typical on the South Side, where homes didn't come with garages, it was parked in the front yard, which we treated as an extension of the house. Amá and Roque took turns sipping from metal cans of beer, and I watched their cigarette smoke dance in thin, blurry clouds as they bent to place the cans on the floor, away from my view.

"*Que quieres?*" Amá asked, annoyed. I began to tell my story, but she cut me off before I could finish. "*Eres una pendeja y una bruta. Como vás a pensar que ese señor tan bueno mató a Jesús Cristo?*" she howled at me accusingly.

"*Entonces quién mató a Jesús Cristo?*" I asked. Amá placed her cigarette on the car's ashtray, and she and Roque both sat silently for a few moments, before turning to face me in such a way that I felt I was the killer, not Mr. Leibowitz.

"*Sabrá Diós quién mató a Jesús Cristo,*" Amá yelled.

"*No seas necia; siempre haces muchas preguntas. Vete a la casa!*" she ordered.

Las tienditas in Taft's South Side, like Don Pancho's dance hall and his Taft Mercantile Store were big moneymakers, too, especially during the cotton season. My cousin Miné and I stopped by the Taft Mercantile Store almost daily after school. We concentrated on the penny candy, but the store offered everything from cotton picking sacks to fresh-cut meats. One day my cousin and I walked into the store where we found one of Don Pancho's sons in the butcher shop area. He was busy cutting large chunks of red meat with a meat cleaver that looked like it could cut a horse in half. Don Pancho's son was deeply concentrating on his cuts, never looking up even for a second while large chunks of red meat fell away from the enormous cleaver. We walked around the counter trying to steal his attention, but his arm continued rising and pounding the cleaver into the meat. As we stood, tiptoeing and peering over the glass to catch the man's eye, the whamming suddenly ceased, and before we knew it, he appeared from behind the counter in his blood-soaked apron.

"*Que chingados mirán?*" he scowled. We jumped, startled by his sudden appearance.

"*Vayánse a la chingada de aquí!*" he ordered.

We ran out of the store, laughing so hysterically that we were nearly mauled over by a car speeding down Davis Road.

It was typical of Miné and me to burst out into hysteric, uncontrollable laugher at the drop of a hat. We found humor in the smallest things, from a dead rat in the street to the curly moustache on a Mexican man or the yellow, tobacco-stained teeth in an Anglo's mouth. We once broke out into a fit of laughter at the sight of a postal clerk's greasy, balding head. I laughed so hard I peed on the hardwood floor of the Taft Post Office. We were thrown out of there too.

At the end of the four-block business district sat the Taft Baptist church—the largest, most imposing brick structure in town. Like so many others in south Texas, Taft's downtown was surrounded by churches. There seemed to be as many Baptists on the North Side as there were Catholics on the South Side, and on Sunday the Baptists spilled in droves from the doors of the church.

Taft Baptists captured my attention because the Baptist church sat next to the only town park I longed to play in. Every day on my way to the school, I saw the same two swarthy Mexican men cleaning the park; one pushed a lawnmower, while the other followed behind to trim the hedges and gather litter and debris. After school, I would usually stop with a few of my classmates to enjoy pecans off the ground, in the shade of the trees that bore them. We chased after squirrels to keep them from taking all of the nuts and roared with laughter as we watched them climb the trees to get away from us. But when we tried to use the jungle gym and the swings the Anglos who lived across from the park rushed out of their homes to chase us away.

"Shoo! Shoo! Get out of here, you dirty little Mexicans," they ordered. We hurriedly left the park and ran toward Green Avenue. Like militia, the mostly older Anglos would watch over us until we disappeared into the downtown district; this continued throughout my elementary school years, until one day I gave up trying to enter the park.

In the center of the business district was a movie theatre, originally named the Rialto. During the early 1950s it was renamed the Leland theatre by its new owners, a tall balding man and his petite but temperamental wife. She sold the tickets shouting at us to have our money ready while her husband hurriedly ushered everyone toward the double doors leading to the first floor seating area. Those seats were reserved for the Anglos and Mexicans, while a large sign that pointed toward the Mezzanine was posted on the building's side entrance. It read, "For Colored People Only." Amá took my brother and me to the movies almost every Friday night. She favored films with Clark Gable and Cary Grant, and I had probably seen all of their movies by the time I was twelve years old.

Interestingly, the only person the theatre owners seemed to tolerate was their six year old granddaughter. The little girl had a habit of running up and down the aisles tossing her head back and forth while her long blond braids swayed from one side to the other. She randomly stuck her tongue out at selected members of the audience and for some reason I was usually her target. I thought many times of pulling her braids more than once but I knew that was one battle I wasn't going to win, my Amá loved going to that movie house.

In 1954, the Leland Theatre advertised a movie about the Siamese twins, Daisy and Violet Hilton, from San Antonio. The twins were conjoined, attached at the back. Much to my surprise, when Amá took me to see their movie, *Chained for Life,* the sisters showed up in person! They happily greeted everyone in the movie house, and signed autographs in their floor-length, backless dresses and matching shawls. The silky fabric of their dresses made a swishing noise as they followed each other's footsteps inside the theatre. I pushed through the crowd and followed close behind, as if I was part of their entourage. Could they possibly be attached by flesh? Fascinated by the oddity of their human form, I leaned in closer and "purposely" slid my hand down their backs. The twins let out a scream, and I jumped back, adding a frightened scream of my own as I ran to Amá's side at the snack stand, safe from the pandemonium that ensued in the theatre; the other patrons began screaming too while they ran in different directions as if the movie house was on fire. I stood and watched innocently waiting for the excitement to die down.

If Taft was prosperous, its layout was a picture of everything that is good and bad; as in so many towns in south Texas the railroad sliced through town and served to separate the Anglos from the Mexicans. The North Side was prosperous, tidy, and populated with Anglos. There were a small number of Anglos that lived on the South Side, but their homes were located in a remote area closer to the railroad tracks rather than deep into *el barrio.* Most of them were just as poor as those of us on the South Side yet there wasn't much social contact between us even if we were basically in the same financial boat. It seemed the poorer they were the more hurtful the words were that spilled out of their mouths toward us Mexicans. The only way I learned to fight back was to call them, "white trash."

The houses on the North Side were beautiful and architecturally unique. Some were single-unit brick ramblers that seemed to stretch an entire block, while others were split-level Cape Cods, but most fascinating to me was that they all had indoor plumbing. I thought everyone had an outhouse like we did! I was impressed at the paved streets, tall, leafy trees, and perfectly manicured lawns that looked like those I admired in my sister Delfina's home-style magazines. Even the pets were fatter, perkier, prettier, and cleaner on the North Side.

The South Side was populated with Mexicans, of whom more than half lived below the poverty line. The bumpy roads were narrow and rough, covered with *caliche,* a surface mixture of clay and salts. The one-story houses were made of low-grade lumber and cheap metal, and most of the cars in front of them all along West Pecan Street were clunky old rust buckets.

My favorite house on the North Side sat toward the northern end of Green Avenue, painted white with shiny black shutters and a sprawling lawn like none I'd seen on either side of town. It reminded me of the White House, where President Eisenhower lived. I once saw the owners sitting in their first floor solarium, sipping drinks and watching television. I wondered what kind of people they were. The man who tended their garden was the father of one of my classmates Alfredo. Many times I wanted to run up to Alfredo's father and ask him what the house looked like inside, but he kept to his work, head down, busily trimming the hedges that graced the perimeter. I kept my dream of living in the big, white house on Green Avenue to myself, mostly because I was afraid that others would try to crush my dream like my friend Helen did one day on our way home from school.

"You are dreaming too big, Graciela. *Estás loca!* You and I will never live in a house like that," she said laughingly. *You're wrong,* I thought, but deep down I felt we were doomed by which side of the railroad tracks faced our homes. Maybe, Helen had a point, but at least I could dream.

The pets in our neighborhood were scrawny, sickly, diseased, and unlucky to be alive! The only healthy dogs on the South Side were those that had signs in front of their master's homes that read "BEWARE OF DOG." My brother was one of a handful of pet owners who had a pet for companionship. *Como Tú* followed Enrique everywhere he went and even slept under his bed at night, which was not common in South Side homes. One warm, sunny day, *Como Tú* ran after a junky old pickup truck driving down the road near our house. The dog let out a few muffled yelps as he was trapped beneath the wheels of the truck. The driver brought the truck to a stop. Enrique ran, crying toward the dog, trailed by his best friend, Gaspar; Gaspar's youngest sister, *La Quatita;* and me. Enrique knelt down but *Como Tu* was dead. He began bawling, picking up *Como Tú,* who was covered in *caliche* and blood. By this time, Amá burst out of the house at the sound of Enrique's bawling.

"*Ya basta*! *Era no más que un perro,*" she admonished.

Enrique wiped away his tears with his shirt and asked if he could bury *Como Tú* in the backyard.

"*Ház lo que quieras; no más para de llorar,*" Amá ordered.

My brother ran inside and returned with one of Amá's dish towels draped around his shoulders, announcing he was wearing the dish towel to look like the cape Father Joe wore when he presided over funerals. The four of us took turns digging a hole big enough to fit *Como Tú*. When it came time to lay his dog to rest, Enrique lifted the lifeless mass of bloodied fur and gently placed him into the hole. We took turns spreading the earth over my brother's big, yellow friend, and as the last patch of black earth was placed over him, I wept along with my brother Enrique . . . even though I had never cared much for *Como Tú*.

Amagrande joked that people on the South Side owned dogs more to keep *los de la Atalaya*-Jehovah's Witnesses, away from their homes than as protection from burglars. She was quick to point out that, "*nuestro mismos Mejicanos,*" committed most of the few break-ins on the South Side and if they dared to break into her home she'd use Buelito's *pistola* against them.

For those of us who didn't own a dog, *los de la Atayala* could be a relentless pain in the rear. They showed up every Sunday on the South Side, swarming down the streets in dark, two-piece suits, each with a Bible tucked under one arm. They stood out in *el Barrio* since the men on the South Side wore suits only to a wedding or a funeral, and while most of us practiced Catholicism religiously, I wouldn't have known a Bible if it fell from the sky and landed on my head. Father Joe took it upon himself to read from the Bible and interpret its message to his congregation, never really encouraging us to read it. Father Joe put the fear of God in us if we allowed *los de la Atayala* into our homes. During most Sunday masses, he warned, "*Se van ir al infierno si permiten que los de la Atalaya entren en sus casas.*"

We knew when *los de la Atalaya* arrived on the South Side by the warning shouts, "*A la madre, ahi vienen los de la Atalaya!*" Every able-bodied person dropped what they were doing and ran inside their homes as if they heard the devil was arriving. The only noise anywhere around was the slamming of doors and clicking of locks; by the time *los de la Atalaya* reached West Pecan Street, it was like a ghost town, not a soul in sight. It seemed *los de la Atalaya* knew exactly what they were dealing with and came prepared. But converting a South Side Catholic into a member of *los de la Atalaya* was no more going to happen than a slimy frog was going to turn into a gentle, handsome prince.

I got used to seeing *los de la Atalaya* on the South Side, but I never got used to the fear of God that Father Joe tried to instill in us if we allowed them into our homes. But the only person on the South Side who wasn't afraid of Father Joe it seemed was Amagrande. She allowed *los de la Atalaya* into her home serving them coffee and graham crackers—the same graham crackers Amagrande wouldn't share with me, because she said they were a part of her special diabetic diet. Amagrande sat in her rocking chair listening intently to a pair of Anglo men tell their version of the Bible in broken Spanish. After they'd leave Amagrande tried sharing with Buelito and me what she had learned from *los de la Atalaya*. Buelito walked away, waving his hands up in the air. I had no choice but to sit and listen to Amagrande go on about the Christian faith according to *los de la Atalaya*.

Chapter 2

La Revolución

*"Poor Mexico, so far from God and so close to the
United States."*
Porfirio Díaz, 1840-1915
President of Mexico (1876-1880 & 1884-1911)

Since the beginning of time rulers of kingdoms or countries have been forced out when their subjects or their voters lost confidence in their leadership. Sometimes such a transition is orderly and precise, while at other times it results in prolonged wars and massive civilian devastation to countries' social and political structure. The Mexican Revolution of 1910 was one of the most extraordinarily violent historical events to take place in North America, taking many lives and changing the face of Mexico's political structure for over eighty years. Still, had it not been for the Mexican Revolution, Amá's parents in all likelihood would not have immigrated to the United States, and I might have much less reason to write this book. In school I was taught more about the American Revolution than the Mexican Revolution. I felt more in tune as an American to understand the causes and effects of the American Revolution on my country, America. Our textbooks mentioned the Mexican Revolution only briefly, something about poor Mexicans fighting affluent Mexicans, led by a bandit named Pancho Villa. When Buelito told the story, though, he never called Pancho Villa a *bandido*. In fact, he praised Villa more often than not.

"Villa era un hombre muy luchador. Si, había veces que no pensaba las consecuencias de sus actos, pero fué un hombre que luchó por lo que creía," Buelito said more than once.

I once asked Buelito, "Wasn't Pancho Villa a bad man?"

"Lo que él hizo, lo hizo en el nombre de la revolución," Buelito declared proudly.

Buelito was born in 1881 in Villa la Madrid, a tiny village in northern Mexico close to Monclova, Coahuila. His father, Matilde San Miguel, and his mother, Victoriana Sanchéz, owned a small ranch where they raised horses and other animals. It was at his parents' ranch that Buelito learned to ride horses, a skill that would prove to be helpful when he rode alongside Pancho Villa en *la revolución.*

Buelito stayed in touch with Mexico through weekly Spanish newspapers he bought from the Taft Mercantile Store. The political stories of Mexico interested him the most, but he would sometimes scan the gossip section, or try to get a rise out of me with a tidbit from Mexico's biggest comedian, Cantinflas.

At first glance Buelito wouldn't necessarily be confused with having been a captain in Pancho Villa's army. Buelito was a small man, very slight, distinguished by his fair complexion, his *whiteness.* His wiry frame didn't reveal any war scars; until he lifted up his right pant leg to show the scar of the bullet from one of General Pershing's soldiers. The one scar was Buelito's badge of honor, a long gash across the inside of his right knee. The old wound looked like a road cutting through a map; and perhaps it was a map, the long trail of Mexican history in North America in which Buelito played a minor but important role. A soldier's bullet struck Buelito's leg when General Pershing, under orders from President Woodrow Wilson, led a U.S. Army force into Mexico in 1916—to capture Villa after he and his army staged a raid on Columbus, New Mexico. Buelito almost lost his leg from an infection that developed while he hid from *los gringos*—as he called Pershing's soldiers—in an abandoned railroad boxcar for several days.

Most evenings Buelito's friends and a collection of grandchildren gathered on my grandparents' tiny front porch, which was nothing more than slabs of old rotting wood carelessly nailed together. Buelito talked for hours about his role *en la revolución* and only trailed off a bit when he emptied the loose tobacco from the blue tin Bugler can to make himself a cigarette. He'd continue the story as he carefully poured the tobacco into a small, thin sheet of white paper. He paused only long enough to lick the paper; continuing his story while pinching the two sides of the paper together, then rolling it between his hands into a finished cigarette. His friends did the same thing, making their own cigarettes and smoking one after another throughout the evening. The porch became a haze of gray smoke, forming itself into imaginary ghost figures.

Buelito kept us captive with his stories. The excitement in his voice made the Mexican Revolution come alive. He told of so many men who died during the *la revolución* that I had a difficult time keeping up with who killed whom and for what purpose. Never mind, that in the beginning I didn't pay much attention, since at the age of five, I was more interested in climbing trees than I was in listening to a history lesson about a revolution that had taken place almost thirty-six years before I was born and in a country that was far away from my imaginative reach. But since I spent most of my formative years with Buelito and Amagrande, I was helplessly sedated with heavy doses of Mexican Revolution stories.

At story time with Buelito, I felt safer than at any other time. He'd snuggle me in his arms and kiss my forehead lovingly at the end of the evening, and I remember the roughness of his thick, white whiskers tickling my face. When I fell asleep in his arms, he'd carry me into the house and lay me down on Amagrande's bed. I credit his storytelling for setting the stage for the fanciful dreams I would have as a young woman.

During Buelito's stories he talked about the important men of the revolution, referring to them only by their last names—Huerta did this, Carranza did that, Villa did that . . . . In later years, I learned that Mexico had been plagued by one upheaval after another since being invaded by Spain; however, none was worse than the Mexican Revolution, the beginnings of which arose after Benito Juárez, the first Indian president of Mexico was reelected for a fourth term. During his presidency, Juárez struggled to keep his country from being taken over by the French government. This happened at a time when America was engaged in its own civil war and wasn't in a position to help protect its neighbor from foreign aggression. Yet, Mexico with its small rag tag army managed to fend off the strong army of Napoleon III until America came to help after the American Civil War ended in 1865. Rather than taking on America's mighty military, Napoleon III fled, leaving without Prince Maximilian whom he had tried to impose as emperor of Mexico. Maximilian was captured by Juárez's army and executed in 1867. Juarez came under heavy criticism from the Mexican conservatives for his role in allowing the French to create such upheaval inside Mexico. So when Juarez was reelected for a fourth term, Porfirio Díaz and his follower, Miguel Lerdo de Tejada opposed his victory and began to raise the idea of a revolt.

The revolt was brought to a temporary halt when Juarez died suddenly in 1872 and Lerdo succeeded him as president. By the end of 1876, Porfirio Díaz, a so-called reformist, who essentially began the revolution, was elected president after defeating Lerdo, who had run for a second term. Díaz was elected on the promise that he would establish a democratic government, stimulate the economy, and redistribute land to the indigenous population. However, he helped only a handful of wealthy Mexican families and gave special privileges to foreign investors—most of whom were American. Toward the end of his reign, nearly half of the land in Mexico was owned by fewer than three thousand families, none of whom were indigenous.

In 1910, when Díaz and his vice president, Ramón Corral, were reelected, Don Francisco Madero, a wealthy businessman and "spiritualist" from Coahuila and his followers (my Buelito and his family among them) declared that the election was fraud and thus was null and void. Recognizing the serious jeopardy his presidency was in, Díaz resigned in 1911, to be succeeded by Madero. Buelito seemed overjoyed every time he told me about witnessing his friend, Madero take the oath of office on November 6, 1911. But, Madero was president for less than two years when his army commander in chief and supposed friend, Victoriano Huerta, assassinated him. In the aftermath of Madero's assassination, Mexico saw death and destruction once again.

President Huerta had barely taken his hand off of the Bible before he began imposing a reign of tyranny on Mexico. His actions against the people of Mexico caused an unlikely partnership to develop between Pancho Villa, and Alvaro Obregón, a former rancher, who became an enormously talented war general. Together, the two men joined Madero's followers in the quest to oust President Huerta.

Buelito's shoulders stiffened whenever he mentioned Huerta and his fists clinched while he warned, "*Ten cuidado con tus amigos.*

Mira lo que le pasó al Presidente Francisco Madero, su mismo amigo Victoriano Huerta lo mató."

History tells us that Pancho Villa's revolutionary efforts began to lose steam around 1917, after Mexico's 1857 constitution was revised to include some of the revolutionists' economic demands. And, two years later when Emiliano Zapata was killed by Colonel Jesús Guajardo of the Mexican Army, *la revolución* essentially died with him.

By the end of 1920, three Mexican presidents had been assassinated and thousands of Mexican citizens had been killed in a ten-year period. When President Venustiano Carranza was assassinated on May 21, 1920, thousands of revolutionaries and their families fled, causing the most expansive exodus ever from Mexico into the United States. Buelito, Amagrande, and the five children they had between them, like so many others, ended up in south Texas, which, for Mexicans, was probably the most hostile place on the planet.

I often wondered why my grandparents chose Texas as the place they'd call home. Perhaps their decision had to do with distance, since their home state of Coahulia was only a few hours from the border town of Eagle Pass, Texas. When I got around to asking Buelito, he simply said that he wasn't thinking about the destination so much as about a quick and safe passage out of Mexico into the United States. But during the 1920s my grandparents learned soon enough that south Texas was more a war zone than a safe haven for Mexican revolutionaries. The Texas Rangers had been formed to fight off Indians and cattle rustlers, but terrorized innocent Mexicans instead; an estimated five thousand Mexicans were killed by Texas Rangers in the Rio Grande Valley from 1910-1919. It became typical for Texas Rangers to drive through south Texas towns with dead Mexicans draped over the fenders of their cars. Who knows why the Texas Rangers killed so many Mexicans. Maybe it was because they could or as stories went, they killed because Villa and his army had left a bad taste in the mouths of the Anglos living along the Texas-Mexico border. Yet, there were other stories that gave rise to this kind of hatred which was blamed on the legendary "Big

Foot" Wallace, who joined the Texas Rangers for one reason: "to kill greasers." It was said that "Big Foot" Wallace wanted to avenge the deaths of his relatives that died in the Goliad Massacre of 1836. (Depending on who is telling the story today, it might have been a massacre or it might have been an execution.)

The Goliad Massacre occurred when Colonel James W. Fanin and his Anglo Texans met General José Urrea at Coleto Creek, near the San Antonio River. Overwhelmed by the Mexicans, Fanin surrendered, assuming that he and his men would be treated as prisoners of war. But General Santa Ana, the man who overran the Alamo, declared Fanin's men pirates under Mexican law and ordered their execution by a firing squad. Unfortunately, this act exacerbated existing hatred, in men such as Big Foot Wallace, whose declaration "to kill greasers" was happily carried out by many of the Texas Anglos, especially in south Texas, where signs that read, "Niggers, Wetbacks and Dogs Aren't Welcome" were commonplace.

Buelito and his friends traded old and new stories about the many innocent Mexicans killed by Anglos, such as the story about one Aureliano Castellano, who was shot eight times and burned to a crisp in January 1896, in Goliad, Texas, for no reason other than that he was romancing *una Americana*.

"No tengas novios Americanos porque a tí te puede pasar lo mísmo que le pasó a Castellano," Buelito warned.

Chipita Rodriguez was another victim of Anglo prejudice who became a legend in the Mexican-American community. Chipita ran a way station in the San Patricio County area during the mid-1800s. A trader by the name of John Savage stopped for dinner one August afternoon in 1863, and while Savage ate his dinner, Chipita stepped outside. When she returned, Chipita found her only son standing over John Savage's body, which lay lifeless on the front porch. Chipita claimed that her son ran from the porch, jumped on Savage's horse, and took off to heaven knows where, never to be captured. Chipita was arrested after John Savage's body was found floating in the Aransas River, though no one could provide information or testify how it got there. Chipita's trial ended in a guilty verdict from a jury that included only one Mexican-American. Supposedly the only words Chipita said during her trial was "Not guilty!" when her verdict was announced. She was convicted even though the prosecutor didn't produce any evidence that Chipita had killed John Savage. The jury asked for clemency, but Judge Benjamin F. Neal disagreed, making Chipita Rodriguez the second woman to be executed in the state of Texas, after a Negro woman had been executed a few years earlier; Chipita was put to death by hanging on Friday, the thirteenth of November, 1863.

Buelito and Amagrande weren't prepared to face the degree of prejudice that existed in south Texas. Amagrande admitted that she had been mistreated, before, in Mexico, but stressed that it had more to do with being poor than simply being Mexican. Buelito, on the other hand, had been born into a well-to-do ranching family. His family's prosperity had given him a leg up in Mexican society. Yet in south Texas, they were both unwelcome Mexicans, and Buelito said it turned out to be a far worse place than he had imagined. On many occasions Buelito thought of returning to Mexico, but he no longer had a place to go home to, he lost ties with his family when he took up with the household maid. Furthermore, Buelito couldn't see a future for himself in the new interim government of Adolfo de la Huerta—not one of his favorite people in Mexico.

Buelito and Amagrande initially settled in Austin, a small college town in central Texas. Buelito met up with some of his fellow Mexican revolutionaries, who warned him about the Texas Rangers, upon his arrival there.

Buelito and Amagrande soon discovered that the Texas Rangers weren't the only ones beating and mistreating people of Mexican descent. Buelito told me about one incident after another where he and his family were turned away from eateries and movie houses by *los Bolillos*. In one incident Buelito recalled an event he said had caused him more pain than the bullet that struck his right leg. That was when he took Amagrande and their six children, aged two to fifteen, to a restaurant in Lubbock, which in the 1920s was nothing more than a small farming town in west Texas. Buelito said he was the first to walk into the restaurant, and no sooner had he walked in than a tall Anglo man marched up and waved his hands in Buelito's face.

"Fuera de aquí mojados!"

Buelito said the tall Anglo man's pale, white face turned a deep red color while he forcefully shoved Buelito out of the restaurant.

"Lo quería matar al gringo miserable," Buelito angrily recalled.

Buelito hated walking away from *el gringo miserable*. He hadn't been afraid to fight against President Díaz and his army in Mexico, but in Texas, he found himself helpless and heavily outnumbered in a part of the country that didn't much care for Mexicans. He admitted that he was afraid to fight back, for fear he and his family would be arrested by the Texas Rangers, or perhaps even deported by *la migra*. Buelito said he often thought of the phrase *"Prefiero morir de pie que vivir de rodillas,"* made famous by fellow revolutionary, Emiliano Zapata, to inspire him to fight back against *los Bolillos*.

Yet, ultimately Buelito allowed the Anglos of south Texas to define him; he didn't learn to speak English, didn't try to blend in with American society, and didn't become an American citizen. He chose to exist in the past, telling stories about his Spanish ancestry and Mexican life until the day he died. It was disappointing for me, to say the least, that my grandparents chose to accept discrimination from the Anglos in their daily lives, rather than to fight against the over the top racism of south Texas. In their own way, they tried to instill this acquiescence in their children and grandchildren.

Chapter 3

Mi Familia

*"You Don't Choose your Family. They are God's Gift to
you, as you are to them."*
The Most Reverend Desmond Tutu, 1931-
Archbishop Emeritus of Cape Town

For my seventh birthday, Amá gave me a kaleidoscope. The varying colors and changing designs fascinated me. The more I twisted the scope, the more the sets of colors changed and so did the patterns. The continually shifting combinations of color, shape, and size reminded me of Amá's family. The family that raised and influenced me came in varying skin colors and shapes. Just because we were all of Mexican ancestry didn't mean we were of the same color of skin, the same facial structure, or the same physical figure. We come in tall, average, and pint-size. Some of us have short arms, skinny chicken legs, and wide derrières; some have round, square, or heart-shaped faces. Our pigmentation ranges from light to deep olive coloring, a reminder of our *Mestizo* background. Those of us with darker coloring often heard snickers that there must have been *un Negrito* in our past. There are as many failures as there are successes in my family which consists of; revolutionaries, public servants, school dropouts, farm laborers, short order cooks, domestic help, drug addicts, circus performers, wife beaters, cotton pickers, schoolteachers, exotic dancers, prison guards, and prison inmates.

Yesirreee! God picks the womb from which we come crying. Our only choice is to respect God's decision and make the best of the situation. Of course in the beginning, none of us knows any of this. But who in his or her right mind would dare get into the ring with God and try to fight against him anyway? Only those that don't believe in God that's who. That's not me. I am a true believer that God almighty exists. I understand that Jesus Christ died for our sins and accept that he is the son of God. The scripture clearly points out that we are our brothers' keepers and that we should honor our fathers and our mothers. So like them or not, I had to embrace all of my family members on my mother's side; my father's family was not in the picture.

Our family believed that friendship, like charity, should start at home. Rarely did family members venture out and bring outsiders into the family circle. Only through marriage did this circle widen. Family outsiders were considered interlopers who couldn't be trusted. "Don't bring outsiders into this house and, don't ever say anything to anybody about our family!" Amá constantly ordered.

I was so much on edge all the time about Amá's preoccupation with privacy. Although, every once in a while I'd sneak in a friend or two to play the card game Crazy Eights. The loser had to drink a glass of pickle juice. But that turned out to be more treat than punishment, since my friends and I loved drinking pickle juice. My family circle started and ended with my maternal grandparents, whom I called Amagrande and Buelito. Amagrande made the family circle go, and it was she who kept the circle tight as a noose, so no one could enter it other than her immediate family.

During his story telling evenings, Buelito talked not only about his revolutionary days but also about the Spanish side of our family's ancestry. He said that in Spain, los San Miguels were *muy importante*, knighted many times by Spanish royalty in the medieval period for their bravery and courage. Buelito's milky white skin, sharp nose, and light brown hair revealed the place of his ancestral lineage: Spain, specifically Catalonia. Every now and then he'd pump his fist up in the air and declare, "*Yo soy Catalán!*"

He boasted that his Spanish ancestors were responsible for the death of Satan, because San Miguel was derived from Michael, the archangel warrior and conqueror of Satan. Buelito devoted much of his life to studying, fantasizing and telling stories far back into his Spanish ancestry—even though it was Mexico where he was born and raised.

While Buelito's family history painted a portrait of bravery and sophistication, Amagrande's background was more fundamental. The two of them began a lustful relationship a year before the Mexican Revolution began in 1910, when Amagrande worked as a maid in the home of Buelito's parents. Buelito was a recent widower, whose wife died while giving birth to their only son, Jesús; Amagrande was a single mother of two children with different fathers, neither of whom married her. Her eldest child Manuel was five who had been fathered by Amagrande's physician. Her second child, Elvira, was two years old and we didn't know much about her father other than he was married *con una infeliz* according to Amagrande.

Amagrande spent all of her young life cleaning up after the wealthy families of Cuatro Ciénegas, where she was born in 1885, and the tales of these times in her life were disturbing to hear. She was sent out doors to eat her meals, made to scrub wooden floors on her knees, and slapped and shoved when her cleaning didn't meet the standards set by the mistress of the household. But after serving up so many of these tragic stories, she'd lighten up and laughingly boast that she got even with her cruel employers by spitting into the food she prepared for them.

Amagrande said that Buelito's family treated her nicer than any other family. While at the same time revealing the hurt she felt when the San Miguels fired her when they learned she was pregnant with Buelito's child (my Amá). Subsequently, the San Miguels disowned Buelito, asking that he leave their home and take his *India* with him. From there, they went on to stay with Amagrande's mother, Nicolasa, until they moved to America in 1920. Nicolasa had the rough edge of an old goat not to mention her personal relationships that stretched a mile long, evidenced by the many children she had with different men. Amagrande liked to brag, that unlike her mother, she hadn't bedded down with just anyone. *"Yo no me ocupo en cualquiera, el padre de mi hijo Manuel, es un doctor de medicina!"* she'd say proudly.

Often times, Amagrande mentioned that I didn't look like the rest of my family adding that I favored the Flores family that lived in a white house around the corner from our house. One day when I was about eight years old she told me out of the blue, *"Si tienes papá pero no se casó con tu Amá y no te quiere,"* Amagrande declared.

I learned many things that day but mostly I learned that Adan Flores, one of the Floreses' youngest sons was my father. Amá met Adán Flores through her younger brother Víctor around 1945, and they had little, if anything at all, in common. Amá was a twice-divorced, Mexican-born mother of four children aged four to eleven; Adán was American-born, single, and living with his parents. Their relationship, like that of my grandparents, was based on lust more than love. Adán was born on May 25, 1925 in Portland, Texas, a small seaside village which sat between the port city of Corpus Christi and the rich, flat lands that stretched all the way to San Antonio with Highway 181 connecting the two.

Except for a few added small shops, Portland was the same in the late 1950s when Amá began taking me to shop in Corpus. Yet, it was in Portland that my dreams to another world began to form. It was from Portland that the lights of the town illuminated for me another way—a road leading to another type of life outside of Taft. Every time we drove through Portland at night and toward Corpus, I became fascinated with the dancing harbor lights along the Corpus Christi Bay. I wondered how far the harbor lights stretched and what was at the other end of the bay. Meanwhile, the stars above the wide Texas sky sparkled like diamonds and twinkled, as if teasing me to reach up and grab them. When Amá and I saw a shooting star, we called out, "Falling!" and Amá excitedly ordered me to make a wish. I'd close my eyes tightly and hurry to make my wish before the falling star disappeared into the gulf. Amá warned that it was bad luck to reveal my wish to anyone. Each time, my wish remained the same, to find a way out of Taft in search of some enchanting, far-away place.

Adán was one of eleven children born to Don Félix J. Flores and Doña Aurelia Treviño Flores, who came from a long line of farm laborers. In the late 1920s, the prospect of a large, lucrative cotton crop in Taft stole the Floreses from Portland. They bought a small piece of land from the same CF-Pasture Company that Buelito purchased his. Their three-room, white wood-framed house sat at the busy corner of Davis Road and Algodon Street. The house was surrounded by clusters of bright, red bougainvilleas. The spacious front lawn was dominated by long, heavily paneled trucks, which were owned by Adán's four older brothers. They worked as farm contractors, ferrying farm laborers from Taft to west Texas and beyond. The white house looked enormous to me each day as I passed it on my way home from school. I marveled at the constant flow of human traffic in the grand, Flores home.

In the early fall of 1945, Amá took her four children and went with the Floreses to pick fruits and vegetables in Big Spring, Texas. Somewhere in the flat agricultural land of Big Spring I was conceived.

I was relieved to learn that some person out there was my father and he was alive despite Amá having told me when I was seven years old that my father was dead. It happened when I came home from school one day and told her that my first grade teacher wanted to know information about my father; his name, when he was born . . . . Amá screamed,

"*Tu papa esta muerto!*"

"*Que le importa a tu maestra si estay tu papa muerto or vivo?*" she continued angrily.

"*La escuela necesita la información de todos los estudiantes,*" I timidly answered.

"*Nomas dile que tu papá esta muerto y se acabó,*" she replied annoyed.

The next day in class before I had a chance to sit down, Mrs. Huber called me over to her desk. She again asked about my father. I responded in a whisper that he was dead. But she wouldn't let it go, wanting to know when and where he died. Students began to pour into the classroom, and I quickly grew more embarrassed at my teacher's questions as my classmates all stood by their desks to listen in on our conversation. The light gray moustache above Mrs. Huber's red lips stood on edge as she continued to interrogate me in front of the class while I stood frozen beside her desk, staring at the floor, speechless—my tongue lying dead in my dry mouth. Exasperated, she dismissed me to my seat, where I made my way, briskly and still staring at the floor. I took my seat with a fleeting sense of relief, hoping at once that Mrs. Huber's inquiries about my father's death were finished, but just as I began to get comfortable, she waved a small card above her head.

"Graciela, don't forget to ask your mother when your father died, and when and where he was born," Mrs. Huber bellowed from the front of the classroom.

I thought all day about how to ask Amá these questions, but all that my mind could register were images of Amá's terrible temper: Both of her nostrils and even the tiny, dark mole at the tip of her nose seemed to grow three sizes larger when she was angry. Amá didn't believe in spanking, but her dark brown eyes could turn a colder glare than an angry lioness, and that, along with her razor sharp tongue, was sufficient disciplinary weaponry in her book. I waited until she was in a good mood and then jumped at the chance to get an answer out of her.

"Amá, mi maestra quiere más información de mi papa," I said cautiously.

"Dile a tu maestra que no pregunte más," Amá retorted unamused.

"Pero ella quiere la información," I insisted.

"A mi no me importa que quiera esa vieja," Amá hollered.

The next day I put the onus on my teacher; if she wanted to know more about my father, she was going to have to go to Amá herself and find out. Mrs. Huber never called Amá, and my school records continued to reflect that my father was dead. But despite Amá's repeated insistence that he was, I wasn't convinced.

I'd often seen a handsome, slender, swarthy man, whom I came to know as *"El Prieto,"* staring at me from behind the screened door at the entrance to the Floreses' home. I sensed his dark, mysterious eyes following me along Davis Road, and often he stepped out of the front door as I turned to disappear down West Pecan Street. Convinced by Amá's tales of my father's death, I hurried along, not sure what to think, until Amagrande unraveled the mystery.

I learned from Amagrande that a few weeks before I was born, Amá went to the Floreses' home to ask Adán for financial help, but instead was met by Adán's six sisters and their mother, Doña Aurelia. Doña Aurelia stood at the door and refused to let Amá inside, rounding up her daughters to cooperatively push Amá down the porch steps. Amá clung to one of the pillars along the stairs to keep from tumbling to the ground, cradling her bulging belly all the while, to guard against the threat of impact.

"Cuando nace tu bebito, que le testen la sangre, para saber si Adán es su padre,"

Doña Aurelia screamed.

Amá filed a paternity suit against Adán Flores after I was born, but Adán refused to acknowledge that I was his child at the hearing in the Sinton County Courthouse saying, *"Esa niña puede ser de cualquier fulano de tál."* The judge ordered Amá to pay for the blood test and return with the results.

I was about one year old when Amá learned that Adán had married a young girl from the coastal bend area. After that, Amá stopped trying to get my blood tested, continuing work at the old Green Hotel to help to support me and her other four children.

As Amagrande talked on, it occurred to me that being the illegitimate daughter of Adán Flores—*una bastarda,* as my brother Enrique taunted—was easier news to take than being adopted, which Enrique also liked to tease me about. For too long, he had me convinced my real mother was a big fat *Negra* because my skin was so dark. I tried to find my "real" mother among the strange women we saw whenever we drove through *el barrio de los Negros* and through the line at the Leland Theatre leading to the door "For Colored People Only." When we were at the theatre, I would turn to look from my first floor seat up at the Mezzanine to try and find the one *Negra* that resembled me, but all I could see were white eyeballs dancing against the darkened figures crowded into the balcony area.

I felt good to know that Amá truly was the woman I knew as my Amá, and it even felt good to know I had a father, even if he didn't want me.

A short time after the revelation of my illegitimacy, I found myself being trailed down Davis Road by a wine-colored car while I walked home alone. The man frowned as he brushed his thin, dark mustache back and forth above his thick lips. His slick, black pompadour was as neatly combed and shiny as my brother Enrique's and I wondered if they both used the same hair jar, with the red roses on it. When I realized the dark man with the thick mustache was following me, I began running and nearly lost my balance trying to race the stranger to my house. As I ran inside, I looked back only to see the car come to a stop in front of our house.

"*Amá ahi viene un señor muy prieto persiguiéndome!*" I announced excitedly. Amá stood in the living room, staring out the window, and we watched together anxiously as the dark man slowly made his way up to our front porch.

"*Ese hombre es tu papa,*" Amá said.

"*No esa ti a quien busca, es a mi!*" she said proudly.

"*Quedate aqui, ahorita vuelvo,*" she whispered.

Amá stepped out to the front porch to speak with the man. They spoke so loudly I could hear every word they said.

"*Lo único que quiero es ver a la niña,*" the man pleaded.

"*No le testado la sangre, así es que no sé si la niña es tuya o no,*" Amá shot back.

"*Como que no es mi hija? Se parece igual a mí y a mi familia!*" he tried to reason.

"*A mi no me importa a quien se parece; vete de aqui, y no vuelvas jamás,*" Amá ordered.

My heart began racing rapidly when I realized that the man in front of me, a mere stranger, was actually my father—the same man I saw so often standing at the door to the white house on the corner. I was afraid to know him, and Amá forcefully cautioned against my ever speaking to him.

"*Ese hombre tiene su esposa y dos hijos; él no tiene ningun uso para tí,*" she proclaimed.

A small part of me still wished to see the man in the wine-colored car again after that, even despite Amá's warnings, but I would not see him again until 1972.

We were ordinary people, yet our family's archive was filled with one scandal after another. It seemed there was some kind of dirt on just about everyone in the family, including me—after all I was illegitimate. Like many other families on the South Side, we all kept pretty close, rarely letting outsiders into the family circle, but unlike most, we did not all gather at our grandmother's each Sunday for a big meal and gossip session. Our Amagrande was a large, strong-willed Indian woman who did not suffer fools lightly. It was she who ruled the roost, making a doormat even of her husband, a survivor of the Mexican Revolution. She verbally abused him almost daily, calling him *sordo* so frequently that it seemed as if that was his given name. There was only one instance anyone could recall when Buelito stood up to Amagrande, firing a few rounds from his old pistol into the air to quiet her. Everyone scattered, including Amagrande. But once the commotion died down and the gun was put away, Amagrande's verbal abuse toward her husband continued until the day he died.

The only times we gathered in my grandparents' house were when out of town relatives visited. On such occasions the house was so packed with kin folks that we younger ones were sent outdoors to play to make room inside for the adults. The kitchen was too small for anyone to do anything except stand or take one of the four chairs around the rickety old wood table.

The men were fed first, followed by the women, then the teenagers, and finally the children—we were lucky to find any food left! Sometimes, when all the food was gone, Amagrande would dig out leftovers consisting of a strange, spicy, Mexican dish I didn't much care for.

There wasn't any socializing at the dining table because Amagrande said the dining table was a place for eating, and not for talking and laughing. After every meal, the women routinely helped clear the table and wash the dishes, while the men stepped outside to smoke cigarettes, pick their teeth, while belching away their dinner. Buelito didn't stick around with the men to make small talk; he preferred to sit on the porch surrounded by his grandchildren telling endless stories about his life in Mexico.

When I was five, I began sleeping in Amagrande's bed, where she revealed to me many of our family's darkest secrets.

"Te voy a decir algo pero prométeme que no le vas a decir a nadie," Amagrande whispered.

By the time I was nine years old, I knew the shape, size, and color of every skeleton in our family closet as well as the size and shape of the closet itself.

My grandparents' journey into America started on a bumpy road and it pretty much stayed that way. They initially settled in Austin. After about two years there, my grandparents moved their family to the town of Floresville, where they lived for almost seventeen years, picking and planting fruits and vegetables on the ranch of Mariano Flores (no kin to me, or to Don Francisco Flores de Abrego of Canary Island descendants, for whom Floresville was named).

They thought America was going to give them an opportunity to have the life and work they couldn't get in Mexico. The United States of America was going to be their "Heaven on Earth.' Once they arrived in America they dropped any illusions about the kind of work they'd do. They were unskilled workers who capitalized on their energy and their physical strength to earn enough money to stay in their new surroundings.

The summer after Amá completed third grade, she began working alongside Amagrande and Buelito in the fields, joining her older half siblings, Manuel, Jesús and Elvira—Adelina and Víctor were too young to work. Amagrande told Amá not to expect to be returning to school in September—she would continue her education among the agricultural fields of Floresville. Amá told me that she had liked school, but would not miss *las Polacas y Alemanas*. They routinely pointed and giggled at the one tattered cotton dress and same old pair of worn out lace-up shoes Amá wore day in and day out. Amá said she felt dirty and different from her classmates, with the only curly black mop against a roomful of neat yellow braids.

Amá continued to work alongside her parents on the Flores ranch until 1930, when she turned fifteen years old and married Pedro Treviño, a twenty one year old man she'd known less than six months. Years later, Amá admitted she was never in love with Pedro, but agreed to marry him at her mother's urging, "*Ya es tiempo que te cases; si no, te vas a quedar a vestir santos.*"

Buelito gave her away, out of pride more than anything else. Pedro's fair skin and hazel eyes were winning characteristics in Buelito's eyes—he saw dark-skinned people as *puros Indios* and didn't much care for them—even though he himself married Amagrande, a woman who was as Indian as they came.

Pedro and his family owned a small grocery store they turned into a *cantina* after the end of the American Prohibition in 1933. By 1935, the growing business at the *cantina* demanded that Pedro spend increasing amounts of time away from his family, leaving Amá to raise two toddlers practically alone while expecting a third. Their first child, Refugia, nicknamed Cukita died when she was six months old. Amá blamed herself for Cukita's death and never really released herself from the guilt. As Amá told the story it was an unusually cold night for south Texas. After she tucked six month old

Cukita into her crib, Amá worried that her light blanket would not be warm enough. In the middle of the night, Amá and Pedro woke to Cukita's loud crying. As Amá started to slowly inch away the warm bedcovers, and rise up out of their metal-framed bed, Pedro held her back onto the bed.

"No le hagas caso, es chiflada," he coaxed.

"Déjame ir a ver por qué llora la nina, puede ser que tenga frio," Amá pleaded.

"Ya te dije que no le vas hacer caso a esa chiflada." Pedro ordered.

Pedro put all of his weight on top of Amá and held her down. Amá struggled in their bed, trying to break free, while Cukita lay crying in her crib so intensely that Amá feared she might choke. As the night wore on, the baby's crying eventually subsided to silence. Already delighted at proving his strength by holding Amá in her place, Pedro gleefully said, *"Que te dije? Era chiflada, no necesitaba nada."*

When the sun came up and Amá was free of Pedro's force, she hurried out of bed toward the baby's crib. Cukita's eyes were closed, but when Amá picked up the baby, her body was stiff. Her body colder than the air Amá had breathed the night before while Cukita sobbed to death.

"Quería matar a Pedro," Amá recalled, holding back tears, when she told me the story.

"Pero fuí una cobarde," she said sadly.

Their marriage was tarnished irreparably thereafter, but knowing that divorce wasn't an option, Amá stayed with Pedro. Amagrande warned Amá when she got married that she had to make the marriage work because she didn't have a place in her home anymore. According to Amá, Pedro drank too much and was physically abusive from the first day they were married. Family rumors suggested that before her marriage Amá might have been violated by a relative, causing Pedro to feel *engañado* by Amá's suggestion of purity.

Amagrande told the story that in Cuatro Ciénegas, if a man found he was *engañado*; he'd return his new bride back to her parent's house and proceed to hang a rounded plate on the front of the house with a hole drilled through the center. Pedro didn't return Amá to her parent's house, but his abusive behavior during their short live marriage only served to fuel the flame of the family rumor. Still, her complaints of his ill treatment were all but ignored the first time she approached her mother.

"*Tu tienes que aguantar*," Amagrande ordered firmly.

Amá stayed with Pedro long enough after Cuckita's death to bear three more children. Their third child Jesusa was barely one year old when Amá decided to leave Pedro. She had no idea where she was going to live or how she was going to take care of her children. Her only hope was that Amagrande and Buelito would help. They were reluctant at first but when they learned the truth about Cuckita's death, Amagrande screamed, "*Este mismo momento vas a dejar á ese perro.*" Amagrande and Buelito helped Amá gather the children and whatever belongings they could before Pedro arrived home from work. Later that night Pedro came to my grandparent's house looking for Amá but Amagrande refused to allow him inside or to talk with Amá.

Amá and her three young daughters stayed with Amagrande and Buelito until the following year, when Buelito heard that a neighboring town had *mucho trabajo*. Ironically, the town Buelito chose to settle his family in had been founded by a kin of William Howard Taft, the United States president who grew tired of Pancho Villa's cross border raids and established a policy of hot pursuit.

My grandparents initially moved into a two-room cabin with four of their children (Elvira was married, and Manuel was in boarding school in Mexico), three grandchildren, and Amagrande's mother, Nicolasa in a building that had once housed laborers of the Taft Ranch.

Later on Buelito purchased for $100, less than one-tenth of an acre from the CF-Pasture Company, just a stone's throw over the town's city limits. Although there were plenty of pretty houses with good land on the South Side, with indoor plumbing and big, leafy trees for cool shade in the midst of wide-open flat land, Buelito preferred to buy a small lot where he could build his own house.

Living in tight quarters with Buelito and Amagrande were Nicolasa; Jesus, Buelito's son from his first marriage, Adelina, their unmarried teenage daughter; and Victor, ten years old; but their land was at least twice the size of the home they were crammed into, so

Amá built a two-room addition on the other half of the lot for herself and her three young girls.

Of my three half sisters, the eldest, Delfina could be the hardest to know and at times could be abusive. She was short and overweight, and had a burning temper just like Amá's. I hated when she'd drag me off to Rodriguez's Beauty Salon, which was located in a separate room off of the Rodriguez home, whenever she felt my hair needed to be curlier than it already was. I'd sit for hours under a large wheel that looked like a space ship, while the beautician used long, black cords with clips at the ends to curl my hair so tightly that it stuck to my scalp in tiny springs. Thankfully these vain expeditions didn't last long. Delfina got engaged at seventeen years old and got too preoccupied to worry about my hair. But Delfina didn't get married then. One week before the wedding, her fiancé came with his parents to finalize the wedding plans and during the conversation as was customarily done, he asked my sister if she was a virgin. My sister lowered her head rather than answer and at that that point her fiancé and his parents stood up and announced there would be no wedding, storming out of our house as if it was on fire. Afterward, Delfina's love life took one bad turn after another.

Delfina was married in 1955 at the age of twenty-two to a man twenty-one years her senior, a widower with three children. Since he was much older than almost anyone in our immediate family except my grandparents we called him by his senior title, *Don*. Don Ramon's youngest daughter was being raised by an aunt and uncle, but his two other children, a girl in her early teens and a preteen boy, came to live with their father and his new wife in their three-room rented house. Delfina resented her step children the start. She exaggerated their misbehavior to her husband, often prompting him to, in particularly, beat the boy with a wide leather belt. After they'd been married a couple of years, Delfina warned me in the presence of her husband and stepchildren not to ever marry a man with children.

Don Ramón could be easygoing. He taught me history lessons about Mexico, but I mostly enjoyed playing Mexican bingo with him and his son. On many a Friday night, we'd gather in their tiny kitchen, where we sat on metal flour canisters around an old wooden bench they used as a dining table.

"*Ahi viene el catrín, Chelita,*" Don Ramón happily announced as he threw out a bingo card depicting a slim, mustachio man dressed in formal wear. I placed a dried pinto bean on the bingo square that matched the card, but I rarely won.

My middle sister, María, cared for me from the day I was born. She carried me in her arms throughout the neighborhood as if I were her very own, and I even took to calling her Mammy, thinking she was my real mother until my brother Enrique told me I was adopted from *una Negra*. Amá said Maria saved my life one day, by lifting a black spider out of my open mouth as I napped.

When I was five years old, María married a man she had met through mutual friends only one month earlier. We knew him as "*Maracas,*" a strikingly handsome man from Mexico. I was standing between María and Maracas *en el puentecito* that spanned over the ditch in front of our house when *Maracas* asked, "*Te vas con migo, María?*"

"*Si,*" María answered promptly. I wept for days after María left. She was my sister and my mother all wrapped into one. After María left Amá sent me to live with Amagrande and Buelito, but I ended up staying much longer than I expected sharing Amagrande's bed until I turned twelve.

Shortly after they were married *Maracas* began seeing other women, and he became nortoriously unfaithful. Regardless, María refused to leave him, until the police did the job for her. *Maracas* was rumored to be selling marijuana, but when the police raided his home, they only found two marijuana joints in the pocket of a coat he wasn't even wearing. Nonetheless, he was sent to prison for two years, but after one year he was deported back to Mexico for good behavior. Interestingly, the day Maracas was sentenced I was shocked to see Amá and María weeping as if there had been a death in the family. I asked Amá why she was crying when Maracas had brought more pain and suffering than pride to our family. "Cáyate el hocico, she screamed.

After his arrest, while pending sentencing, my family discovered that *Maracas* had told one lie after another. The official name he used was actually taken from the American dead brother of his best friend. He had us convinced that his family members were dead but of course that was not true. We learned he had a large family in southern Mexico that included a father, a stepmother, scores of half siblings, and a very close aunt and uncle that had been searching for him for years. Needless to say, his official birth name in Mexico was very different from the one he used in America. So, legally speaking, María was married to a man who had sometime in the past gone to the great beyond. There weren't any survivors' benefits to collect, nor was there much of anything else to claim on her dead husband's behalf. It's as if she had been single all along.

After *Maracas* got out of prison María made several trips to Mexico to visit the so-called "husband." But after awhile it became clear that their relationship wasn't going to work while they lived hundreds of miles apart. *Maracas* didn't waste any time in remarrying. He was after all a single man in Mexico. This time he married under his birth name to a Mexican woman with whom he had four more children. María never remarried; subsisting on government assistance for the remainder of her life.

The youngest of my three older half-sisters, Jesusa was nine years older than me, and spent most of her teenage years at Don Pancho's dance hall. Don Pancho's was **the** social gathering for all of us on the South side. Every Saturday night rain or shine the girls sat on small makeshift wooden benches next to their mothers or fathers or both, while the boys stood at the entrance waiting for the music to begin so they could ask the girls to dance. Since our Amá chose not to escort Jesusa to Don Pancho's like all the other parents, I ended up with the task. Jesusa's bubbly personality made her one of the more sought-after dance partners, and she would squeal with excitement at the number of boys who had asked her to dance by the end of each Saturday night. There was no way I could compete with the excitement of the dance hall and the ever-growing list of cute boys in Jesusa's life, and so she never paid me much attention.

Jesusa loved Don Pancho's dance hall so much that she chose to elope from there with her boyfriend Nacho one, cold winter night in 1956. My sister's best friend Delia woke me while I slept on one of the benches at Don Pancho's to tell me the news. Delia led me out of the dance hall into the dark empty street while I sobbed trying to figure out why Jesusa had left and didn't bother to tell me anything. When we arrived at my house, I told Amá what happened but all she could say was, "*Que tiene esa pendeja, irse con ese arrastrado!*"

Nacho was one of nine children, and known more for starting fist fights at Don Pancho's than holding down a job. But a few years later Nacho surprised Amá and everyone else in town when he picked himself up, as they say, by his bootstraps, at least long enough to be elected the first Mexican-American constable in San Patricio County. His election in 1968 raised tensions between Mexican-Americans and Anglos in Taft to such a level that Dr. Hector P. García, a nearby civil rights activist and medical doctor, was asked by Nacho to come to Taft and help quiet things down. But after one more reelection, Nacho gave up law enforcement politics. As time went by, alcohol ended his marriage to my sister and contributed to his early death.

My brother Enrique enjoyed being the baby of our family until I came along on June 11, 1946, but even before then, he wasn't always the spoiled brat I knew him to be. From the time Enrique was two years old until he was five, his father, Candido was severely ill with tuberculosis. During those years, Candido wasn't in any condition to take care of Enrique while Amá went to work. His way of taking care of his son was by tying him to the bars of the metal bed he shared with Amá. When Enrique soiled his diapers Candido whipped him but kept him tied to the bed until Amá returned from work and released him. Sometime after Enrique's fifth birthday, Candido, whom Amá married after she became pregnant a few months after having met him, went away somewhere to die, but no one in my family remembers where.

The effects of Enrique's abusive early childhood revealed themselves vividly as he got older; he was angry most of the time, and liked to take his anger out on me. Why he chose me is anybody's guess. Perhaps because I was much smaller than anyone else, or perhaps it had to do with my having taken his place as the baby of the family. Whatever the reason, his verbal and physical abuse against me was constant and willfully deliberate. He tried to seriously hurt me more times than I care to remember. Once, when I was six and he was twelve, he jumped me from behind, threw me onto Amá's bed, placed a pillow over my head, and sat his body on top. The more I struggled and gasped for air, the harder he pushed down on me with his body weight. I could hear muffled cackles and laughter from him and Gaspar as I fought to get free. I began to suffocate under the hot, bulging pillow. So I pretended to pass out; holding my breath and remaining still; only then did he release me.

"Ya bastarda, ya te puedes ir," Enrique said laughingly.

He bullied my three sisters too, and though they were much older than he, they were just as terrified of him as I was. Whenever he spotted one of them talking to a male friend, he'd break up the conversation and order my sister to go home. Enrique had no problem exercising the freedom given by Amá's constant declarations: *"El es el hombre de la casa, el puede hacer lo que el quiera, y valemas que hagan lo que el dice."* Enrique used his *machismo* power to abuse my sisters and me yet, all we ever wanted was a brother to love and to protect us.

On the rare occasion that Enrique felt like being civil, we might stay up all night listening to a country western station, singing along to our favorite song, *Jambalaya*, by Hank Williams. Our off-key shrieks could be heard throughout the neighborhood when we got to our favorite part: *Sonofagun, we'll have big fun on the bayou.*

During the summer, Enrique and I would take showers outdoors with a rubber hose, and at night we slept outdoors, studying the Milky Way and the other twinkling stars above the wide, open Texas sky. Every Saturday, we went to the Leland Theatre, just the two of us, to watch western movies and eat crispy fried chicken that Amá cooked in the kitchen of the Johnsons' café.

We even took to dressing up like the cowboys in the western movies. I talked Amá into buying me a Rex Allen cowboy shirt and a pair of Gene Autry mid-calf brown leather boots so that we could dress up like the cowboys in the films. Enrique looked like Roy Rogers in his sharp, pointy-toed cowboy boots and neckerchief. Of all of the movie heroes we saw, my favorite was Lash La Rue: His all-black wardrobe and slick whip-lashing technique made him look tougher than the other cowboys. Enrique kicked my legs and pulled my hair all the way home from the theater when he heard me say I liked Lash La Rue better than his favorite, Rex Allen, and when we got home he banged his fists on my head to clear it of Lash La Rue.

Enrique was my hero even though he beat me up and called me names. I even took to imitating the way he and Gaspar urinated by the side of road, though I ended up with a warm river of liquid down my legs. Enrique and Gaspar filled up Seven-Up bottles with their urine and passed them out to their friends as treats on hot summer days. But I didn't tell on them. Instead, I watched along with Enrique and Gaspar as the gleeful victim's face quickly turned sour after the first gulp. I trailed behind Enrique and Gaspar, up and down West Pecan Street, while they cackled at their own antics.

More than anything, I loved climbing trees with Enrique, Gaspar, and Gaspar's sister, La Quatita. We would imitate Tarzan's jungle yells while hanging from tree limbs. Once, I ate more berries from a mulberry tree than my brother, Gaspar, and La Quatita combined. By the end of the day, my hands, lips, and tongue had turned a deep purple color and I would have to spend most of the night in *el escusado*. Whenever Amagrande saw me climbing trees, she'd yell for me to get down. "*Eres una cabra; bájate de ese árbol! Se te mira todo el mundo!*"

She said I should sew dolls' clothing, like my cousin Miné, but playing with dolls, let alone making clothes for them to wear, could not have been further from my mind. My ideas of fun were shooting BB guns and riding bicycles. The only doll I ever had, I got for Christmas at six years old, and it barely survived the holiday season. Before our Christmas tree came down, most of the doll's yellow hair was missing, and what was left looked brittle and tangled. One of her limbs was torn off, her dress was in shreds, and her shoes were discarded, as I didn't see any reason why a doll should wear shoes. When Amá saw the doll's awful condition she scolded me, reminding me she had driven all the way to Corpus to buy me my doll and swore she'd never buy me another doll and she didn't.

Another year, Enrique and I both received Red Ryder BB guns for Christmas. We'd take shots at anything airborne and moving—we mostly ended up killing tiny innocent birds that didn't bother anybody.

Enrique made real good grades and at the same time, he excelled in sports. But at sixteen he eloped with his girlfriend, María, who was three years older. I was against the marriage from the start but Amá explained to me that if she didn't allow Enrique to get married, María's life would be ruined forever. She said the same thing could happen to me. "*Sería un escándalo si tu te vas con un muchacho y despues no se casa con tigo!*" Amá said.

"I don't care, you can't let him get married," I said harshly.

"*Que va decir la gente si Enrique no se casa con María?*" Amá argued helplessly.

"Who cares what people say, it's his education and future that counts," I countered.

"*Que educación, ni que educación. El tiene que mantener a su esposa, y si no quiere ir a la escuela, ese es su negocio.*" Amá angrily declared.

On the South Side, there were many couples forced into early teen marriage by parents that didn't want to take their daughters back after they'd spent a night with their boyfriends, whether there was intimacy or not. They were seen as *mujers usadas* whose actions brought shame to the family.

Amá said I sounded wiser than my eleven years. I persuaded her to talk with Enrique about getting married so young and dropping out of school, but he refused to sit down long enough to listen to Amá's advice. His sole argument was that he was going to end up bagging groceries at the Piggly Wiggly regardless of whether he had a high school diploma. A few months after my brother married María, the high school coach came to our house, looking for Enrique. He offered him a position on the high school varsity football team and promised that if Enrique did well, the coach would help him get a college scholarship. That was the type of offer and support I had heard only Anglos got, yet Enrique refused the coach's offer.

Enrique became a father by the age of eighteen, and before he turned thirty five he and María were the parents of four children. For the most part Enrique and Maria chose to live one day at a time. They, like other members of my family, used God as an excuse not to take responsibility. "*Lo que Dios quiera eso haremos!*" These were words spoken too often in my family about things that they could and should have tried to change. Unfortunately, my brother's life was not atypical. His way of life thrives on the South Side.

I curiously but sadly watched the mistakes of my three half sisters and half brother. It was like watching an airplane fall from the sky and being unable to prevent the crash. Those mistakes were among the ones that I had to avoid if I was going to break into the culture of advancement within America, and I knew it wasn't going to be easy.

Chapter 4

Separate Tables

*"I have a dream that one day this nation will rise up
and live out the true meaning of its creed: We hold
these truths to be self-evident, that all men
are created equal."*
Rev. Dr. Martin Luther King, Jr., 1929-1968
American Baptist Minister

In 1908, the Green Hotel was built about eight miles due west of Taft, primarily to accommodate the officials accompanying President William H. Taft the following year, upon his visit to the Taft Ranch. The hotel looked more like a Southerner's plantation than a commercial building, with its dormer windows and tall, white columns. The Green Hotel quickly became famous throughout Texas for its exceptional food—due, mostly, to Mr. Joseph F. Green, Superintendent of the Taft Ranch. Mr. Green and his wife had been so impressed in their travels to Europe by the quality of the food and service that they returned to Texas having recruited several noteworthy chefs and attendants to come and work in the Green Hotel. But once the Sinton and Taft families began to sell off the Taft Ranch, the hotel business saw a slow decline.

In 1922, the hotel was relocated to Taft, and 17 years later Amá went there to work only to be told that Mexicans and Colored people weren't admitted to dine in the hotel restaurant, and that she ought not to get any ideas about bringing her family in. Amá, like most people on the South Side, had grown accustomed to the prejudice shown to the Mexicans in Texas. Yet, somehow she thought Taft was going to be different. But she found out soon enough that life in Taft was just as harsh if not worse than what she had previously experienced. Mexicans and Anglos didn't socialize nor did they live together. She told me the story of Army Sergeant Mike Morales, a highly decorated soldier in World War II who couldn't buy a house on the North Side in 1949 because the developers wouldn't sell to a Mexican-American. Sergeant Morales left Taft, and reenlisted in the Army where he went on to earn more medals as a soldier in the Korean and Viet Nam Wars. But no matter how many medals Sgt. Morales earned defending his country, he wasn't allowed to live on the North Side of town.

Raising three children and expecting another, Amá knew that the Green Hotel was as good as it was going to get for her.

I often wondered why residents of the South Side, including my own family members, never stood up against their oppressors. Amá explained that she and many others on the South Side worked as maids and farmhands to the wealthy landowners who ran the town, and they needed to keep their employers happy if they wanted to feed their families; troublemakers would be fired on the spot and immediately replaced by the next in a long line of eager-to-work Mexican-Americans.

In the early 1950's the Green Hotel was shut down, and was sold off in parts to the residents of Taft. Tío Mike and Tía Lina bought a small section which included a big, enchanting front porch and four large rooms. Trucks with huge cranes moved their piece of the property to the South Side, located across from the Catholic Church. I couldn't wait for Amá to take me inside Tío Mike's big house. Seeing it from a seven year old eye, the house seemed much bigger than it actually was but it was certainly bigger than most on the South Side, its rich history evident in the shiny, wooden floors and especially high, wide windows. The regal, white columns on the grand porch led to a spacious and airy living room and in the kitchen—the roomiest I'd ever been in—Tía Lina watched the busy street through the large window above the sink while she washed dishes.

For a while, some of our family would gather every Saturday night at my aunt and uncle's house. Tío Mike talked about the beautiful city of Paris he visited as a soldier during *la Guerra Mundial*. He sipped one beer after another while spilling stories about faraway places that only served to captivate my imagination about where I might one day travel. I mostly passed the time playing with my cousins, Miné and Angelina, the only ones I knew on the South Side who played with Tinker Toys. The instructions told us we could build just about anything with the small, wood pieces, but try as I might, I never did manage to construct a single darned item.

On our way home one evening, Amá told me never to tell Amagrande about our visits, to Tio Mike's and Tia Lina's. She was afraid her mother would be angry. Amagrande didn't approve of family gatherings without her being the center piece. Her habit of spreading hate and dissention among her daughters and grandchildren was well known and her insults toward family members were even more habitual. Once, one of our relatives brought her newborn child to meet Amagrande, and, in typical fashion, she took one look at the baby and said, sarcastically, "V*álgame, Dios! Ese niño parece que le dió una aguantada a Cristo*!" But that was Amagrande; always using words that hurt more than helped. She badmouthed one daughter to another; drawing a wedge among them which served to raise tension among all members of the family. Her behavior left little room for any kind of love or trust to develop among us.

After the Green Hotel was shut down, Amá went to work as a dishwasher at the Johnson's' Café in 1951. The Johnsons had moved to Taft with their three children from Corpus in the late 1940's and opened up their café in 1947, which picked up the hungry clientele left over after the decline of the Green Hotel. As business took off, Mr. Johnson taught Amá to cook and bake, and soon, she had taken on duties as the morning shift, short order cook, and baker. The café's menu varied from day to day, and Amá quickly became famous throughout the area for her skillful and delicious dishes. On Sundays, her roast turkey with cornbread dressing drew just about every Taft resident to the café, and her meatloaf with gravy, whipped potatoes, okra with stewed tomatoes, stuffed bell peppers and short ribs, in their delectable sauce, made it onto the menu daily. Some customers traveled 18 miles—all the way from Corpus—for Amá's fluffy biscuits and giant size, glazed donuts.

During the day, the café was constantly bustling with farmers, ranchers, and business owners. In the evenings, many of those same men brought their families to the café for dinner. The first time I stopped at the café on my way to school was in 1952. Amá led me to a dingy room at the back of the restaurant, stocked with heavy sacks of flour, giant cans of fruits and vegetables, and restaurant equipment. While there was no sign at the café reading "For Coloreds Only," local Blacks knew that if they wanted to get served, this back room was where they'd have to go. That first day, I took my seat at a small, rectangular table, where a group of Black men sat sipping coffee and eating doughnuts, and not a one of us said so much as a word. But, the next day, each of the men introduced himself.

"Good morning, young lady," one of them said cheerfully.

"You sure are a mighty pretty little girl," another piped up.

Too shy to look them in the eye, I stared down at my doughnut instead, but after a few morning visits; I began addressing the men by their first names. Donnie, Mack, Buddy and Willie were some of the café's regulars, with whom I'd have to wait while Amá used her food-stained apron to clear off the table she used to make the biscuit and pastry dough. Like me, the men were eager, to dig into the tasty glazed doughnuts, and none of those in our back-room breakfast party seemed to mind the poor conditions around us.

Most of the café's Black customers worked in town shining shoes or cleaning the schools and shops along Green Avenue. Amá volunteered to those who'd care to know that the Johnsons did not hate *los Negritos*. They were merely accommodating *los Bolillos de el pueblo* who preferred not to eat with *los Negritos. Los Bolillos* could stay out front, as far as I was concerned, as I looked forward to my mornings with *los Negritos,* laughing along at their hilarious, playful exchanges. Sometimes our bursts of laughter rumbled through the pantry, prompting Amá to scream from the kitchen, "*Ya callénse el hocico!*" It was easier for her to speak Spanish. But what Amá didn't realize is that she was inadvertently teaching *los Negritos* Spanish, which they ended up speaking very well; before long, their Spanish was even better than mine! They learned plenty of Spanish curse words, too. One time, one of *los Negritos,* burned himself on a bit of coffee that was still too hot, and screamed, "*Ay, Chingado.*"

I found it all very amusing, and the men were so kind and fun to be around. The table we gathered around was too high for me to reach my food, so there was always *un Negrito* who'd place his overcoat on my seat to give me a boost. But there was one man at the Johnsons' café I wouldn't call friendly to anyone. He shined shoes in the barbershop across from the café, and I would come to know him only as the Shoe Shine Man. He mostly kept his pockmarked face down, eyes averted, speechless, and without even a hint of a smile. The lively chatter among us fell silent whenever the Shoe Shine Man entered the room. The gruff manner and self-entitled tone he took with Amá when ordering more doughnuts, more sugar, more this, and more that bothered me, but Amá told me to pay him no mind.

"*Los Bolillos no quieren a los Negritos, y a él menos; yo creo que ni el mismo se quiere*," she said, in a sad, defeated observation of truth.

The Johnsons allowed Mexicans to dine in the front room of the café, but Amá told me she didn't want me taking up space traditionally occupied by the farmers and ranchers of the Taft area. She was quick to mention that these men had grown accustomed to their own personally designated seating and didn't take too kindly to finding that someone had taken **their** seat.

Sometimes Amagrande would treat me to anything I wanted from the café as my reward for accompanying her to the doctor's office. Amagrande had many ailments—diabetes, arthritis, glaucoma, cataracts, and constant diarrhea—so we were at the doctor's office and the café often.

I dreaded those trips to the doctor's office, where the strong stench of chemicals and medicine choked us both immediately as we walked through the doors, and the few windows benefited only *los Bolillos* sitting in the bright, cozy waiting room. As soon as we entered the white, stonewashed building, the soft-spoken Anglo girl behind the front desk greeted us cheerfully and quickly redirected us toward the stuffy, hot, windowless room behind the door reading, "For Coloreds and Mexicans only." I had a hard time understanding why we Mexicans were allowed to eat and watch movies with the Anglos but weren't allowed to share the same room in the doctor's office

"Ya'll need to move into that room until Celeste or Yolanda calls your name, ya'll hear?" she'd say in her sweet demure Texas drawl. There must have been a lot of unwell Blacks and Mexicans, because that room was always packed, full of young, pregnant girls, crying babies, and crusty old men and women. With only a few seats available, I often ended up sitting or lying down on the cold, hard tile floor, staring around into space, like all the rest of the unseen, without anything to read or even rifle through. Many times I thought of striding into the waiting room for *los Bolillos* and grab a handful of the books and magazines lying unread, but Amagrande warned that, *"El doctor Yenkens nos vota de aquí."* Instead, in the summertime, I tried to pass the time with my *Weekly Reader*, but it proved to be a thin read. I'd just about memorized it front to back by the time we'd walked out of the building.

Those afternoons dragged on and on, as Celeste or her younger sister Yolanda called out the name of one *Bolillo* after the next before calling anybody out from our cramped quarters. Celeste and Yolanda were impressive in their starched, white nurses' uniforms; they were the only people I knew on our street who'd graduated from Taft High School. I never took so many naps in a place as in the doctor's office.

Amagrande preferred to be treated by Dr. Jenkins, whose dark hair and thick moustache stood out among the prominently fair, blond-haired German and Irish population. At first, I thought he might be Mexican, and still wished that he were, so that I could proudly say that my hometown had a Mexican doctor. One time, we thought Amagrande was going to die, so Amá borrowed a telephone from the Esparzas next door to call Dr. Jenkins and tell him that Amagrande was too ill to make the walking trip to his office. I remained in Amagrande's bedroom when Dr. Jenkins walked in. But both Dr. Jenkins and Amagrande asked me to leave. As the door slammed shut I pressed my ear against the wall to hear their conversation, but Amagrande's voice was barely audible, only the doctor's husky voice came through loud and clear. He spoke Spanish and it was puzzling to me that Dr. Jenkins could speak Amagrande's language but she couldn't speak his.

"Como se siente, Lazara?" he asked.

After a very long time, Dr. Jenkins emerged from Amagrande's room. He walked out straightening his jacket and combing back his hair. After he left, I tried to get Amagrande to talk about Doctor

Jenkins's visit but she just laughed and only offered how handsome he was.

Amagrande and I ate among Taft's wealthiest ranchers and businessmen along the counter at the Johnsons' café. The counter seats were too high and uncomfortable, but Amagrande preferred them over the booths. She liked to sit among the men, perched on one of the rotating seats, drinking coffee, which she did in a most unusual way. Dressed in her *luto*, Amagrande poured her coffee out of the cup and onto the saucer. She made loud slurping sounds, prompting everyone in the café to stop what they were doing to stare. Amagrande set the saucer down long enough to take deep drags from her hand-rolled Bugler cigarette. She was the only woman at the counter who smoked cigarettes, the only one who drank coffee from a saucer, and the only one dressed like she was from another planet.

The food and the ambiance weren't the only things good about the Johnsons' café. Sometime around the age of seven, I developed a crush on the Johnsons' youngest child, who was my age. His yellow hair and blue eyes captivated me. At the café, I attempted several times to lock eyes with him but he always turned away. One day after school I followed behind him on Green Avenue. We were both on our way to the café. I ran ahead of him and eagerly drew a heart-shaped design on the sidewalk, where I scribbled, my name and his. I ran across the street to wait for the boy's reaction, but it turned out to be my most embarrassing moment when, raising his head up after reading my message, had the look of someone who had been fed a spoonful of castor oil. That was the first time my heart was broken, and it took me a very long time to get over the little boy's rejection.

The workload at the Johnsons' café got heavier during cotton season. Every Saturday afternoon there'd be a line of customers that stretched from the café's rear entrance to Green Avenue. The out-of-town cotton pickers ordered so many hamburgers and French fries that there were many times Amá would run out of ground beef and potatoes. Many times I heard Amá tell her customers to order from the main dining room where they could sit down, but they refused, preferring to eat inside their cars.

Sometime in the early 1950s a young couple from Alabama, Mary and John Smart, began working at the Johnsons' café. John Smart was hired as the short order cook for the afternoon shift while his wife Mary worked as a waitress in the main dining room. At first Amá didn't see much of the new couple, but when their shifts overlapped they began to know each other.

A year or two after they started work at the Johnsons' café, both Smarts told Amá they were planning to open a restaurant of their own in Taft. When they offered her a job as the morning short order cook for a few more dollars than the Johnsons paid, Amá asked her boyfriend Nene and me what she should do. The three of us gathered around our tiny kitchen table eating supper while Amá verbally weighed the pros and cons of taking the new job. Nene and I listened to Amá argue with herself about not wanting to leave the Johnsons. I felt that Amá thought she was never going to have to leave the Johnsons' café. She seemed lost and frightened at the prospect of having to tell the Johnsons she was leaving them. Amá felt she was betraying the Johnsons and stressed that they had taught her everything about cooking and baking. They treated her well too—better than any other employer she'd known. But Amá said that the Johnsons couldn't match the Smarts' offer. Amá's dilemma frightened me. What if things didn't work out with the Smarts? Could she return to the Johnsons? I was afraid for Amá, but when Nene spoke up after sipping a few beers, I felt a sense of relief.

"No lo pienses más y vete a trabajar para los Smarts, yo te ajudo si no trabajan las cosas," Nene urged.

At the end of the evening Amá told Nene and me that she'd made up her mind to leave the Johnsons. She reasoned that she didn't think the Johnsons' café was going to survive the business that the Smarts were going to take from the town and from travelers on Highway 181. And the pay raise that the Smarts were offering would make it easier for her to pay bills and buy a new car. The next day Amá told the Johnsons about her plans to leave. They didn't seem surprised to hear the news but as Amá expected they were hurt and then became angry. Amá and the Johnsons parted friends but their relationship was never the same, nor was business at the Johnsons' café, although the café did remain open for another ten years.

The Smarts' café took off like a rocket. They got the cook that attracted the locals and drew in the many tourists and visitors that traveled on Highway 181. Their restaurant started as a small operation but after a couple of years, the Smarts moved into a bigger building in the late 1950's. On opening day, the crowds spilled out onto to the street. All day customers streamed in and out of the open house.

Sometime during opening day, I got the chance to meet the two young Smart sons. The older son was about thirteen years old. I found him to be extremely good-looking. His medium-built physique, straight light brown hair, and dreamy dark eyes made me take a second look. But after my bad experience with the Johnsons' young son, I erased whatever thoughts I had about the Smart boy. Mr. Smart introduced me as Catalina's youngest daughter to the two young boys, but they hurriedly brushed past me without speaking.

Everything seemed to go well on opening day until a young teenage Mexican-American boy sitting at a back table with his friends kept calling out to Mr. Smart by his initials, J.B. Mr. Smart ignored the young teenager until he realized the boy was going to go on calling him J.B. all day if he didn't stop by the table and say hello. After shaking hands with all the boys around the table, Mr. Smart walked straight into the kitchen, looking as though someone had slapped his pronounced beet red face. He went on a tirade, complaining to Amá about the young snot-nosed kid having the audacity to call him by the name only his closest friends used. After Mr. Smart left, Amá scolded me in such a way that I thought I'd been the one that had insulted Mr. Smart. She ordered me never to refer to an older person by their first name, nevermind by their initials.

Amá said the one thing she liked about the Smarts was their old-time manners. Yet she complained about the way they treated Black people. "*Que podemos esperar? Ellos son de Alabama, donde no quieren a los Negritos, ni pintados.*" The first thing Mr. Smart did when he opened his larger, new restaurant was post a sign reading, "We reserve the right to refuse service to anyone." Those kinds of signs popped up all over south Texas in public dining places. Like the Johnsons, the Smarts allowed only Anglos and Mexicans in the main dining room, not Blacks. But that didn't seem to bother the local Blacks. When Amá moved with the Smarts every one of the

Blacks that had once patronized the Johnsons' café followed. *Los Negritos* and I picked up where we had left off at the Johnsons' café. We shared our breakfast in the back room of the Smart's café.

When I turned twelve, I began filling in when the regular dishwasher didn't show up. I washed dishes and took food orders from *los Negritos*. The usual crowd I'd known over the years came every day, including the unfriendly, grumpy Shoe Shine Man. One morning the Shoe Shine Man ordered his usual doughnut and coffee. On my way to deliver his order, the doughnut fell onto the dirty cement floor. I bent down to pick up the doughnut, and assuming no one had witnessed the incident, I dusted the doughnut off on my apron and placed it back on its plate. I served the Shoe Shine Man the doughnut along with his cup of hot coffee and just as I began to walk away, he angrily, said, "You think I didn't see you drop that doughnut, do you? You take that doughnut back and get me another one."

I gently picked up the plate and returned to the kitchen, where Amá had finished stacking a large platter of freshly baked doughnuts. I thought for a minute about whether to return the old doughnut to the Shoe Shine Man or give him a fresh one. But all I could think of was the way he treated Amá; he spat orders with an angry tone I didn't think she deserved. I walked to the back and served the Shoe Shine Man the same old doughnut.

"That's better. Don't ever let me catch you pulling that stuff again," he angrily ordered. The other men around the table looked up at me and smirked when I winked at them.

I knew that what I had done to the Shoe Shine Man wasn't very nice. But it was one small way of my getting even for what he'd done to Amá over the years. I didn't feel that it was up to me to try and figure why the Shoe Shine Man was so angry; maybe it was his job, maybe it was his home life or maybe it was the fact that he was a Black man living in a place where his color meant more than his character. I didn't think he liked being called boy or nigger any more than I liked being called wetback or dirty Meskin. We were both trapped in human suits that brought us a painful challenge every day. But the way I figured, it was up to people like him and me not to get caught up figuring why our color offended most Anglos in Taft. Maybe it was too late for him. But even at my young age, I realized that I wasn't going to allow negative experiences to dictate my future.

In the final analysis, the Shoe Shine Man taught me much more than he or I realized at the time. His attitude, rude as it was, taught me to stand up for my rights, which I figured was what the Shoe Shine Man was trying to do for himself all along.

The Smarts' café prospered even as it denied front room service to Black people. During the late 1950s and early 1960s, there were many sports teams who stopped at the café as they traveled to the coastal bend area from the northern part of the state. It became customary to see the Anglo team members, the coaches and their staff, dine together in the main room, while allowing their fellow Black team members to eat their food inside the school bus or in the back room of the café. There were many times Amá couldn't hide her anguish over seeing one black player after another being turned away. She'd complain to me as if I was in any position to change things. But one fall evening in 1962 Amá came home more exuberant than I'd ever seen her.

"No vas a creer lo que pasó esta noche?" she excitedly asked.

It turns out that a football team from up north stopped at the café after a game in Corpus. The mixed team of Blacks, Anglos, and Mexicans walked in and when they tried to sit down together, Mr. Smart turned away the Blacks. This time, the head coach took his staff and non-Black team members aside. According to Amá, the coach returned alone and told Mr. Smart that if he didn't serve the Blacks, he and the rest of his staff and team players wouldn't dine at his café. Mr. Smart stood his ground; allowing the entire coaching staff and all of the team members to walk out in solidarity. Amá couldn't contain her excitement about what she had witnessed. She said that if more Anglos and Mexicans stood up for the Blacks like those she witnessed, things were going to change for *los Negritos*. Amá didn't know it, but she was witness to the coming of a new era of equal justice that was about to take over Taft and the rest of America.

I was nine years old when Emmett Till was brutally murdered in Mississippi in 1955 because he whistled at a white woman. Till's murder triggered the civil rights movement, which led to the eventual passage of the Civil Rights Act of 1964. Yet, no one in my family or anyone in my school, teachers included, mentioned his murder. As a young woman I didn't participate in any civil rights activities, and that was because there weren't any protests to speak of by Blacks or Mexican-Americans in Taft up until the time I moved away in 1965. I cannot speculate why we Mexican-Americans along with the Blacks didn't protest against the racism that we endured. Maybe we were more docile and timid than we thought; maybe we weren't ready to protest, maybe we just didn't want to stir up trouble, or maybe it was because we were aware of the powerful Ku Klux Klan that existed in nearby Sinton. In my case I was more caught up in my self-identity about being illegitimate and growing up on the South Side where I didn't know how my life would unravel from one day to the other. Yet, I knew that in time I'd have to find a way to fight for my civil rights. Eventually, it was Black Americans that began to show me the way. Their will and their determination to have equal footing in America only served to energize me. The Black Americans' struggle to fight for civil rights became my struggle soon enough.

Chapter 5

School Life

"The joy of learning is as indispensable in study as breathing is in running. Where it is lacking there are no real students, but only poor caricatures of apprentices who, at the end of their apprenticeship, will not even have a trade."
Simone Weil, 1901-1943
French Philosopher

My three older sisters used every trick in the book to keep from going to *La Escuela Zavala*, which was located only a few yards from our house. My oldest sister, Delfina, was a fifth grader; the middle sister, María, was in the third grade; and the youngest of the three, Jesusa, was a second grader when all three decided to skip class. When Amá discovered that her daughters hid behind our grandparents' house until school let out she didn't get angry. *"No vayan a la escuela si no quieren ir, con el tiempo ustedes son las que van a perder,"* Amá told them.

Our Amá wasn't the type to force anything on us, including an education. She was an emotionless wreck who appeared only mildly interested in our lives. My belief was that her emotional detachment from us, including my brother whom she favored, was due to losing her six-month old child because she had failed to overcome her husband when he stopped her from helping the crying baby. Amá's way of paying attention to us was calling us *bad names*. We were basically left to form our own path through life.

The cruel and hurtful words of the racists around me were bad enough but the hurt that Ama's words inflicted almost daily were, to say the least, harder to take. My sisters coped by breaking our Ama's golden rule—running off much too young with boys much poorer than them. My brother didn't have to worry; Ama's razor sharp words were saved only for her four daughters. I coped by losing myself in the world of Hollywood. Flipping through movie star magazines, I envisioned myself a famous movie star, attending Hollywood parties, and signing autographs to my fans. I even took to fantasizing that the famous 1950s actress, Dorothy Malone, was my mother. Ms. Malone never realized that her world of Hollywood and the world I created around her, allowed me to escape from my challenging environment on my own terms.

I could've easily gone the way of my sisters. But the Catholic school saved me, well, almost. In 1951, the South Side's Immaculate Conception Church took over the old Zavala School that had been built during the 1920s. *La Escuela Zavala,* named after Lorenzo de Zavala, the Interim Vice President of Texas in 1836, was one of two schools built in Taft specifically for Mexican-Americans. The other was a private boarding school sponsored by the Presbyterian Church. The Pres-Mex initially sought out to teach poor Presbyterian Mexican girls but in time it became an exclusive boarding school for mostly upper class girls from Mexico and the Rio Grande Valley. The whitewashed stucco building with its Spanish tile roof greeted travelers who took Highway 181 from up north toward the coastal line. The Pres-Mex closed in the late 1950s, leaving behind an academic life that many on the South Side wished they could have afforded, including my Amá. *La Escuela Zavala* also closed in 1950 to make way for Mexican-Americans to integrate the North Side school system. That happened four years before Oliver L. Brown, a Black pastor, joined a lawsuit in Kansas, *Brown v. Board of Education of Topeka,* that allowed Blacks to go to an all-white school.

I was five years old when I was enrolled as a kindergartner in the Catholic school. Father Joe was the school principal and the nuns from our church became the teachers of grades K-eight. I liked the school because the teachers could be sweet motherly nuns; there were fun things to do during recess, and especially because I could get there by myself in a matter of minutes since it was only half a block from our house.

All the students except the kindergartners were required to wear school uniforms. The boys wore navy pants, white shirts, and navy ties. The girls looked scholarly in their navy jumpers, crispy white cotton blouses, and black and white oxford shoes. I couldn't wait to wear a school uniform.

My class began each day with prayers followed by religious instruction and for what was left of the day we learned the alphabet, but mostly we learned about the birth of the baby Jesus. During our mid-morning break the nuns handed out an assortment of freshly baked cookies along with ice cold RC colas. Every student's favorite teacher was Sister Carmen. She was the Mother Superior who taught seventh and eighth graders. I looked forward to the day I'd be in Sister Carmen's class.

But my Catholic education started on a slippery slope and ended in a quick death. In fact, I didn't even get to finish my kindergarten year at *La Escuela Católica*. It started with a simple question from my classmates.

"Graciela! Does Sister Juana wear panties? Yes or no?" a classmate asked.

I ignored the question and continued playing hopscotch. A second classmate yelled the same question. Before long, I was surrounded by a group of classmates taunting me to find out whether Sister Juana wore panties under her heavy skirt. I kept playing hopscotch but my classmates were relentless.

"I don't know and I don't care," I answered to nobody in particular.

"I dare you to find out," someone else hollered.

"I double dare you to find out!" another voice rang out.

That was it! No one was going to double dare me to do anything. I charged at my target much the same way a bullfighter went after his bull. I imagined my classmates yelling, *"Olé!" "Olé!"* as I gathered enough strength to lift the nun's long flowing black skirt up off the ground. The heavy fabric of the skirt seemed to weigh a ton yet I managed to lift it up, only to end up trapped in Sister Juana's heavy clothing. I tried holding on to the nun's legs, but her thick, black, slippery stockings caused me to lose control.

"Ayayay!" Ayayay!" Sister Juana screamed.

As Sister Juana and I danced around the playground to gain freedom from one another, the thick square heels of her shoes crushed my toes. The deep pain paralyzed me under Sister Juana's skirt. Daylight became a dark inferno. I tried frantically to free myself from the nun's hot, smothering clothing, but the weight of the fabric kept me trapped between her legs. The more I fought to escape, the more my body became entangled in her clothing. We both sounded like a pair of strung out rock and roll singers, screaming at the top of our lungs. Finally, after much twirling and whirling on the school's playground, we both crash landed on the hard, dry, Texas soil.

Before the dust had a chance to settle on the playground, I found myself sitting across a small, rickety dark wooden desk from Father Joe. His reputation for a quick temper played out that day. I must have heard the word "sin" one hundred times, "hell" another one hundred and "purgatory" at least twice as much. The tone and length of Father Joe's lecture convinced me that I couldn't say enough novenas to save myself. Father Joe evoked the names of Jesus, *La Virgen de Guadalupe,* and some saints I had never heard of to make his point that I was in serious trouble.

It didn't help my case that only a few months earlier, Father Joe had baptized me along with a group of screaming babies. I walked to my baptism with Amagrande and a godmother that was conveniently available, but without a godfather. During Sunday mass, Father Joe said that everyone should be baptized during infancy or we'd end up in purgatory. It seemed Father Joe was always warning his congregation about ending up in purgatory regardless of what we did. I didn't know where purgatory was located but it didn't sound like a very happy place to be; at least that is what Father Joe had us believing. As I walked inside the church flanked by my Amagrande and my *madrina* Chepa, I felt very much at the front door of purgatory. The three of us made our way to the front of the altar where we stood with our heads bowed among the screaming babies and nerve-wrecking parents. Suddenly, the swishing sound of Father Joe's robes made the three of us raise our heads only to find him standing so close to us I could smell his early morning breath. He glared directly at me and asked in the angriest tone yet, *Por qué están bautizando a esta niña tan grande?"*

A dead silence swept throughout the church. Amagrande and my *madrina* Chepa lowered their heads and stared at the floor while I chose to stare at the statue of Jesus nailed on a cross that was displayed at the base of the altar. The body of Jesus was half-naked except for his bottom, which was protected by a white cloth that resembled a baby's diaper. Blood streamed from the thorns embedded in his forehead all the way down his face and chest. His hands and feet also had blood streaming from them where the nails had been driven there by the Roman soldiers. I felt so ashamed to look up at the suffering Jesus. I was convinced that because I walked to my baptism, Jesus would be as angry as Father Joe assuring me of a trip to purgatory. Father Joe ranted and raved about my age and when he learned that I didn't have a godfather, he ranted and raved even more. I had never seen Father Joe as cross as he was on the day of my baptism. But on this day while I tried to explain about my incident with Sister Juana, he was angrier still.

Amá had a run-in with Father Joe earlier in the school year, having to do with my school dress. Next to racing her two-tone brown Nash along Highway 181 against known and unknown motorists, Amá's favorite pastime was clothes shopping. When Amá found a piece of clothing she liked she'd buy two or three of the same item. On one shopping trip to Levine's in Corpus Christi she bought me three cotton dresses, one yellow, one blue, and one green. The knee-length dresses had a row of sunflowers sewed on their spaghetti straps. Amá excitedly told me I could wear all three of the dresses in a week's time. The first day I wore one of the dresses My teacher, Sister Vicenta took me aside.

"Niña, dile a tu Mamá que este vestido no se usa en La Escuela del Padre José," she said.

I ran home to tell Amá Sister Vicenta's message.

"Dile a esa monja que no se meta en lo que no le importa, Amá said angrily.

The next day I wore another one of the dresses. But before the school day ended, Father Joe called me into his office. He wrote hurriedly on a piece of white paper which he inserted in an envelope and sealed it.

"Dale esta carta a tu madre," he ordered.

Amá tore up Father Joe's letter after reading it. She sat down at the kitchen table writing a letter of her own.

"Toma, lleva esta carta a ese padre necio," Amá ordered.

The next day I stopped by Father Joe's office dressed in the third dress and handed him Amá's note. I didn't know what the note said but I knew enough not to wait around for Father Joe's reaction. Before the end of the day, Sister Vicenta waved a white envelope in front of my nose and told me to deliver it to Amá. The note was from Father Joe. The note-writing battle between Amá and Father Joe waged on. In the end, Father Joe won. My three summer spaghetti strap dresses were saved for walking trips through the South Side with Amagrande.

My Amá could be as stubborn as a mule. But she admitted she was no match for Father Joe, who was unequivocally the most powerful person on the South Side. Yet her *orgullo*, along with her stubbornness didn't allow her to negotiate with Father Joe. As priest of the Immaculate Conception Church since the late 1940s, he ruled with an iron fist. Almost ninety nine percent of the South Side residents were Catholic and whether we wanted to acknowledge it or not, we fell under the sphere of Father Joe's influence.

Father Joe was a short, slim man who rarely expressed a smile. His serious and often sour personality was no match for that of the friendlier and jovial Irish priests that filled in for him. Father Joe blamed his congregation for everything bad that happened on the South Side. But he provided an opportunity for us to redeem ourselves. He established a "Special One Dollar or More Collection Basket." At every Sunday mass, Father Joe ordered us to fill the basket. He warned that if we didn't drop at least a one dollar bill, God was going to punish us.

The South Side residents earned some of the lowest wages in the entire state of Texas, yet we managed to drop enough dollar bills into Father Joe's Sunday special collection to eventually get him a new church and a new rectory. There were times, not often, I used some of my weekly allowance to drop a one dollar bill into Father Joe's special collection basket believing that my contribution was going to save me from purgatory and possibly earn me one more step toward heaven.

Father Joe's lifestyle was a lot better than that of the rest of us on the South Side. I saw the first color television set in his rectory. Sometimes I peeked through the glass panel window and found Father Joe sitting on a leather recliner, sipping red wine from a sparkling crystal goblet. I wondered whether the wine was the same he offered during communion. The wine we drank tasted more like the vinegar that came from pickle jars. Father Joe sold us just about everything, including, at one point, holy water. He sold corn dogs at the church-sponsored baseball games. He boasted about cooking the corn dogs himself from a "family secret" recipe. I figured if Father Joe wasn't going to succeed in getting us to drop one dollar in the special collection basket, he was going to find his way into our wallets through the "family secret" corn dog recipe.

There wasn't a carnival or circus that was allowed to pitch a tent on the South Side without approval from Father Joe. During Sunday mass he told us many things, but how to lead our lives was the better part of it. He emphasized that married couples should use the rhythm method of birth control. He cautioned that if any other form of birth control was used, God was going to punish them. The rhythm method? At the age of nine, I thought I knew how children were made. Add to that the idea of rhythm, a la dancing, and I had the most impossible picture of not making a child.

I avoided telling Amá about my incident with Sister Juana. But Father Joe helped me out when he stopped by Amagrande's house on his way home after school. When I spotted his car in front of Amagrande's house, I ran behind a nest of oleander trees next to the house and pressed my body against a nearby window to listen in on the conversation. I couldn't imagine what was going to happen to me but I was as frightened as I'd ever been in the first five years of my life. As Father Joe and Amagrande talked, Amá, called by Amagrande, joined in the conversation. The three sat in Amagrande's front room while Father Joe did most of the talking. After a few moments Father Joe stormed out of the house and had barely started the car engine when Amá's voice bellowed throughout Amagrande's house.

"*Que* no friegue," Amá barked.

"*Que no friegue* were typical words spoken in our family. They were used against those that brought trouble to our family.

Father Joe was a holy man, not a troublemaker. When that phrase was used in our home the message it sent was that the person saying it wasn't willing to negotiate or to compromise or to apologize. Negotiating over something, never mind compromising, wasn't done in our family. An apology was as foreign to my family as the word itself—it was never used. The idea that any one of our human acts resulted in us having to apologize for something we did was seen as defeat.

In the end, Amá's *orgullo* stood in the way of allowing her to negotiate, compromise, or apologize to the person who held the upper hand. Amá stubbornly refused to acknowledge Father Joe's power while holding on to her pride, and for what? So that I could be the first and only five year old, expelled from Father Joe's *Escuela Católica*. So in September 1952, instead of walking a few steps to *La Escuela Católica* I walked one mile and a half to enroll in the Taft Elementary School. The school was located on the North Side of town-*el barrio de los Americanos,* where the Anglos lived.

As I reluctantly began the walk with Amagrande, she pushed at me, *"Andale niña, camina rapido, que ya vamos tarde,"* she urged. Amagrande's command to hurry along was lost on me. But so were the songs of the birds, so were the barks of the dogs and so were the drones of the jets from the Naval Air Station in nearby Corpus Christi, which seemed to dominate the blue skies every day of the week. The only sound I heard was the beat of my heart. I worried about what was going to happen to Amagrande and me when we approached *el barrio de los Americanos*. Were the Anglos going to chase us out of their neighborhood? Who were *los Americanos*? What were they like? A hundred questions raced through my mind.

I needed Amagrande more than I wanted to admit. Yet, I felt somewhat resentful that Amá wasn't with me on my first day of school. I knew she was working at the Johnsons' café. Yet I couldn't help but feel that Amá didn't love me and that was a feeling that would stay with me for many years.

To make my day worse, I was embarrassed to be seen with Amagrande. The *luto* she wore made her look odd and strange. And her behavior was unpredictable. Amagrande belched loudly before a meal, during a meal, and after a meal! She broke wind with carefree ease. The strong gaseous smells forced unsuspecting souls to pinch their noses as they scurried away. She did what she wanted to do, whether in Father Joe's church, at the Piggly Wiggly or at the counter of the Johnsons' café. I envisioned Amagrande lifting up her skirt to take a pee in the school yard, as she had done in other public places. I hated my first day of school!

I hadn't been exposed to many *Americanos* before my first day of school. I knew them as *Bolillos, Gabachos, Pan Blancos, Gringos*, Americans, and Anglos. At first I thought the names were attributed to different kinds of people. But I came to find all the names referred to one group, white Caucasians. Amagrande and Buelito spoke about *los Americanos,* as if they were better than anyone else on earth. "*Ellos no son como nosotros los Mexicanos,* they often stated. My grandparents seemed preoccupied with the color of a person's skin. The way they talked about *los Bolillos* had me convinced that their pale skin, yellow hair, and light-colored eyes made them better than us Mexicans.

I desperately searched for a familiar face on the school grounds. But all I saw was a large crowd of white, pale-faced people. Except for my friend *la Bolilla,* I hadn't been exposed to people with such pale skin. I couldn't keep from staring at *los Bolillos*. They momentarily interrupted their own conversations to stare back at us, giggling and pointing at Amagrande. Amagrande stood out in the crowd of well-dressed women. Most had their yellow hair pulled back in ponytails. Some wore their hair short like men. Their shoes and handbags matched the color of their dresses. The sparkling jewelry they wore around their necks, on their earlobes, and on their wrists made them look elegant.

While I was mesmerized by the likes of *los Americanos,* my cousin Miné popped out from the crowd, trailed by her mother, Tía Lina. Miné's tall skinny white frame towered over the much shorter blond boys and girls. Never had I been so happy to see her. We ran towards each other. "Eight," she said excitedly (This is how south Texan Mexicans say Hey to one another). "Eight," I answered back. We were careful not to show too much emotion towards one another since Amagrande didn't approve of such displays.

The human line of parents and students stretched along the side of the school building. Mrs. Roberts, the school principal, waited at the front of the line to direct us to our new classrooms. I was relieved to reach Mrs. Roberts's desk. She muttered a few words to Amagrande, but although Amagrande, had a strong and compelling spirit, she couldn't comprehend a lick of English.

"Can't you speak English?" Mrs. Roberts asked.

I was too embarrassed to help Amagrande.

"What about you? Can you speak English?" Mrs. Roberts turned to ask me.

Words wouldn't come. My shaking hand placed a set of documents that Amá told me to give to *la vieja* on Mrs. Roberts's desk. While Mrs. Roberts thumbed through the documents the long beads she wore around her leathery wrinkled neck swayed across her chest. After reviewing them, she hurriedly placed the documents in a folder that, she shoved into Amagrande's chest.

"Andale! "Andale!" she said in broken Spanish and waved us away from her desk. I was surprised to hear Mrs. Roberts speak Spanish. I wished Amagrande could speak English so I wouldn't have to always translate for her.

The classroom was filled with students that looked like me. Their olive features made me feel at ease. Their dark eyes danced merrily as they followed Amagrande and me making our way toward the teacher's desk. My new teacher was a young-looking Anglo woman. Her short, strawberry blond hair sat like a cap on the top of her head. She wore a dark-colored matching skirt and jacket. Amagrande handed her the folder. The teacher glanced up and down at Amagrande before taking the folder. The red nail polish on her fingernails glistened as she flipped each page. Mrs. Nance laid down the documents and told me to take any empty desk. She waved in a scooting motion to Amagrande. While I searched around for a desk, Amagrande made her way out of the classroom. I laid my things on a desk at the back of the room and immediately ran toward one of the windows that faced Green Avenue. I stared out onto the street until Amagrande exited the building. Mrs. Nance's voice commanding me to sit down rang obscurely into thin air. I was lost in my thoughts about Amagrande leaving me. As I watched her oversize black smock turn into a tiny speck along Green Avenue, uncontrollable tears streamed down my face.

I cannot remember when it occurred to me that Mrs. Nance's classroom wasn't a first grade class. My classroom was called "primer." It was a special class designed for Mexicans whom the school identified as being non-English proficient. The special attention we received was a slow process of teaching us the basics, because somehow we were supposed to be slow learners since we didn't speak English. Yet, not one student in my class was tested to determine whether we were slow learners, nor did anyone in the school system test our English proficiency.

During the winter months our class size doubled when the children of migrant workers returned from their seasonal work. But by early spring, the migrant kids were taken out of school to help their parents pick crops in other parts of Texas and the United States. Some even traveled as far away as Ohio. One classmate left me thinking there were several states named Ohio when she happily announced she was leaving school to go with her parents to *los Ohio states a trabajar*."

I wondered what it would be like to travel with the migrant workers to faraway places. But that thought quickly evaporated when I heard a teacher say, "Those kids aren't ever going to amount to anything if they keep being taken out of school."

During my primer year my brother was a seventh grader. His classroom was one floor above mine in a two-story building called the Green Avenue building. The Anglos called my brother Henry, the English version of Enrique. They liked him because he was good in sports. But even so, the Anglos didn't befriend my brother any more than they did us Mexicans who didn't play sports. On our way back from lunch, my class met my brother's seventh grade class and some other higher grade classes on the stairway as they made their way to the cafeteria.

"Hey, you damn wetbacks, outta the way!" several of the Anglos yelled. The first time I heard them, I ran to tell my brother while he waited in the cafeteria line.

"*Vete de aqui,*" Enrique yelled angrily.

There were times my classmates and I brushed against the Anglos on the stairway.

"Ugh! You dirty little wetbacks. Get away! Get away!" they hollered.

The Anglos brushed their hands and arms against their clothing as if they were cleansing themselves of our human contact. There was one especially vocal girl among the group. She was a tall slim girl with a head full of curly red hair. Appropriately, she was known around school as "the redhead." A mass of freckles covered her entire face, and her deep green eyes were the color of the marquee at the Leland Theatre.

I grew tired of being called a wetback day in and day out. My classmates did too, but they didn't seem to want to make an issue of the name calling as I did.

"Let's say something back to the redhead," I told a group of my classmates.

"We can't say anything back to *los Americanos*," someone shouted.

One day I decided to fight back. But my nervousness was so intense that my knees almost buckled while I made my way to confront the redhead. She and a group of girls stood in the hallway chatting as I made my approach.

"Hey, redhead, come here," I demanded.

She and the other girls turned to stare at me. Their laughter rang throughout the hallway, while they looked toward one another. I got closer to the group and called her name again.

"Redhead, come here," I repeated louder than before.

By this time, whatever fear I had was overtaken by the anger I felt from their laughing at me. The redhead sashayed boldly toward me. I looked up at her freckle-filled face and peered directly into her sparkling green eyes. She stared me down and asked.

"What do you want with me, you ugly little wetback?"

I gallantly tiptoed to make direct eye contact with her. Within a matter of seconds, I lofted a gob of spit at my target but missed her forehead. My warm spit splattered over her eyes and nose instead. The redhead's high-pitched screams startled me. I jumped away from her and made a mad dash for my classroom, followed by a small group of classmates, leaving the redhead screaming on the second floor hallway of the Green Avenue building. The redhead's girlfriends quickly formed a circle around her. As I dashed down the hall, a couple of angry-looking Anglo girls followed me.

"We're gonna get you wetback," they announced angrily.

I walked away, shaking more than when I first spat onto the redhead's face. My classroom was unusually silent when I entered. The eyes of everyone in the room seemed to follow my every step.

"*Hijole* Graciela, you are in big trouble," several classmates warned.

I hadn't expected my classmates to abandon me. They complained as much as I did about the redhead's ethnic slurs. I didn't expect anything good to come of my spitting at the redhead, yet I was unsure what was in store for me—that is, until I saw the redhead's teacher stomp into the classroom and make her way to my teacher's desk. She whispered into my teacher's ear and after a few seconds, both raised their heads to look in my direction. The frowns on their faces revealed that I wasn't exactly going to earn a gold star that day. The redhead's teacher stared me down as she sped out of the classroom. My teacher, in the meantime, took a white piece of paper and began writing rapidly. She folded the paper and placed it in an envelope.

"Gracie Ella, take this note to Mrs. Roberts," Mrs. Nance ordered angrily.

You could hear a pin drop as I made my way out of the classroom. Mrs. Roberts was a small, slim woman, but she had a reputation for being tougher than nails. The sound of her high-pitched, nasal voice alone made the elementary school students scatter. I found Mrs. Roberts sitting behind her wooden desk, looking content in a gray-colored skirt and matching jacket. She greeted me with a smile. The ends of her thin gray hair rested at the tips of her earlobes. That and her prominently square jaw made her look mannish. Her leathery, wrinkled neck was graced by a long pearl necklace. I handed her my teacher's note, and rather than locking eyes with her, I lowered my head, which Amagrande said was a sign of respect.

"Take a seat," she said warmly.

While she read the note, I stared down at the floor, thinking about ways to escape from what was sure to be some form of punishment. When I looked up, Mrs. Roberts's earlier smile was gone and the more she read, the more her face turned sour. By the time she finished reading, Mrs. Roberts's hands were visibly shaking.

"Stand up." she ordered angrily.

Mrs. Roberts pulled out a long, wooden ruler from a gray cabinet that stood behind her desk. She gripped the ruler while she walked around her desk to meet me. Her wrinkled skinny hand was covered with brown spots. She held the ruler tight to strike at me and at that point I lost myself on Mrs. Roberts's brown spots to avoid feeling the pain of the ruler's blows against my body. Mrs. Roberts delivered rapid and powerful blows to both my arms and legs. I grimaced at every blow, but I refused to cry.

On my way back the windows of the Green Avenue building were covered with human faces staring at me. For days afterward, I heard many comments made about my incident with the redheaded girl.

"Did you hear about the dirty little Mexican who spat on the redhead's face?" one student after another said. I made school headlines that day. Since the day Taft was incorporated from the Taft Ranch no Mexican-American had stood up to an Anglo. I made Taft history all right, but it wasn't without a great deal of emotional pain. I was ostracized by my classmates, and even by my own brother. Yet, I didn't have any regrets about spitting on the redhead's face, not even after Mrs. Roberts took the ruler to me. Still, it bothered me that neither my teacher nor Mrs. Roberts asked why I had spat in the redhead's face.

What bothered me more was that my brother took the side of the redhead girl and all of the Anglos. He acted like a *lambiache*. For days, Enrique stayed away from me in the schoolyard, treating me like a total stranger. To begin with, Enrique rarely spoke to me unless he absolutely had to, and since he never absolutely had to, we rarely spoke. Amá entrusted Enrique to keep my school lunch money. He was supposed to hand me the lunch money while I stood in the cafeteria line but after the incident with the redhead Enrique threw the coins on the ground instead, dashing off like an Olympian runner. Only the clinking noise of the coins dropping against the cement sidewalk alerted me that my lunch money was nearby. Many times I missed lunch because Enrique threw the coins on the grass instead of on the sound-making sidewalk.

Enrique ate in the school cafeteria too. But when I approached his table, he waved me away.

"*Vete de aquí pendeja*," he growled.

I attempted to sit at other tables, but they were filled with Anglos who yelled, "Get out of here you dirty little Mexican." I carried the heavy, metal, food tray throughout the cafeteria until I found an empty chair which was usually located at the "losers' table," called so by the Anglos and even by my brother. I made up the losers table along with the so-called bookworms, the slow learners, and kids who had serious medical problems. One time, one of our tablemates suffered a seizure. He fell on the floor and foam began spilling out of his mouth. Everyone near our table screamed and ran from the sick boy.

"Ugh, he's spitting foam," someone yelled.

"It's contagious! Get away from him," another person warned.

After that, no one wanted to come close to our table for fear that we too had our tablemate's disease.

After the spitting incident the redhead stopped calling my classmates and me wetbacks. In fact a few months later, the redhead and her family moved out of town.

I knew I was headed for an identity crisis when Mrs. Nance pronounced my name Gracie Ella instead of Graciela. She had a difficult time pronouncing other Spanish names too. My classmate *Esperanza's*, first name came out sounding more like S Per Ansa, while her pronouncement of the last name *Rodriguez*, sounded more like Rod Ree Jay. My school future lay in the hands of a teacher who didn't demonstrate much knowledge about the culture of her new students and because of that I was sure I was going to fail. However, I passed and ended in *el Maestro García's* first grade class.

El Maestro García was the only Mexican teacher in the Taft Independent School District. But his class was known to be made up of Mexican students who performed poorly, who couldn't speak English, and who were mostly migrant workers. I protested and so did my cousin Miné. We made such a ruckus going into el *Maestro García's* classroom that Mrs. Roberts called Tia Lina to take us out of the classroom.

El Maestro García was well known in town, mostly for preparing the tax returns of South Side residents. Every April the line of cars, including my Amá's, ran from *el Maestro García's* front lawn all the way down Davis Road. But regardless of the teacher's talent in filling out tax returns and his pleasant personality, I didn't want to be in his classroom. After my Aunt Lina met with Mrs. Roberts, Miné and I were admitted into Mrs. Florence Huber's integrated classroom which was mostly filled with wide-eyed blonde-headed kids. There were two other Mexican kids in the class, but they ignored Miné and me. I took a seat behind a tall, lanky Anglo kid that turned around to stare with his mouth wide open the entire morning. My skin color and my curly, black hair made me an oddball among all the fair-skinned kids, including my cousin Miné, whose skin was almost as fair as that of the Anglo kids'. No matter, I was determined to survive Mrs. Huber's class.

It didn't take long for me to realize that *los Americanos* didn't mix with Mexicans off or on the school grounds. But one day out of the clear blue sky, *una Americana* asked me to play on the swing. Maggie was one of the brightest *Americanas* in my first grade class. She lived in a large, enchanting, brick house located across from the junior high school. During the winter, Maggie wore the prettiest wool caps over her strawberry blonde hair. So when Maggie invited me to "bump" with her, I couldn't climb on the swing quickly enough. Maggie sat on the swing while I straddled my legs over her lower body. Our faces met each other as our strength allowed us to "bump" the swing high up in the air. Our laughing screams echoed throughout the schoolyard. But suddenly our swing was jerked to a quick stop. One of the teachers pulled me off of the swing, grabbing one of my arms, and leading me away.

"Listen, you little Mexican, don't ever let me catch you playing with Maggie or any of her friends. Maggie's mother doesn't want her playing with Mexicans and neither do any of the other parents," the Anglo teacher warned. She then shoved me forward and told me to go play with the other Mexicans.

In school, I wanted to be a part of everything, whether it was appearing in school plays, going on school trips, or trying out for the spelling bee. But I came to learn there were limitations for me because I was Mexican and sometimes that limitation came from my own fellow Mexicans. I loved singing *Texas My Texas* every morning, but one of my Mexican classmates told me to shut up and stop acting as if I was *una Americana*.

On a school train trip from Taft to Sinton one of the teachers told me to sit with my cousin Miné, not the Anglo students. And after seeing a Mexican-American girl from Corpus appear on the Howdy Doody Saturday show as the area's spelling bee champ, I thought

I could become a spelling champ too. But when I told my fourth grade teacher of my interest, she advised me to think about doing something else.

I tried out for school plays, but that was a losing proposition too. I quickly learned that the teachers had their pets and most of the time it was they who got the leading roles. The lesser roles were saved for us Mexicans but not even those did I get a chance to do. When my second grade teacher asked the class which of us wanted to appear in the school play *Cinderella,* I was the first to raise my hand. But she already had her pick. She chose a poor Anglo girl to play the raggedy Cinderella and a very pretty blonde girl whose parents lived on a large ranch to play the enchanting Cinderella. I wasn't given a role, not even to play one of the mice that chase after Cinderella when the clock strikes midnight. The girl that played the pretty Cinderella was one of the prettiest girls in elementary school and my second grade teacher made it her duty to remind us of that almost every day in class. "Cheryl is a real beauty!" she stated day in and day out.

After school, I'd run home and scrub my body with lots of soap, hoping that my skin would turn milky white like Cheryl's. I kept my dark brown eyes cast down for fear I'd attract undue attention from the teacher, who seemed enchanted with Cheryl's looks. My curly, black hair was covered with a dark heavy scarf most of the time so the teacher wouldn't compare my unruly mop with Cheryl's soft, straight, blond hair or that of the other Anglos girls in the class.

Indeed, Cheryl was a pretty girl and it was she who helped me make a discovery about Anglos and Mexicans that turned my tide in school. My grandparents had drilled into me so much superiority talk about *los Americanos* that I began to believe I was inferior to them. Sometimes I wondered why I bothered going to school. Why bother placing my hand over my heart to recite the Pledge of Allegiance? Why bother singing, *Texas My Texas* and for that matter why bother learning anything in class? I was convinced that nothing I did in school was going to be good enough unless I looked like Cheryl.

Yet, there was something that nagged me. If *los Americanos* were indeed superior to Mexicans then that superiority would have to be tested, proven and settled in no place other than the toilet bowl. For some reason, I envisioned Cheryl and all the other *Americanos* dropping nuggets prettier than the ones I dropped. So, to test the superiority of *los Americanos,* I decided to chase Cheryl into the restroom one day to see if her bathroom droppings were different than mine.

"Cheryl! Hurry! I need to make number two!" I screamed. "Don't flush! Don't flush! I will do it for you," I said excitedly.

Before Cheryl had time to answer, I jerked open the stall's door. As I went in and Cheryl rushed out, there to my surprise and immense happiness was a pile of brown nuggets floating in the toilet bowl. They weren't gold nuggets, or prized diamonds, or sparkling gemstones; they were brown nuggets just like the ones I dropped! Hoorah! That revelation convinced me that Cheryl and I were on equal footing. I felt that I could keep up academically with *los Americanos.*

My friends and classmates from the South Side were dropping out of school like dead bugs, and everyone assumed it was just a matter of time before I did the same. However, for the first time, I felt I could do some of the same things *los Americanos* did and if I studied hard enough, I could possibly do things better than they did. After my discovery, I ignored my teacher's daily ritual of praising Cheryl's beauty. And when my grandparents ordered me to step out of the way for *un Americano* to pass through, I ignored their command. Nobody knew the shitty little secret I kept about the supposed superiority of *los Americanos.*

By the time I reached the sixth grade, more than half of all the Mexican-Americans that began the first grade with me had dropped out and I could understand why they did. *Los Americanos* made fun of our Spanish-sounding names. They made fun of our Spanish accents. They made fun of our clothes. And they made fun of our food. Since most of the South Side students couldn't afford to eat in the cafeteria, they brought their lunches of flour tortillas stuffed with pinto beans, which they ate in the classroom. *Los Americanos* laughingly crowded around them while they ate their lunches. It got to the point where they ate their lunch meals directly out of the brown paper sacks, leaving no space between sack and mouth, so their tortillas wouldn't show. The unwanted attention to our dark skin, our Spanish accents, our clothing, and our food became too much for many South Side students. Yet, some dropped out because their parents simply couldn't afford to send them to school. And then there was the factor of speaking Spanish in school. Anyone caught speaking Spanish on the school grounds was sent home for three days. If you were unlucky like my classmate Lucia and you missed a quiz or a test during that time, the teacher automatically gave you a zero. Lucia's grades unfortunately were so low she gave up trying to catch up and dropped out. I had another classmate Marta that was sent home when the teacher found lice crawling down her forehead. Our teacher used a ruler to examine Marta's head for more lice while the rest of the class watched in shock. The teacher rolled her eyes and asked that we stay away from Marta until her head was clean of lice. After that day Marta never returned to school.

There so many things that I witnessed the first six years of my school life, some of which left me frightened and sad. There was a third grade classmate who one day asked if she could walk home with me. She was a sweet girl who, along with me and other girls our age, offered flowers to *la Virgen de Guadalupe* at the Catholic Church on Tuesday evenings. That day, as my classmate and I walked out of the school building, the janitor waved to us while he cleaned the floor with a large machine. When we stepped out the front door, my classmate suddenly stopped and ordered, "Wait here. I am going back to the classroom to get something." While I waited, the buzzing of the floor cleaner stopped and the building began to clear out. I didn't know what to do; walk home alone or wait for my classmate.

I decided to walk back into the dimly lit building to find my classmate, but there wasn't anyone inside our classroom. As I made my exit, I heard low voices coming from the classroom across the hall. I slipped in quietly and noticed in the adjacent supply room a pair of black-and-white oxford shoes on tiptoe facing a pair of dark, worn-out rubber shoes. The upper part of their bodies was hidden by a portable blackboard, behind which they were standing. I tiptoed quietly toward the blackboard and peeked around the corner. The same man who was moments before was polishing the floor was bent down, pressing his lips against those of my classmate, while one of his hands was lost under her skirt. I became paralyzed, unable to move much less think what to do next. I walked backward out of the room and sprinted down the hallway. As I darted out of the building

I heard my classmate shout for me to stop. Her appearance made me more frightened still: Part of her dress was tucked up against her waist, and the barrettes that held back her short, wavy, brown hair looked loose, while her face was flushed.

"What did you see?" she asked anxiously.

"Ah, nothing," I answered quickly, without looking her in the eye.

"He gives me money and candy," she said excitedly. If you want to share in on the money and candy, I'll tell him," she added.

"No!" I said loudly.

After that day my classmate approached me several times to ask if I wanted to share in the candy and money from the old man. But every time I answered the same until she finally saw fit to leave me alone.

My friend Helen was the saddest casualty of all. Although I must admit her misfortune had nothing to do with the prejudice that befell most of my classmates. In Helen's case, she was the victim of Mexican-on-Mexican crime which could happen as often as that from the Anglos.

I first met Helen in the schoolyard during a recess softball game in the fall of 1957. She stood behind me while I swung the bat at record speed. My swing struck Helen with such force that she ended flying up in the air and crash landed on the ballpark's tough ground. Her loud scream echoed throughout the school yard. The other players and I ran toward Helen, frantically examining Helen's injury. Her lips looked as if they'd been stung by a bee. I worried that the bat might have knocked out some of her teeth, but thankfully the extent of her injury was a big fat gashed lip and nothing more. After school, I followed Helen home to make sure she was okay. We walked home together many days after that day.

Although Helen towered over me like a giant, she and I agreed that we had much in common. We both liked school and enjoyed playing softball. We proudly pointed to the identical moles that graces the right lower sides of our olive square faces as our marks of beauty; teasing each other about the possibility that we might be related.

As our friendship blossomed I came to the sad realization that Helen's home life was anything but happy. Helen came to live with her aunt after her mother dropped her off and fled to heaven knows where. Helen didn't seem to know the whereabouts of her mother or for that matter whether her father was alive or dead. Her aunt was known on the South Side for her high-strung temper and for the string of boarders that slipped in and out of a one-room shack located in the back of her house. Helen's aunt beat her but she made me promise not to tell anyone. "If she finds out I am telling you, she'll throw me out of the house, and I have no place to go." Many times I found Helen washing clothes on a washboard. The knuckles on her hands were bruised from the pressure she applied to the washboard's metal ridges. She cleaned up after her aunt, her younger cousin, and even the boarders.

Helen and I remained friends throughout the fifth grade. When school let out for the summer, I didn't see much of her. By September I was anxious to meet up with my new friend, but Helen wasn't in my sixth grade class or in any of the other sixth grade classes. A few weeks later, I spotted Helen in a beat up, old car sitting up in the front seat with a much older, heavyset man, whose hair was whiter than my Buelito's. Helen lowered her head when the car passed me on West Pecan Street. I wondered what she was doing in the car alongside the strange, older man. And, the next time I saw Helen she was riding in the same beat up car with the same man, but this time, she held a baby wrapped in a blanket. Amá told me the man with Helen had a wife and five children in a nearby town but that during the week, he worked in Taft and rented a room from Helen's aunt. Sometime during his stay at her aunt's house, the older man took liberties with Helen and took her as his own. Helen ended up living with the old man in the one-room shack he rented from her aunt.

I was a senior in high school the last time I saw Helen. She sat slumped down in the front seat of the same beat up car alongside the same older man. This time, their car was filled with so many children that I couldn't count them all. Helen's tired, sad face turned away when she spotted me on the road. I wept for Helen that day more than I had the first day I saw her with the old man. I took a step back to memory lane, when I first met Helen, and recalled how innocent and happy she seemed. I remember her telling me of her dream to graduate from high school. But her dream was broken, and her life was shattered beyond repair—which I saw happen before my very eyes. What did Helen do to deserve such a cruel life? Why is life fair to some and not others? Helen had so much to offer and so much promise, yet her life ended before it had a chance to begin. I wondered if she would have been better off being run over by a car on Davis Road than suffering the way she did.

I did a lot of praying that day. I prayed for Helen but mostly I prayed for myself, that my road would continue smoothly from the disturbing and tragic realities around me.

Chapter 6

Adventures with Amagrande

*"Children have never been very good at listening to
their elders, but they have never failed to imitate them."*
James Baldwin, 1924-1987
American Writer

Amagrande and Buelito helped Amá rear me. But it was Amagrande who influenced me more than any other member of our family. It was she with whom I spent most of my early childhood years. We slept together, we ate together, and we traveled everywhere together.

Amagrande met Buelito in Mexico during the early 1900s and a few months later, she became pregnant with their first child, my Amá. Amagrande's past which included giving birth to two children out of wedlock, sank any chance she might have had of being accepted by the more proper San Miguels of the state of Coahulia. Yet, she trekked every year to Monclova, Coahuila to visit what was left of the San Miguel clan. Amagrande chose a different grandchild every summer to accompany her on the trip to northern Mexico rather than her husband, who happened to be the "real" relative of the people she visited. I wondered why she visited Buelito's family one summer after another when it seemed clear to me they didn't much like her.

Amagrande's oldest son, Manuel, lived in Monclova too, but Amagrande rarely visited him. Maybe their strained relationship had more to do with him saying to her one day, *"Me da verguenza que usted sea mi madre."*

It was no secret that Tío Manuel preferred to be in the company of his father, a well-known physician in Monclova, but his stepmother discouraged it. Tío Manuel straddled two lives: one of poverty and uncertainty, and the other of wealth and comfort. In the end, Tío Manuel wasn't able to keep up with the demands of his father's lifestyle, and ended up depending on Amagrande for financial assistance, suffering from alcoholism, and marrying a girl from a poor Mexican family. Yet when he visited Amagrande, Tío Manuel's self-importance fooled us all about the real life he led in Mexico.

Every time I'd hear that Tio Manuel was coming to visit my Amá said angrily, "*Ahí viene ese perro de vuelta.*" Amá complained that Tío Manuel visited their mother only to take money from her. Perhaps she was right because Amagrande didn't allow anyone in her house when Tío Manuel visited—maybe that was so we wouldn't see her wait on him hand and foot and fill his billfold full of American currency. During his visits, Tio Manuel didn't have much to do with the rest of us. The only time we caught a glimpse of Amagrande's eldest son was when he brushed past us on the way to *el escusado.*

By the time I was twelve years old, I'd been to many places with Amagrande. Our trips took us to different parts of south Texas, and they were always interesting and, more often than not, downright embarrassing. If we weren't hopping on the Greyhound bus to Corpus, we rudely called on her friends and neighbors unannounced. Or we paid visits to every church denomination on the South Side, but most of all we went to more funerals than your average undertaker. My favorite time with Amagrande was our trips to Mexico. I was ten years old when I took my first trip to Monclova. It was the most memorable and the most embarrassing. Our trip began in Taft, where we boarded a Greyhound bus. Every seat was filled with young and old people, most of whom were Mexican like us. I liked riding in the Greyhound bus; the inside always had a fresh, aromatic smell. The slim, gray dog that was painted on the side of the bus signaled adventure to me. The rides were so smooth that I usually fell asleep watching my reflection in the large glass windows.

But on this bus trip to Monclova, things began to unravel before we were out of Taft's city limits. Amagrande began pestering me to tell the bus driver to stop so she could relieve herself. I pretended not to hear, but she kept on. *"Dile al chofer que necesito ir a el escusado,"* she barked.

The roar of loud laughter permeated throughout the bus. I leaned over to whisper that we would be approaching the Sinton station soon and she could pee there.

"Pendeja, para que vinistes conmigo, si no me vas ayudar!" she declared angrily.

I reluctantly got out of my seat and slogged down the aisle with my head down so none of the riders could see my blushing red face.

"Andale, apurate!" Amagrande yelled.

The bus driver waved his hand for me to get back into my seat.

"Take your seat, young lady!" he snapped.

"Sir, my grandmother wants you to stop the bus so she can use the bathroom," I pleaded.

"What? Are you loco? Get back to your seat," he commanded.

As I made my way back, my heart was beating like a loud drum while every person in the bus focused on me. I leaned down to tell Amagrande what the bus driver said but she interrupted and screamed, *"Eres una pendeja! Quítate de aqui."*

Amagrande jumped up from her seat, shoving me aside with such force that I landed on some passenger's lap.

"Get back to your seat, Señora!" the bus driver commanded.

Amagrande didn't understand a word the bus driver said to her except *"señora."* She stood, gripping the rail, while everyone on the bus stood up to watch the scene unfold.

"Yo tengo que orinar! Yo tengo que orinar!" Amagrande cried.

I tried holding Amagrande's hand but she yanked it away threatening to urinate in the bus unless the driver stopped. Amagrande refused to sit down; leaning on one foot and then on the other while placing a hand between her legs. The driver threw up his arms and steered the bus toward the side of the road. Every passenger sprung forward from their seat when the driver slammed the brakes. When the door swung open, Amagrande flew out toward the side of the bus. Every passenger peeked through the windows to get a closer look. They elbowed each other and giggled when Amagrande dropped her oversize white panties, and squatted to relieve herself.

I waited by the door to help Amagrande up the steps but she pushed my hand away. "Ya *no te necesito más*." she bellowed.

I sheepishly trailed behind her toward our seats, where we sat quietly until the bus driver announced our arrival in San Antonio. The city rocked with excitement; the streets filled with heavy traffic, the tall buildings, the large crowds all fascinated me. But we had to quickly board another bus that took us to the border town of Eagle Pass about two and a half hours away. The trip was uneventful. Other than a dead armadillo or two on the side of the road, the flat south Texas terrain was uninspiring; it helped us to fall sleep. We arrived in Eagle Pass too late to catch *la Flecha Roja,* the Mexican bus to Monclova.

Amagrande didn't have a plan where we would spend the night. She mentioned a family she had met years earlier that rented rooms. *"Yo creo que viven junto del Puente,"* she said. The two heavy suitcases we carried weighed us down in the scorching heat, while we searched frantically for *una familia Mejicana que renta cuartos.* We went house-to-house, knocking on doors, asking whoever answered if they rented rooms or if they knew someone who did.

Just when the sun started to sink down into the flatland of Eagle Pass, we found the family that rented rooms sitting on their front porch. The landlords were an elderly couple that looked to be about Amagrande's age. The heavyset man and his gray-haired, petite wife fanned themselves with newspapers to cool down from the raging Texas heat. Their home was a sprawling wooden monstrosity surrounded by huge pecan trees whose shells we crunched beneath our feet as we made our way up the front porch. I became excited at the thought that Amagrande and I were going to sleep inside the couple's beautiful, spacious home. But instead, the man led us to the back of his house, where a cluster of three old, dilapidated tiny shacks greeted us.

"Cuantas noches estarán aqui ustedes?" the man asked.

"Nade más que una noche," Amagrande answered.

The man demanded he be paid in cash. Amagrande took a wad of bills from a tightly wrapped handkerchief hidden inside her brassiere.

The man pointed us toward one of the shacks that sat a few yards behind his home. When we entered, the wood floors cracked under our feet, while a swarm of large, black flies and mosquitoes immediately attacked. The old man led us to a small, rusty metal-frame bed that was covered with a stained, light blue, chenille bedspread. The bed rested between two large windows that were hoisted open by a wooden pole. The only other piece of furniture in the room was a weathered wooden table that had a small, round tin pan and a dirty glass pitcher on top. The old man told us we could wash our faces by filling the pitcher with water from the outdoor faucet. He pointed to a small wood building the size of our outhouse back in Taft that we could use to shower.

After the man left, Amagrande and I walked to the shower room, where we encountered a group of young Mexican men converging between the two other broken-down buildings. They looked as if they hadn't shaved or showered in years. Dressed only in long khaki pants, they followed our movement like a pack of vultures. Their exposed chests revealed tattoos of the Virgin Mary and other symbols I couldn't make out. Their wolf whistles were barely audible over the loud, accordion-type Spanish music blaring from a radio. I recognized the voice and music of Agapito Zuñiga, who often played at Don Pancho's. I couldn't understand how Agapito Zuñiga's music could be heard in Eagle Pass, Texas; I thought his music was heard only in Taft. Amagrande and I each took a turn watching out for the men while we hurriedly showered. On the way back, the men yelled, *"Orale, masotas para donde van? Quieren una cervezita?"* they asked flirtatiously.

Amagrande grinned back at the men, reminding me of a joke she had told me about a grandmother who is on a stage coach trip through Mexico with her two teenage granddaughters. Three robbers stop the stagecoach and order all of the ladies out of the coach. After they rob the women, one of the men suggests they should take liberties with all of the women.

"Sir, you can do anything you want with us but please leave my grandmother alone," one of the young girls pleaded.

The girl's grandmother interrupts.

"He said everyone!"

When we arrived back in our tiny room, it was so dark inside that we couldn't see our hands in front of us. I was hesitant to enter, but Amagrande pushed me inside, telling me I should only be afraid of the devil, and she was certain he wasn't in there. We somehow found our way to the bed and both jumped on it with our clothes on, pulling the stinky, urine-smelling covers over us. The tiny bed forced our bodies to press against each other. I tried pushing Amagrande's heavy arms and legs away but it was no use; I lay under her heavy weight all night. Amagrande's weight and her loud snoring, plus the busy traffic of men passing and stopping by our window, kept me awake all night.

In the morning, we left without washing our faces or brushing our teeth because Amagrande wanted to get on the first bus to Monclova. But we missed the bus because she preferred to walk across the International Bridge rather than pay for a taxi. On our way across the International Bridge, I saw a large number of Mexicans walking into the United States. Amagrande said the Mexicans went to United States to work for better pay.

Once over the bridge we were inundated with beggars. I'd seen only one beggar before, and that was in Taft. Enrique and I were on our way to school when a scruffy-looking man with a dark beard approached us in the backyard. The stranger asked us for a quarter. But Enrique told him to get off our property. The stranger scooted toward the home of one of our neighbors.

"He's a hobo!" Enrique proclaimed matter-of-factly.

"What's a hobo?" I asked.

"Hobos are men who live in railroad box cars, stupid. They jump out in certain towns, where they beg and stay only a short time. Sometimes they end up in big places like Los Angeles and New York," he explained further.

I couldn't imagine any train running through such a tiny town as Taft that could end up in big cities like New York. After that encounter, every time I saw a train speed through Taft, I wondered whether one day I would ride it to a faraway place like the hobos did.

But the beggars in Mexico were not hobos; they were young women and children. The young women's sun-baked faces made them appear old, like Amagrande. Some carried babies tucked in multi-colored wraps that swung around their waists and up under their breasts. As we passed by them, they pleaded, *"Por favor, ayúdennos, no tengo para darle de comer a mis hijos."*

Their children were dressed in dirt-stained underwear and went barefoot. They eagerly ran up to us with their tiny hands cupped.

Amagrande, who probably still had the first nickel she had ever earned, surprised me with her generosity. She handed me a few coins to distribute among the beggars too. I couldn't help but think that Amagrande pressed the few coins into the hands of the beggars because she thought God was going to punish her if she didn't, rather than because she wanted to help the beggars. My family lived on guilt 24 hours a day. We conducted our lives day in and day out based on whether we thought God was going to punish us for what we did or didn't do, so that is why I thought Amagrande was being so generous.

As we walked down the street, distributing coins, the soft voices of the young girls trailed down the street, *"Muchas gracias, y que Dios los bendiga."* I felt a step closer to heaven hearing them ask God to bless me and remembered the nun's words during catechism class: "Should a person come up to you for help that could be Jesús, Mary or Joseph in a person's form. God is watching you all the time and you should help those that ask for your help," the nun warned.

We arrived in Monclova very late into the night. Amagrande admitted that she didn't remember how to get to the house of *Lola la Partera*, Buelito's younger sister. We ended up staying at the first hotel we saw, a small, clean one-story building where we shared the bathroom with the other guests. As she customarily did with sales people, Amagrande tried to bargain with the hotel manager for a lower rate. But the tall, dark-haired, less-than-friendly man refused to bargain, demanding she pay the stated rate or leave. Amagrande reluctantly removed the tightly wrapped handkerchief from her brassiere, pulling out the huge wad of dollars bills once again.

The next day we began our search for *Lola la Partera*. Amagrande said it wouldn't take long for us to find Buelito's younger sister, because everyone needs a midwife.

"Vamos a buscar a una persona en el camino que parece que sabe más de la vida que no más de su culo," Amagrande said. We stopped one stranger after another but none of them had heard of *Lola la Partera*. Most of the people laughed at Amagrande's question, while hurriedly walking away. Sometime in the late afternoon, we came upon a park on a busy street where we found a cool spot under

a cluster of shady trees. A pestering street vendor pressed us into purchasing a glass of *jugo de tamarindo*. I took a quick gulp of the milky, white acidy beverage and almost threw up. But in Mexico, *jugo de tamarindo,* which is made from tamarind seeds, is sold daily by the gallon. The sunny afternoon was turning into nightfall when we came upon a middle-aged woman at the park who knew *Lola la Partera*. We found Lola's house in a quiet neighborhood not far from downtown Monclova. A young girl not much older than me answered the door. She was dressed in a neatly pressed black dress with a crispy, white linen apron tied around her tiny waist.

"*Yo soy la cuñada de Lola la Partera*,' Amagrande said anxiously.

"*Pasen,*" the girl said hesitantly.

The house was peaceful and smelled of fresh cut flowers. The girl led us through a long hallway that spilled into a spacious room full of young girls with bulging bellies. They sat in small wood chairs dispersed throughout the room surrounded by soothingly potted and hanging plants. We took a seat among the pregnant girls. A yellow parrot caged in an adjacent room made us pop up from our seats when it began chattering loudly. I thought the bird would never stop singing and talking in Spanish. But when *Lola la Partera* walked into the room, everyone stopped talking, including the loud, chattering bird. *Lola la Partera* embraced me and asked that I call her Tía Lola. Then she turned to Amagrande and offered her a firm handshake. Tía Lola didn't look like any of my relatives back in Taft: Her complexion was milky white and her blue eyes glistened like sapphires. Her young assistant offered Amagrande and me a glass of warm goat's milk and some *pan dulce*. I took an immediate dislike to the goat's milk but I was too thirsty to toss it away as I had done with the *jugo de tamarindo* earlier that day. During our meal, Tía Lola reacted with surprise when Amagrande told her we would be staying for a month. "*Aquí?*" Tía Lola asked stunned.

The month of July came and went before we knew it. During our stay, we managed to stay out of Tía Lola's way, while she delivered one baby after another. We occupied ourselves by visiting Amagrande's relatives. One of those relatives was her youngest and only living brother; we found him living in a horse barn among the horses he took care of for an affluent Monclova family. Amagrande and her brother hadn't seen each other for almost 30 years, yet they didn't display much emotion when they met; they shook hands and that was about it. Amagrande's brother tipped his hat when she introduced me. He towered over us like a giant. His complexion was a light chocolate color like Amagrande's. He had a head full of black hair, but the deep lines on his face revealed a much older man. Amagrande's brother invited us to sit on the haystacks that filled part of the barn where he slept. It was awkward watching Amagrande and her younger brother try to make small talk. After a few minutes of mostly staring into space, Amagrande stood up to leave and pressed a couple of coins into her brother's hand. "*Toma este dinero es para que te compres algo de comer*," she said somberly.

Amagrande's brother looked at the small amount of coins and shook his head lightly as he led us out of the barn.

On another day we took a city bus to visit the family of Tío Manuel. We found Tío Manuel's wife, son, and daughter living in a two-room house located in a poor section of Monclova. Tío Manuel lived alone, in yet an even smaller structure a couple of blocks away, but that day we didn't see him. As was customary with Amagrande, we arrived at her daughter in-law's house unannounced, but in this case our host didn't seem to mind. Other than writing Tío Manuel's wife a letter, there was no way we could have let her know of our pending visit. We arrived around lunchtime and found Tío Manuel's wife cooking while her teenage son lay in bed awake. The tiny place had a soaked, earthy smell, the result of the wet dirt floor we were standing on. Tío Manuel's petite wife, María, welcomed us with a less-than-enthusiastic embrace. She walked barefoot on the dirt floor, swatting flies out of the house with a white rag. When she cried out to the flies, her mouth revealed much needed dental work. María wore a flimsy cotton dress that revealed saggy raisin-size breasts. She offered to make lunch for us, but Amagrande quickly said we couldn't stay long. It was a good thing; the kitchen was so tiny there was space for only the wood-burning stove and a small rectangular wood table surrounded by three fruit crates that served as seats. A swarm of large black flies sat on the mouth of a glass pitcher filled with goat's milk that, María insisted, "*Es muy bueno para la niña.*" Amagrande and I stood in the front door making small talk with

María, while her two children remained in bed. We left in less time than it had taken us to locate María's house.

After our visit to Tía María's house, I wondered how Tío Manuel, whose father had educated him in private schools and sent him to college, ended up the way he did, along with his family. He wasn't a favorite uncle but just the same, I worried that he and his family didn't have enough to eat.

The impoverished lives of Amagrande's relatives haunted me all the way back to Taft. I wondered how my own life was going to turn out. Would I graduate from high school? Who would I marry? Would I have children? My thoughts about my future foreshadowed anything about the trip when we left Monclova on that hot, steamy day in July of 1956. I couldn't stop thinking about the wide economic disparity that existed between Amagrande's relatives and Buelito's. I couldn't imagine having a household full of servants like Tía Lola. Thinking about what lay ahead for me was scary as hell!

After our trip to Mexico, life with Amagrande continued as usual. She had many friends on the South Side and somehow managed to take me along to visit all of their homes and stores by the time I was 10 years old. Amagrande never called ahead; we just showed up, she knocked on the front door, and sometimes even the back door, until someone answered and let us in. She spent the afternoon chatting and drinking coffee with her friends, while I took naps on some strange person's bed. I liked visiting Amagrande's friends. They treated me to delicious food and always told me how pretty I was. Some of the old women enjoyed pressing their fingers into my dimples, which sat like small craters on each side of my face.

I liked going to *la tienda del reloj* the best. The owner of the mom and pop store, an elderly, skinny woman offered me a different kind of snack every time we visited whether it was an ice cream cone, a chocolate moon pie, or a handful of penny candy. The store got its name from the huge clock that hung on the back wall. Many in the neighborhood went to the store just to stare at the clock's large hands that made a loud tick tock noise every time they moved and I was no different staring at it as if it was some strange creature from another world.

But of all of Amagrande's friends, there was one I didn't care to visit. It was an old woman who dressed in black from head to toe and had a, small mountain of a hump on her back that frightened me. She seemed to walk on all fours, because she had a stoop-like posture, while her arms dangled and swayed, almost touching the floor. The constant frown on her face disappeared when Amagrande and I appeared at the house she shared with her daughter, son-in-law, and their many children.

Sometimes we accompanied the old woman to the South Side Baptist church to hear her son-in-law, preach the good Lord's word. *El Ministro* preached for such a long time that I ended up falling asleep on Amagrande's lap. But almost every Thursday, Amagrande and I willingly went to the church to witness the ever-entertaining baptisms and to partake in the delicious meals prepared by the church ladies. While Amagrande and I ate our food from paper plates, we amused ourselves by watching young and old get dunked in a large rubber pool. The pool, sitting on the church stage, looked like a giant lake. Painted on the wall behind the pool was an outdoor scene, giving the illusion the people were baptized outdoors. One time, a grown woman slipped and fell into the pool. She began screaming that she was drowning, flailing her arms and legs, splashing water all over the stage. Amagrande and I were bent over with laughter while everyone in the church gave us dirty looks.

The Baptist church wasn't Amagrande's only stop. Even though she was a Catholic, Amagrande liked visiting other churches on the South Side. If we weren't having supper with the Baptists on Thursdays, we were jumping up and down with the Pentecostals on Wednesdays. On Tuesdays, Fridays, and Saturdays, Amagrande took me to offer flowers to *la Virgen de Guadalupe* at the Catholic Church. On Sundays I helped her entertain *los de la Atalaya*. Monday was a day of rest unless there was a special revival going on at the Pentecostal church.

For some reason Amagrande took me to the Pentecostal church more than any other. One hot, muggy, summer night, when I was about six years old, I had an experience that left me feeling more frightened than saved. The one-room Pentecostal church was located two blocks from our house, and on our way up West Pecan Street, the chants of the people were unusually loud, as was the music. The church was overflowing with people jumping up and down and making strange noise with their tongues, while others banged on tambourines. As soon as we took our seats in one of the first-row pews we heard the pastor announce that it was a special night because several *hermanos y hermanas* were embracing Jesus Christ as their savior. I was sitting next to Amagrande, tapping my toe to the beat of the tambourines, when a short, dark, heavyset woman appeared out of nowhere. She stood next to me with her arms raised up in the air, making those same strange noises. Suddenly, she lifted me up off of my place on the pew, gripping me by my rib cage. My body was helpless under her tight grip. She ran up and down the center aisle, tossing me up and down, while speaking in tongues. I tried unsuccessfully to pull down my dress to cover my underwear, but my bare legs and white cotton panties were there for the world to see. After more tossing and bouncing than any human could withstand, the woman put me down in front of the makeshift altar. The woman's sweat dripped on my face while she reached down to face me and began shaking me. "*Miras a Díos? Miras a Díos?*" she asked anxiously.

Her hands felt clammy as she slid them up and down my skinny arms. Heavy drops of sweat flowed like a river from her forehead to her chin and down her neck. I shut my eyes to see God but only saw dark space. The woman kept shaking me like a rag doll with both of her hands. "*Miras a Díos, niña? Si, lo miras! Dime que si lo miras?*" she insisted. I figured the only way for her to stop shaking me was for me to answer in the affirmative.

"*Sí,*" I whispered.

"Oooooooh! "Oooooooooh!" She hollered.

The heavyset woman picked me up again off of the floor, carrying me down the center aisle of the hot, steamy room.

"*La niña a visto a Dios! La niña a visto a Dios!*" she announced over and over.

The entire congregation jumped up from their seats. Tambourines clamored, while every person in the room raised their arms in the air, stomped their feet, and made loud strange noises with their tongues. I frantically reached for Amagrande to rescue me but she ignored me, clapping and stomping her feet, along with rest of the Pentecostals.

After that night, I figured that my going to the Pentecostal Church or any other church wasn't necessarily going to earn me a ticket into the pearly gates. I made my move to put a halt to Amagrande's church invitations. One night on our way home after offering flowers *to La Virgen de Guadalupe* at the Catholic Church, I led her through deep, soggy mud puddles that were caused by a heavy rainfall the night before. While I was at it, I decided to put her eyesight to the test. Amagrande told me more times than I wanted to hear that her thick, heavy, coke bottle eyeglasses helped her see. She blamed glaucoma and cataracts for her poor eyesight.

Amagrande walked into the first puddle.

"*Ay, yayay, Ay, yayay,*" she screamed.

I took her hand and led her into a second puddle that was much deeper than the first.

"*Bruta, pendeja, que estás haciendo?*" she asked nervously.

Amagrande's black dress became caked with mud and my white dress was a muddy mess, as were my white shoes and matching socks. After that night, she didn't invite me to any more church visits and I was just as happy.

Amagrande took me on shopping trips to Corpus Christi most Saturdays. One very hot summer Saturday when I was about eight years old we headed to Corpus on the Greyhound bus so she could buy herself a chamber pot. We headed straight to Levine's department store, which sold everything from fashion wear to cotton picking sacks.

"Yo *quiero comprar un bacín,*" Amagrande said anxiously.

The store clerk gave an embarrassing chuckle but quickly collected himself and ran down a couple of aisles, returning with a white enamel pot.

Ese mero es el que quiero," Amagrande announced proudly.

The store clerk gently wrapped the pot and its lid in a light brown paper bag, which Amagrande asked I carry.

"*Está muy grande, yo no puedo cargarlo,*" I complained.

"*No seas malcriada,*" Amagrande scolded as she thrust the package at me.

We had stepped only a few feet outside Levine's when the flimsy brown paper bag tore open. The chamber pot flew like a missile out of the bag, tumbling down Chaparral Street, the Fifth Avenue of Corpus, which was overflowing with shoppers. The strong winds that earned Corpus its nickname "the windiest city in the world" accelerated the pace of the pot down Chaparral Street. The excited shoppers scattered, allowing the pot to run its course while they pointed and laughed. The chamber pot seemed to have a life of its own, rolling endlessly one way down the street while its lid ran in an opposite direction. Amagrande shoved me to run after the pot, while yelling, "*Pendeja, corre a levantar el bacín.*" But I refused to move from my place in front of Levine's. Suddenly, a well-dressed man with a thin mustache jumped from the crowd and began sprinting after the chamber pot. He grabbed it seconds before it would have crashed against the curb and then proceeded to chase after the lid, which was rolling further down Chaparral Street. The man proudly handed the pot and lid to Amagrande in full view of hundreds of Saturday shoppers. I ran off but Amagrande caught up with me, thrusting the chamber pot and its lid into my hands.

Back home we went grocery shopping every Saturday. At the H.E.B. grocery store, Amagrande picked up a banana or two, which she freely enjoyed while she shopped. Afterward, she tossed the peels on the floor while I rushed to pick them up, but she scolded me every time to leave them on the floor.

She'd send me to Julio's grocery store almost every day and made sure I didn't forget her order by tying a string around one of my fingers. I liked running her errands to Julio's, which offered a large selection of penny candy. But one day, the owner's teenage daughter took so much time waiting on me that I ended up peeing on the store's wood floor. I frantically yelled at Mabel to hurry. But it was too late. I felt the hot liquid run down my legs while embarrassingly watching it form a huge puddle on the wood floor.

"*No tienes verguenza, Chela,*" the owner's son, Valentin teased.

"*Válgame, Valentin, ya no aguantaba,*" I answered. I stood in front of the candy counter holding my bag of candy while Valentin brought out a rag mop to clean up while his younger sister Mabel dressed in her usual tight shorts, was so bent over with laughter I thought surely the seams of her shorts were going to rip open. I ran out of the store barely able to hold the two milk bottles Amagrande had ordered. As I made my way up the back steps of her kitchen, Amagrande swung open the door, knocking me down on the ground. The milk bottles fell out of my hands, dropping on the hard earth floor. The crashing sound of glass prompted Amagrande to scream,

"Pendeja! "Bruta!" Lying down covered with broken glass and cold milk, I raised my head to answer back. *"La pendeja es usted, para que me mandaba a mí,"* I said crying.

Amagrande was our matriarch, so respected and so feared that no one dared answer back to her. I expected the worst, but to my surprise Amagrande laughed so hard at my response that her dentures fell out of her mouth, landing on the ground next to me. It felt good seeing her laugh so joyfully and came to realize what laughter can do to change the appearance of an otherwise cross-looking person.

And I can't remember how many wakes and funerals we attended, probably more than any undertaker could withstand. On the South Side, people didn't cry softly when a dear one passed away; they wailed loudly as if someone was sticking a knife into them. The wailing began as a low-pitched cry and crescendo into a high-pitched wail. Once it reached its ultimate volume, one person after another followed, making the same noise. The wailing sounds of friends and relatives spooked me but were more entertaining than watching Howdy Doody on Saturday morning television.

In the South Side the wakes were typically held in our homes and the casket always remained open. In one particular instance, one woman was so grief stricken that she picked up her husband's dead body out of the coffin. She shook the dead man with both hands while asking, *"Por qué te fuíste y nos dejastes solos? Por qué? Por qué?"* The older, heavyset woman shook her husband's body as if he was a rag doll. Her strength was so powerful that the man's hairpiece came loose and ended up on the wood floor. The woman stepped on it while she kissed her dead husband's face, smearing his makeup. It took a group of men to rescue the disheveled body from the wailing woman.

Amagrande feared *La Migra* would deport her and Buelito to Mexico. Although both my grandparents as well as my Amá were legal residents, they weren't American citizens and because of this they feared deportation. I told Amagrande she should become a citizen so she wouldn't fear *La Migra* and so she could vote. But instead of learning how to become an American citizen, Amagrande held forth from her rickety rocking chair, complaining that *El Paul Taxes* wouldn't let her vote.

One day she went on and on about *El Paul Taxes*. I tugged at the hem of her long, black dress wanting to hear about more *El Paul Taxes*.

"*No preguntes más niña. Andale, búscame un cigarro,*" she ordered.

The top drawer of the nightstand next to her bed was cluttered with blue tin cans of Bugler tobacco, packages of thin cigarette slips, and matchsticks. I opened the Bugler metal can and carefully spilled the tobacco onto the thin cigarette paper, then gently rolled the paper between my palms. The tip of my tongue brushed the adhesive side of the paper, which I connected to the dry side. I took two drags to be sure the cigarette was fit for Amagrande to smoke. Tiny puffs of smoke quickly filled the room and just as I was about to take another drag, Amá walked in.

"*En donde aprendíste a fumar?*" Amá asked angrily.

"*No te metas en lo que no te importa,*" Amagrande replied readily.

Amagrande made many a declaration and spun innumerable stories from her rocking chair up until the day she died. No one besides Amagrande was allowed to touch the rocker, let alone sit on it. The rocker sat in a corner of her bedroom embraced by two large windows that provided cool breezes from the gulf that overcame the hot, steamy Texas climate. Amagrande's bedroom known as *el cuarto de Amagrande*, was the central point of family gatherings. The four-poster bed, which she draped with a pink chenille bedspread, was her prized possession. No one was allowed to sit on it except me. I felt contented and protected in Amagrande's bed. The sheets were as soft as the cotton we picked during the summer, and just as white. They smelled of the kind of perfume Amá ordered from the Avon lady. During the cold season, Amagrande and I kept our feet warm by wiggling our toes together until we fell asleep.

But sharing Amagrande's bed wasn't without its drama and entertainment. She suffered from a number of ailments one of which caused her to pass wind so much that the house was often filled with a stinky, foul odor. Her over active bladder made Amagrande get up at all hours of the night to use the chamber pot. She turned on all of the lights while unabashedly allowing West Pecan street a full view.

Amagrande's queen-size bed had a matching dresser, where several of Tío Victor's memorabilia still lay—his army tags and photo, handwritten letters to his parents from faraway lands, a pair of brass knuckles, and an array of Asian trinkets he had picked up along the way during his Army tour in the Far East. The memorabilia lay comfortably at the center of the dresser, as if waiting to be picked over by Tío Victor. The dresser sat adjacent to Amagrande's side of the bed, where she picked up Tío Victor's Army photo every night and gave it a kiss while wiping tears from her eyes. She loved her youngest son more than any of the rest of her children, she once told me.

Another of Amagrande's prize possessions was a five-foot-tall, cedar armoire that stood on the wall across from her bed. She was the only person who could open the armoire, which she did with a key she kept linked to her brassiere with a safety pin. The armoire was mostly filled with documents: her and Buelito's marriage license; their last will and testament, which she amended every time a daughter angered her; and a sundry of other personal items that revealed my grandparents' earlier life in Mexico.

And then there was the money!

Amagrande kept a white canvas bag filled with money tucked underneath all of the documents. How much money was in the bag at any given time no one knew for certain. I saw lots and lots of loose dollar bills whenever she opened the bag to count the money or to lend money to friends and relatives. It seemed every day some man or woman knocked on Amagrande's front door to borrow money. Amagrande didn't show favoritism; she charged all borrowers the same interest rate and each was expected to pay back on the day she designated.

But nothing meant more to Amagrande than a personally signed letter from President John F. Kennedy that praised Tío Victor's service in the Army which she proudly hung on the entrance wall. When a visitor missed the letter, Amagrande would lead them to it and proudly announce, *"Esa es la carta del Presidente Kennedy."* Amagrande told her visitors that if it weren't for *El Paul Taxes,* she would have voted for President Kennedy. For a long time I thought *El Paul Taxes* was a real person. I envisioned an Uncle Sam-like figure—a tall, wiry Anglo man with a long white beard, sharp nose, and angry blue eyes, dressed in a stars and stripes suit. His top hat was covered with glittering silver stars that sparkled like diamonds, while his shoes were long and floppy like those of a clown and covered with stripes in the red, white, and blue of the American flag. I envisioned his tall, angular body at the doorway of the voting booth, stretching out his arms to prevent brown people from entering. I imagined the tall, Anglo man yelling in a heavy Spanish, "Fuera *de aqui!*"

My imaginary characters didn't ask questions, didn't fight back, and left without voting. The more Amagrande spoke about *El Paul Taxes*, the angrier I became. But I got scared too. What if Amagrande was able to vote? Would she have the tenacity to push away the arms of *El Paul Taxes* from the door?

The day I learned the true meaning of the "poll tax," I ran home from school to tell Amagrande. I excitedly said that *El Paul Taxes* was not a real person and explained that the Democrats in southern states had started the poll tax to keep *los Negritos* from voting, and that other states including Texas, followed to keep *los Mexicanos* from voting too.

I thought Amagrande would become an American citizen when the poll tax was outlawed in 1964, but she didn't. Instead, she complained that she couldn't vote because *El Paul Taxes* wouldn't let her.

The older I got the more detached I became from my Amagrande, but the older I got my future without her in my life seemed incomprehensible at best . . . .

Chapter 7

West Pecan Street

"There are no second acts in American lives."
F. Scott Fitzgerald, 1896-1940
American Writer

During the days of the Taft Ranch, West Pecan Street was nothing but a trail upon which cattle and riders traveled to and from. When my family moved there during the late 1930s, there were but a few remnants of the ranch life left such as the ditch that separated our street from the city limits that once served as a feeding trough for the cattle. There were fourteen families that lived on West Pecan Street during the late 1940s and early 1950s. The land was sub-divided into small lots—just about large enough to build one small-size home but most families, in order to house all of their relatives, bought two lots, where they built two and sometimes three homes. Our end of the street—the part west of Davis Road—was only two blocks long but at that time it seemed to stretch on forever. Our house sat on the far west side of the street along with the homes of seven other families. Those seven families became an important part of my early life. They nurtured my spirit and helped influence who I was during those early years.

There was always something happening at the end of our street. The characters came to life in so many different ways. On Saturdays, the khaki-and-white-sleeveless-T-shirt-clad men tinkered with their cars while Spanish music blared from the radio. The women dressed up to go to the grocery store, where they shopped for food that would last a week. And, on Sundays, families came together at their parents' houses. The women cooked a variety of Mexican dishes while the

99

men gathered in the backyard drinking beer and making small talk. We were the only family that didn't do that, because Amagrande didn't believe in such gatherings.

Since West Pecan Street sat outside the city limits, we could own and raise animals on our property. A family, who lived two houses down, owned a cow, which their youngest daughter, *la Bolilla,* and I tried unsuccessfully to milk many times. My grandparents raised chickens which they kept in a coop in their backyard. On special occasions Buelito had the task of picking and killing the best looking chickens. While he studied the chickens to make his choice, I'd run off, not wanting to witness the massacre. I'd seen Buelito many times take a chicken by its neck and wring it until the poor chicken's eyes nearly bulged out of their sockets. One time, Amagrande was entertaining relatives from Floresville so she and Buelito picked out three chickens to feed them. The chickens squawked in terror, running and fluttering, as Buelito chased after them. When Buelito caught the first one, he began by wringing its neck with one hand until the clucking stopped. Afterward, he looked as if he'd been in a pillow fight, covered with chicken feathers from head to toe. Amagrande took the dead chickens and dropped them into a large, cast iron pot filled with boiling water. After they'd been in long enough for their feathers to come lose, I helped Amagrande pluck what was left of the feathers. But neither on that day or any other day that I can remember did I join in on the chicken dinners—I remembered all too vividly the poor things running for their lives from Buelito.

Our life on West Pecan Street reminded me of the Mexican border towns I'd visited with my Amá: Nuevo Laredo, Piedras Niegras and Matamoras. Almost every South Side resident maintained and practiced the customs of their native land: they spoke Spanish, ate food derivative of Mexico, listened to Spanish radio stations, and read Spanish newspapers and magazines. In our home we did the same, except instead of eating the typical food staples of *frijoles rancheros, carne picada con fideo, arroz Mexicano,* and *tortillas de harina,* we ate the type of food Amá cooked at the Johnsons' café. Amá practiced her cooking by serving food I'd never heard of; grits-a mush made from finely ground cornmeal, chicken fried steak, and a gummy vegetable called okra. Sometimes the local ranchers, after a successful quail hunting trip, heaped a crate full of the tiny birds into the backseat of Amá's car. Amá prepared the quail in a wine jalapeno sauce that made the tiny bird taste so rich and wonderful. And when she was in a good mood, she baked a delicious cherry cobbler that left all of us begging for more.

We spoke Spanish at home and when I slipped and spoke English there was always someone reminding me that I wasn't *una Americana*. My grandparents told me that the Anglos were the real Americans; we were foreigners and should act like it. They discouraged me from trying to be too "American." Yet they encouraged me to go to school and to graduate, so I would make something of myself.

Every Halloween night, a large crowd of Anglo teenagers made their way to the South Side to knock down outhouses. They'd hook up the outhouse to the back of their truck and drag it onto Davis Road. Other times we'd find an outhouse lying as far away as Green Avenue, half a mile away. One Halloween night, they knocked down the outhouse of our next-door neighbor while he was inside. The Anglos dragged the outhouse onto West Pecan Street in front of my grandparent's house.

"*Auxilio, Socorro, ayudenme, ayudenme!*" our neighbor screamed frantically.

I wondered who *Auxilio* and *Socorro* were. I had heard the two names in a movie starring Cantinflas where a woman is caught in a fire and yells the same names, except Cantinflas answers by saying, "*Auxilio y Socorro no estan aquí, pero aqui voy yo!*"

Our neighbor was trapped inside with its only door pressed against the ground. He anxiously pounded his fists against the dilapidated wood structure while just about every resident on our end of the street stood motionless, staring at the tiny, wood toilet structure. Finally, someone in the crowd suggested flipping the outhouse so its door faced the dark sky above. He was a large, heavyset man who probably outweighed the structure in which he was trapped; so it took several men and young boys to flip the outhouse. When our neighbor was free, he brushed his giant-size overalls and sauntered off without speaking to anyone in the crowd. He stepped inside his one-room house, where his huge shadow danced against the unfinished, bare walls while his wife and two daughters wrapped their arms around him.

Our neighbor's property lay immediately to the left of our house; only a wire hurricane fence separated his family's compound from ours. Although his family's property was only a tad bigger than ours, it had twice as many structures. He shared a one-room house with his wife, two teenage daughters, and a teenage son. Another son, lived in an even smaller one-room house on the property with his wife and new baby. The oldest son, lived with his wife and their two young sons in a three-room house, the biggest house on our neighbor's property. One of our neighbor's grandsons and I were the same age, but at six years old he was the worldlier. Every time he saw me play outdoors, he'd call me over. When I looked up, he stood behind the front screen door naked as a jaybird. He held his penis, waving it back and forth. But showing the tiny pink penis wasn't enough; his soft voice called for me to kiss it.

Our neighbor spent his day lying on a rickety bench he had made from lumber scraps. He would exchange used glass bottles he picked up along Davis Road for flimsy fruit crates from Julio's grocery store. He carefully arranged the crates around the oak tree; they served as chairs for the daily visitors that streamed in and out of his backyard. The odor from the dirty denim overalls he wore day in and day out reached all the way to my grandparents' backyard. It seemed the only time our neighbor left his space was to visit *el escusado*. Every day, his tiny wife, who reached her husband to the height of his belly button, brought him a plate full of refried beans along with a straw basket filled with flour tortillas and a tall RC Cola.

Our neighbor's youngest son, who was about fifteen years old, was accused of being a Peeping Tom. On most evenings, I'd hear the loud screams of my three older sisters followed by foot stomping that sounded like stampeding cattle in a Roy Rogers movie. The thin wood floors in our house made loud, creaky noises under their heavy stomping. My sisters ran from one room to the other screaming as if their hair were on fire.

For their second act, they were even more dramatic. "*Ave María purísima, ave María purísima, un bulto paso por la ventana!*" they all three screamed in unison. Their third and final act was making a sign of the cross while they ran to every window in the house, looking for *El Bulto!* My sisters' pleas for help from the Virgin

Mary along with their wild screams frightened me more than our neighbor's son whose face popped up from one window to the other. As far as I knew he never hurt anyone. He simply stood next to the window looking for what and at whom, no one could say. We thought that maybe he had a crush on my sister María, but we never had a chance to find out. Our neighbor's son was struck and killed by a car driven by an Anglo from Taft. The story went that the young boy was hitchhiking from Sinton and accidentally stumbled onto Highway 181. That was the end of the Peeping Tom, and my sisters' high flying acts.

Another son, performed for all of West Pecan Street. He got drunk just about every Friday night and he beat his wife in the process. He'd hit her with his fists as if he was fighting another man, except his wife didn't strike back. He dragged his wife up and down West Pecan Street by her hair, while bobby pins flew in every direction. By the end of the beating, his wife's blue chenille housecoat was covered in blood, as were her face and hair.

"Ayayay! Ayayay! Ayeeeee!" his young wife screamed. But no one on our street came to rescue her: not her in-laws, with whom she lived, and not her own parents, who lived nearby. One night Amá got tired of seeing him beat his wife and called Chief Edwards. The chief could be the friendliest and sweetest policeman, but if provoked, he could be one tough *hombre*. When Chief Edwards arrived he found the man on top of his wife, pummeling her face with his fists. The chief forcefully pulled him off of his wife and thrust him against his police cruiser. WHAM! POP! THUMP! The pounding of the man's skinny body against Chief Edwards's car sent chills down my spine. The chief used his fists, pounding the young man's face and chest. He bounced around like a rag doll. By the end of the beating, our neighbor's son lay half dead in front of my grandparents' porch. Chief Edwards kicked him several times while he was down. Blood spilled out of his mouth and nose and looked the color of the catsup that my brother Enrique drenched his fried eggs in every morning. The chief yanked the half conscious man off of the ground and leaned him against the police car, where he placed two newly minted handcuffs on his wrists. Afterward, Chief Edwards threw the culprit into the backseat of his police cruiser and drove him to jail. No one intervened to defend or speak up for the

offender, just as no one had intervened to help his wife when he beat her to a bloody pulp. But our neighbor's family became my family's enemy. They, including the young man's wife, blamed Amá for their son's arrest. The fight between our neighbor's family and my family began in earnest.

Our neighbor's wife, his two daughters, and his daughter-in-law, began tossing their dirty dishwater onto Amagrande's prized white grape vineyard and rose garden. For their part, Amagrande, Amá, and my three sisters fought back by tossing their dirty dishwater onto their family vegetable garden. Even his prized outdoor furniture got caught up in the dishwater crossfire: The fruit crates were destroyed, as was the bench. In the meantime, their grandson's pink penis appeared on the scene more often than not. And the stench from their yard grew stronger by the day. It got ugly!

Our neighbor's son stopped abusing his wife because Chief Edwards made the rounds on West Pecan Street every Friday night. But that didn't last long. Chief Edwards was **gunned down** by a gas station owner on Highway 181 in July 1953, when I was seven years old.

The chief's murder happened after the town's council passed an ordinance that all businesses had to have their lights turned on after hours to deter burglars, because the streetlights were not burning on the main highway. One particular gas station owner refused to obey the new ordinance and threatened that if Chief Edwards showed up at his business, he was going to shoot him. In fact, a witness at the trial testified he had overheard the gas station owner saying, "There goes that S.O.B. I'll get him if it's the last thing I do."

When Chief Edwards got off his motorcycle, the gas station owner shot him four times; leaving him dead between the station's two gas pumps. The station owner wasn't the only bad apple at that gas station. One of his gas station attendants from the North Side was seen sexually attacking his invalid mother by a group of Mexican boys that were doing construction on a nearby house.

We on the South Side wept for days after learning of Chief Edwards's murder. The older residents made a sign of the cross whenever someone brought up his **killing**. Everyone in town who could drive, walk, or crawl showed up for Chief Edwards's funeral. Even, *el panadero con la pata de palo* showed up. He didn't bring his straw basket of freshly baked *pan dulce*, which he sold on the streets of the South Side every morning. Instead, he limped alongside his beautiful wife. It was the first time any of us laid eyes on *el panadero's* wife. The word was that *el panadero* kept his wife by home because she resembled the beautiful Mexican movie star Dolores del Rio and was jealous some man would steal her away. But on the day of Chief Edwards's funeral, *el panadero con la pata de palo* and his wife stood along with every Taftite, wiping tears from their eyes.

Chief Edwards was one of the very few Taft Anglos friendly to us Mexicans on the South Side. He directed traffic on Highway 181 to help us Mexican students cross the busy artery onto the South Side after school. After Chief Edwards was buried, we didn't have anyone to stop traffic for us on busy Highway 181, and our neighbor's son went about beating his wife every time he felt like it.

Even though the South Side wasn't filled with a lot of social activities as those found on the North Side, if we dug enough we could find plenty to keep us busy. In my case, I signed up for just about everything that presented itself on my street. I joined so many groups and played with so many different neighborhood friends that I had difficulty keeping up. I joined the Brownies and loved being one so much that I took to wearing my uniform to school every day until my teacher suggested that I wear it only while attending Brownie meetings. But, Enrique laughingly said the brown uniform over my dark skin made me look like more like a Tootsie Roll than a Brownie so I stopped wearing my uniform and before long I quit the Brownies altogether.

I signed up for piano lessons when I was seven years old. My teacher was a high school student who taught piano to South Side kids after school. The small upright piano was located in the front room of the four-room house she shared with her mother, an aunt, and her younger sister, whom some kids called Aunt Jemima because she resembled the Black lady on the pancake box. I took lessons three times a week along with two other kids my age. The three of us stood to the side of the piano while our teacher's dark, skeletal fingers gently pressed the white keys and then the black keys to show us to how to play.

One of the girls in my class wore pretty pouf dresses with matching hair ribbons. My worn out jeans tucked inside my cowboy boots, my tattered, long-sleeved, cotton shirt with Rex Allen's name embroidered on one of the front pockets, and my unruly curly hair were no match for her ladylike dress and manners. After class, I chased Monica down West Pecan Street, pulled the fancy silk ribbons from her hair, and threw them on the ground. I kicked her shiny patent leather shoes with my boots until she cried for me to stop. It wasn't that I was jealous of Monica; I just didn't see any reason why someone my age had to dress so frilly and be so demure and ladylike.

Monica's neat appearance began to change. The brightly colored silk ribbons that spiraled through her long, yellow braids disappeared, while her bright yellow hair became loose and turned dry and brittle. Her Mary Jane patent leather shoes were replaced with boy-type laced-up boots, while two raggedy cotton dresses replaced her many stylish pouf dresses. Red welts began to show up on her arms and legs. I didn't know it, but Monica had been adopted from a single, unmarried, young girl from nearby Corpus. It took a few years before Monica's biological mother found out about the abuse, and when she did, took Monica back to live with her. After Monica left rumors surfaced that her adoptive father was in fact her biological father; giving rise to why she was abused by her adoptive mother.

One summer, I signed up to go to some camp on the east coast. Amá raised holy hell when she got the bills for all my summer activities, but she paid them just the same, except for the one camping trip to the east coast. Another summer, I inquired about going to Camp Karankawa. The camp was popular with Taft Anglo students, who learned to ride horses, swim, and play a variety of outdoor games during the summer months. What a great way to spend my summer, I thought. But Amá reminded me that I'd probably be the only Mexican at the camp. I envisioned myself singing Kumbaya all alone while the Anglos kept away from me, so I concocted other things to keep myself busy that summer.

The Anglos had the city swimming pool to enjoy during the summer, but we Mexicans weren't allowed to use it. South Side teenage boys used an old excavated hole we called *el pit* that was located on a rural section of the South Side. My brother and his friends swam in the deep hole for several summers until the day Simón, *el chueco* drowned. After that day no one was allowed to swim in *el pit.* Yet, we on the South Side were still not allowed to swim with the Anglos in the town's only swimming pool.

The Esparzas who lived across the street from my grandparent's owned the largest and prettiest house on West Pecan Street. And it seemed their house was filled with visitors from everywhere on an almost daily basis. They bought the first television set on our street and had the first telephone. They didn't let anyone from the South Side enter their home, except to use their telephone, for which we were charged ten cents. One day I needed to call Amá at the Johnsons' café but Doña Cleotilde asked for ten cents before allowing me inside. It was my first time inside the Esparzas' house. The heavy, black phone stood on a small stand at the entrance of their living room. It was the first time I spoke on a telephone and it was odd to hear Amá's voice, which sounded like she was in a tunnel. While I spoke with Amá, I took a quick eye tour of the Esparzas' spacious living room. The gleaming wood floor was partially covered by a fancy, colorful rug, while the high school graduation photos of the Esparzas' daughters, Celeste and Yolanda hung over the mantle of the fake fireplace. Yolanda and Celeste, and my piano teacher, were the only Taft High School graduates on West Pecan Street. As I continued the house tour, the deep, sexy voice of the Mexican singer Chelo Silvas cooed throughout the room. A big yellow-and-green parrot sat in a large cage located in a corner of the room.

"*Quién, es? Quién es?*" The parrot asked over and over.

I later became acquainted with that bird and realized he could say other things besides, "*Quién es?*" One time, I taught the parrot to say "*Chinga tu madre*" and when Doña Cleotilde found out that I was the teacher; she didn't allow me to play with her granddaughter La Bonnie for a very long time.

The Esparza's were well-known on both sides of town. Don Rogelio was a contractor for the local cotton farmers and was the one who went looking for *manos* on the South Side during the cotton harvest season. At twelve years old my Amá sent me off with Don Rogelio to pick cotton. She wanted me to know what real hard work was all about. But my idea of a summer school work vacation didn't include getting up at 4:30 every morning and working like a dog until sunset.

There were three types of cotton pickers on the fields in and around Taft: the hard core migrant workers who could pick cotton faster than a flying bullet, the recreational south Texas types that came to Taft to pick cotton only for the summer; and then there were us locals who sometimes couldn't pick enough cotton in a day to make a handkerchief—we could be more trouble than we were worth.

Our everyday predictable lives were temporarily interrupted when the cotton season began. The South Side came alive! During the late 1950s I spent every summer welcoming the cotton pickers along with other South Side residents. Their caravans, made of large and small panel trucks, station wagons and mid size cars caused a traffic jam on Davis Road. The brake lights of the vehicles blinked like the stars in the heavens as they made their way down Davis Road toward Julio's grocery store. Every person in town had their own reason for welcoming the out of town laborers with open arms. The farmers had extra hands to pick their cotton crop, which made them large profits. And girls like me got the chance to meet new boys. Even Father Joe got into the act. Many of the out of town cotton pickers gave a big chunk of their earnings to Father Joe's Immaculate Conception Church. The Brocamontes family, from central Texas, was one family in particular that came year after year, faithfully giving more of their earnings to Father Joe's Church than anybody else. And because of their generosity, the family was the benefactor of more special blessings from Father Joe than the Pope administered during Holy Week at the Vatican.

In the cotton fields no one came to check our legal status or our ages. But if we didn't pick enough cotton to give Don Rogelio his quota, he'd fire the slow ones. I should have been fired many times over but since I was a friend of Don Rogelio's granddaughter, La Bonnie, he always sent someone to help pick my row of cotton so I wouldn't slow things down. I didn't pick enough cotton to pay for the *pan dulce* and soft drinks I bought on credit from La Bonnie's snack stand, so Don Rogelio cheated on his ledger, writing down pounds of cotton I didn't pick.

Picking cotton was painstakingly laborious and that realization, along with the south Texas heat made me appreciate what the real cotton pickers went through to earn a living. And the Anglo farmers provided nothing more than old run down shacks for the cotton pickers to sleep in. Most of the shacks lacked plumbing and electricity and some even had dirt for floors. Yet, I looked forward to picking cotton each summer and riding in Don Rogelio's truck. As I got older I got to sit on the floor of the truck where my feet dangled barely miss touching the exhaust pipes. There were times that *los Bolillos* chased after Don Rogelio's truck in their cars. The car load of blonde heads raced behind us, honking the horn while *los Bolillos* laughingly threw us the finger. We returned their hand gestures and before long there were middle fingers flashing all over Highway 181.

On Wednesday evenings, the drive-in theatre in nearby Portland charged $1.00 per carload. Don Rogelio filled his panel truck with his hired hands to take advantage of the low price. I was excited to be a part of Don Rogelio's drive-in crowd, but after a couple of trips I became embarrassed at the scene we created. The truck brought jeers and laughter from the movie crowd as we climbed down from the big vehicle which had to be parked in the rear of the theatre to avoid obscuring everyone's view. But like so many good deals, the drive-in $1.00 price tag came to an end because so many movie goers began making their own interpretations of what a carload meant. Some thought it meant loading up the car and the trunk full of people, while others like Don Rogelio interpreted a carload to be the same thing as a truckload of humans.

Something different happened every day in the cotton fields and many times the "happening," was more tragic than funny. By the time I left the cotton fields for good in the late summer of 1964, I had witnessed a handful of children killed by the wheels of the cotton trailers who were left under the trailer by their parents while they picked cotton. And it seemed a snake bit one of us on an almost daily basis. One afternoon, a man's screams rose from among the cotton rows. "*Ayayay! Ayayay*," the man hollered, anxiously. As I looked up, a short, a man with dark-complexion ran down the field with his pants half way down to his knees, exposing his giant buttocks. He flailed his arms in every direction while attempting to raise his pants up. Those closest to him, jerked off their cotton sacks and ran toward him. I was one of those that raced toward the screaming man but I did it more to be nosey than to help. When a group of us reached the hysterical man, we found a long colorful snake slithering away from the place he had been using as a restroom. One of the cotton pickers ran toward Don Rogelio's truck and came back with a hoe that he used to jab at the snake. Blood sprayed everywhere.

"Hijo de su! De buenas que no me picó la víbora chingada," the man declared happily.

If we weren't fighting off snakes, we had to find ways to protect our lunch bags from the same group of boys that walked all the way from town to the cotton field. We knew when the group arrived on the scene. Some voice rang from the middle of the cotton field alerting us, *"Me los voy a chingar a esos cabrones."* When all of us looked up from picking cotton, we could see the group of boys rifling through the lunch bags in the front seat of Don Rogelio's truck where they lay for safekeeping. We'd drop our sacks and run to save our lunches but by the time we got to the truck, only bits and pieces of flour tortillas and greasy Mexican chorizo lay among the shredded brown paper bags. The scene looked as if a bear had gone through our food while Hondo and his friends were off running toward town munching on our food.

While Don Rogelio was even tempered and well liked, his tiny, skinny wife was more feared than loved. Her skinny legs reminded me of the legs on the pink flamingoes that decorated their front lawn. Doña Cleotilde spent most of her time politicking. Every election year, Doña Cleotilde was out and about urging the South Side residents to vote. She didn't have to tell them to vote for the Democratic candidate, because no one in their right mind ever voted Republican; we believed the Republican Party was only for the Anglos and for the wealthy. Days before election time, a line of politicians made their way inside the Esparzas' house. One bright sunny day in 1957, I saw a three-car caravan drive up to the front of their house. A tall, slim Anglo man stepped out of one of the cars wearing a large cowboy hat. Every person on West Pecan Street ran toward the Esparzas' to figure out the identity of the tall, lanky stranger.

"*Ese hombre se parece igual a el Lyndon Johnson,*" someone proclaimed excitedly.

"*No puede ser. Yo creo que es el Ralph Yarbrough,*" someone else hollered.

"*Si, es el Lyndon Johnson,*" the excited crowd hollered in unison.

The tall Anglo man stopped on the street long enough to tip his oversize cowboy hat, and wave to the anxious crowd. It was Senator Lyndon Johnson—alive and kicking on West Pecan Street.

Even though politicians went into and out of the Esparzas' house, I didn't pay much attention to politics until the day my classmate Alicia asked me in the cafeteria line who my parents were going to vote for president in 1956. I was too embarrassed to tell her that I didn't have a father or that my Amá wasn't an American citizen. I avoided answering and instead turned the question back to her.

"Who are your parents voting for president?" I asked.

"Ike! My father fought in World War II and loves Ike. Besides, my father hates Adlai Stevenson because he has been slinging mud at Mexicans," she stated firmly.

Slinging mud at Mexicans! Geez, Louise! That was all I needed to hear. I declared to Alicia right there and then that I too liked Ike.

"Wear this button if you mean it," she challenged.

I proudly wore the "I like Ike" button the entire day at school. But when I got home, Doña Cleotilde spotted me from her front lawn and called me over.

"*Quién te dió esto?*" she asked sternly.

Before I had a chance to let a few words slip out, she tore the button off of my dress. The political button ended up on the caliche covered road, where Doña Cleotilde stomped on it until Ike's his face was distorted and the words "I like Ike" were no longer legible.

"*No sabes tú que solamente los Bolillos ricos apoyan ay el Ike?*" she asked angrily.

After she stomped off, I picked up what was left of my "I like Ike" button and tucked it in my dress pocket. I cried all the way home. It was my first political button but little did I know at the time it would be far from my last.

La Bonnie was my entrée to the Esparza's spacious home and I couldn't wait to visit each day to see what famous and important person I'd find drinking coffee in the living room. It didn't matter that when I called on La Bonnie, Doña Cleotilde made me wait on the white wood swing that hung from the ceiling of their front porch. I was excited to be there and to enjoy the fresh-baked cookies and soft drinks Doña Cleotilde routinely served La Bonnie and her friends. There were three or four of us from our block that routinely played with La Bonnie. Doña Cleotilde held dance contests and rewarded five cents to the winner. We wildly wiggled our tiny fannies and tossed our heads to the left and then to the right to Pérez Prado's mambo music. After awhile, I began to notice that the same girl won every time. I protested. Doña Cleotilde jerked me off of the front porch and led me to the back of her house.

"Ella tiene que ganar, por que su familia es más pobre que todos los demás," she said sternly.

I didn't like the girl that well; that was because her oldest sister had taken me to the family's chicken coop when I was six years old. She pushed me down and forcibly lowered my panties down to my ankles. When the girl bent down and tried to kiss my *cosa,* I jumped up screaming. While I stumbled frantically toward my house with my panties still wrapped around my ankles, her voice trailed behind me, "Come back, you'll like it."

A short while later, the girl and her family moved to another part of the South Side, and an elderly couple moved in after them. Doña Lupe invited me to visit her and Don Juan the first day they moved into the old wooden house. I didn't like to visit them, because Don Juan was a grumpy old man who'd holler at his wife for every little thing.

"Quitate de la ventana, vieja chingada," Don Juan ordered angrily.

Doña Lupe ignored her husband and continued rushing to the window every time she spotted a person walking in front of their house.

Even though I didn't much care for Don Juan, I spent a lot of time with him and Doña Lupe, mostly because of the delicious food they fed me. Doña Lupe liked to dress me up in her jewelry and high heel shoes and used her cosmetics to apply makeup to my face. I ended up looking like a lady of the night by the time she got through with me. That was the only time I saw the grumpy Don Juan laugh, so I was more than happy to have his wife apply makeup on my face. Doña Lupe had statues of the Virgin Mary and Jesus propped up throughout their three-room house. Candles burned next to the statues day and night. She pointed to the small water glass that sat under the Virgin Mary's statue.

"*Vien mira, Chelita. La Virgen se tomó la agua,*" Doña Lupe said excitedly. She believed the glass was dry because the Virgin Mary had drunk the water sometime during the night.

Besides the famous politicians, Don Rogelio and Doña Cleotilde had so many other interesting people visit their home. Among the most frequent guest was a heavyset Anglo woman known as La Mrs. Fike whose only son Billy was my brother's classmate. She was the town's welfare social worker whose job was to ensure that qualified poor, single mothers with children received child welfare benefits. But La Mrs. Fike acted more like a cop than a welfare employee. She did surveillance of welfare recipients' homes from her cream-colored Dodge. For some reason she seemed to focus on one young woman who rented a small house near my Amagrande's house.

One time, Amagrande and I were sitting on the front porch when we saw a young man fly out the back door of the welfare recipient's house just as La Mrs. Fike was driving up. When La Mrs. Fike saw him running up West Pecan Street she gave chase in her new Dodge car. She burned rubber half way up the street, where she caught up with her the man. La Mrs. Fike jumped out of her car and grabbed the youngster by his shirt, tossing him in the backseat of the Dodge. La Mrs. Fike then drove back to the home of the welfare recipient.

From our place on the porch, Amagrande and I could hear La Mrs. Fike scolding the young couple. During her tirade, she made the decision to disqualify the young mother from receiving welfare benefits because her relationship with the young man violated welfare rules. After La Mrs. Fike left, the young girl walked over to us and asked if we knew who turned her in. Amagrande shrugged her shoulders and quickly led me inside the house, leaving the young girl sobbing on the front porch. I didn't feel good leaving her the way we did but Amagrande made it clear she didn't want to get involved in something that would only bring problems with nearby neighbors. She suspected one of them was the informant.

Another frequent visitor of the Esparzas, was the one bad boy of the neighborhood. He was the cousin of my friend *la Bolilla,* but they couldn't have looked more different if they tried. She was as white as Snow White while her cousin's complexion was the color of a dark Hershey chocolate bar. The fathers of *la Bolilla* and her cousin were brothers; the skinny, swarthy-looking brothers looked almost identical. The brothers and their families were migrant workers, but *la Bolilla* and her family used Taft as their base, which is the reason I saw her often.

The boy and his family followed the crops from one end of the state to the other and came to Taft during the summer to pick cotton. When he showed up every smart-thinking South Side resident scattered out of his path. He was known to carry a knife and suspected of even carrying a gun. He wore black from top to bottom and buttoned his long-sleeved black shirt all the way up to his Adam's apple. His baggy black pants sported a watch and chain that hung from a pocket. He wore spit-shined, pointy-toed, black laced-up shoes. We made sure not to look directly into his eyes, which in our culture was a sign of confrontation.

One Saturday night, la Bolilla's cousin made a name for himself on the South Side that was not forgotten for a very long time. No one really knew what led my friend's cousin to attack a cousin of mine on my father's side. Some said that the boy had his eye on a certain girl from the South Side and when he saw her talking with my cousin he went after him with a switchblade. My cousin was unaware that the boy liked the girl—in fact, so was the girl. But just the same, the boy followed my cousin down Davis Road and near Nene's icehouse, he plunged the long switchblade into my cousin's mid-section. The boy kept slashing with such fervor that my cousin's intestines began to spill out on the road. When the crowd saw the intestines protruding from his stomach area, they screamed and ran off as did attacker. My cousin's bloody body was left lying on Davis Road until the ambulance came to pick him up. The perpetuator sprinted up Davis Road toward Highway 181 and was swallowed up in the dark of night. For months after the stabbing there were rumors of his sighting prompting us to keep our doors and windows locked for the first time that anyone could remember.

The sound of ambulances the night of the stabbing seemed louder and lasted longer than usual. It was too late in the night for South Side residents to rush after the ambulance as we were known to do. There wasn't an emergency vehicle we didn't chase. One time the fire department responded to a fire but the Anglo firemen, unfamiliar with the South Side, couldn't locate the place. The fire engines drove madly up and down Davis Road while most of the South Side chased behind in their vehicles and on foot. In the end, the house burned to the ground because the firemen wouldn't stop to ask for directions and those of us who did the chasing didn't offer to help. But on this night, the screaming sounds of the ambulance kept us up most of the night. The next morning a large crowd milled in front of the Esparzas' spilling over into my grandparent's house.

"No sabes lo que pasó anoche, Chelita?" one of our neighbors asked.

"Mataron a tu primo," another neighbor added.

The crowd spoke in a low whisper while looking over their shoulders in case the face of my friend's cousin popped up from somewhere. But he never returned, and miraculously my cousin survived the brutal stabbing.

My cousin was a son of one of my father's older sisters, Nicha. None of my father's family had much to do with me except Nicha, who'd give me a nickel whenever we met on the street.

Tía Nicha always looked elegant. She was the only woman on the South Side who wore a hat and gloves everywhere. She matched the color of her handbag with her shoes, and the black line on the back of her hosiery was always straight. It was as if she had come from some big city and somehow ended up on the South Side of Taft.

After the stabbing, I stopped playing with *la Bolilla*. I was afraid her cousin would show up and stab me too, especially since I was related to his victim. But I also became afraid of another of *la Bolilla's* relatives. A short time after the stabbing, a relative of *la Bolilla's* invited me to play in *la Bolilla's* house. The girl was twelve and I was ten. We went inside the empty two-room house, where the girl asked me to play a game that required us both to slip under the largest bed in the house. I followed her under the double-size bed, where she asked me to lie still. Suddenly, she began to fondle me. I tried to get out from under the bed, but she held me down. The doors and windows of the tiny house were closed, making the temperature under the bed stifling hot, but it didn't matter to her; the much stronger girl kept me pinned down, while she fondled me. I fought to get away and started crying, but only when we heard voices outside did the girl let me go. A short time after that incident, *la Bolilla* and all of her relatives moved away and never returned.

My place of escape from life on West Pecan Street was under the cluster of oleander trees located in the front of my grandparent's house. I lay there flipping through movie star magazines, where I lost myself in the lives of Natalie Wood, James Dean, and my favorite teen idol, Sal Mineo. I suffered a real heartbreak when I discovered that Sal Mineo liked boys, not girls! But that happened long after I became president of the Taft Sal Mineo Fan Club. As president, I received a box full of three-by-five, reproduced signed photos of Sal Mineo, along with a letter thanking me for agreeing to become a president of his fan club. I sold each photo to my classmates for twenty-five cents. My piggy bank grew while my classmates were over the moon with their reproduced, signed photos of Sal Mineo.

I knew fulfilling my dreams would be a huge challenge. In the words of F. Scott Fitzgerald, "There are no second acts in American lives," and I knew that was especially true for Mexican-Americans not only on West Pecan Street but throughout south Texas.

Chapter 8

Mi Casa, Tu Casa

*"Every house where love abides and friendship is a
guest, is surely home, and home, sweet home for there
the heart can rest."*
Henry Van Dyke, 1852-1933
American author and educator

La Quatita came to our house looking sadder than I'd ever seen her.

"My father got a new job. We are moving to another town," she said quietly.

"When? Where?" I asked nervously.

The news struck me as if my place in the world was suddenly pulled away.

"We are moving to Rockport in a few days," she answered sadly.

La Quatita's father's new job was located in a town almost 38 miles northeast of Taft, yet it seemed hours away. La Quatita assured me we would see each other often, but somehow I didn't believe her. For the first seven years of my life La Quatita had been my closest friend on West Pecan Street. In fact, my family, who shied away from bringing outsiders into the family circle, embraced the Garcías more than any others. Fela, the oldest daughter, was the best friend of my sister Delfina and was my confirmation sponsor—*madrina* which meant she was my Amá's *comadre*. But Amá forbade Fela to call her *comadre* because she said the term reminded her of a gossipy person. La Quatitia's older brother, Gaspar, was my brother's best friend. Amá spent most of her Saturday afternoons sipping beer and smoking Camel cigarettes with Ramón and Elvira, La Quatita's parents. Ramón told one joke after the other, while he cooked food

117

on the outdoor grill. Elvira and Amá laughed so uproariously at Ramón's jokes that their laughter could be heard throughout the Garcías' backyard.

I couldn't imagine life without La Quatita. She was my playmate, friend, and protector. When we first met, La Quatita asked that I call her by her birth name, but in time I ended up calling her La Quatita, like the rest of her family. "La Quatita" is an endearment term for twin. La Quatitia's twin sister died when they were nine months old, after the baby contracted a mysterious fever which Ramón and Elvira blamed on someone casting *el mal de ojo* on her.

The best part of my friendship with La Quatita was having dinner with her family. The Garcías were the only family that I knew who actually sat down together for dinner every night. A sense of excitement filled the air when the father Ramón arrived home from work. La Quatita grabbed his lunch box, while her two brothers and sister rushed to hug him and pat his back. Elvira greeted him with a warm embrace and a peck on the cheek. Ramón helped himself to a cold beer while shouting comedic phrases to us all. While Elvira prepared Ramón's bath water, I helped La Quatita set the dinner table. I don't know why I didn't call Ramón and Elvira by the more traditional title of Don and Doña—maybe it was because they were both so friendly and easygoing.

The Garcías' dinners were usually a simple staple of pinto bean soup, ground beef mixed with *fideo* and white flour tortillas. Yet Elvira insisted on using their best dishes for supper and expected that we set them in their proper places. Ramón sat at the head of the table and told endless jokes in both English and Spanish. We had a difficult time keeping our food down from all the laughing we did. At the opposite end of the table, Elvira kept watch over our table manners. She'd give a hard jab at any elbows found resting on the table, and jabbed even harder if we didn't place our napkins on our laps.

Elvira wore the prettiest clothes for supper. She customarily wore a white blouse with a tight black skirt and high heel shoes along with a pearl necklace and matching earrings to complete her ensemble. She wore a crispy, white linen apron to protect her clothing and always wore her jet black hair slicked back into a chignon. Her mouth was filled with gold teeth, which glittered whenever she laughed.

After dinner, Elvira and Ramón sat in their living room smoking cigarettes and drinking coffee. My brother and I, along with their four children, sat on the bare wooden floor enraptured by the stories they told about their younger days in south Texas.

A few days after La Quatita announced that her family was moving, a large, white metal truck roared down West Pecan Street and parked in front of the Garcías' house. I was able to view the Garcías' move from my grandparents' porch. Numerous stuffed chairs, bed mattresses, and clothing were loaded into the truck; when the Garcías' living room sofa landed on the bed of the truck, I sobbed uncontrollably—the sofa was the place Ramón had sat many a night regaling us with funny stories. And when their dining table and chairs were carried onto the truck, I slipped under my Amagrande's oleander trees and sobbed even more. I remained under the trees until all of the household items were moved out of the house. When the truck began making its way up West Pecan Street, the elder Garcías, along with La Quatita and Gaspar, followed in their car. I ran toward the street but the car sped away too soon for the Garcías to see me wave good-bye. I stood alone, engulfed by the dust their car kicked up.

Amagrande's oleander trees replaced the García home after our neighbors moved away. I sat under the trees for days, reminiscing about the delicious meals Elvira had cooked and the many jokes Ramón had told one night after another. I missed my tree-climbing episodes with La Quatita and our brothers the most. The Garcías were my family staple and I felt so lost without them. It was difficult for me to understand how my life had changed so much in so little time. I remembered back to the day the photo on the cover of this book was taken. It started with my sister Delfina taking a photo of La Quatita with her rag doll. I wanted a picture taken with the rag doll too but Delfina refused because she said that the rag doll belonged to La Quatita. I threw myself on the ground, screaming until La Quatita intervened by handing me her rag doll. I grabbed the floppy rag doll, tucked it under my arm, and posed looking more hurt than angry, because I believed Delfina didn't want to take a picture of me, rag doll or no rag doll.

The Garcías' move reminded me of the day their eldest daughter, Fela, eloped with her boyfriend. Both events seemed to affect me the same way. Fela and my sisters, María and Delfina went to see Mexican movies every Sunday at the Rialto Theatre on the South Side. One Sunday, Delfina couldn't go, and for some reason I ended up going with Fela and María. The day was warm and sunny as we made our way to the movie house on Davis Road. During our walk I noticed that a light green car with three men inside passed by us several times. When we reached the Rialto, the green car stopped next to us and a tall, skinny, swarthy man sitting in the backseat jumped out of the car. Fela ran toward him, embracing him tightly. They spoke in a low whisper and after a short while, Fela left the man standing by the car to join María and me.

"*Yo me voy con* mi novio," she announced excitedly.

Fela wrapped her arms around María and me before she dashed off toward the green car. She settled in the backseat with the skinny, swarthy man as the car raced up Davis Road toward Highway 181. I worried that something terrible was going to happen to my *madrina Fela* but María reassured me that she was going to be okay but worried how she was going to break the news to Ramón and Elvira that Fela had eloped. Although we knew Ramón and Elvira as a fun couple, Ramón especially was known to have a temper that could explode louder than a firecracker. María and I never made it inside the Rialto. For me, it was just as well. The Rialto was nothing like the Leland Theater on the North Side. The small building was dark and dingy and most of the seats were torn. We couldn't use the arm rests because they were layered with used up chewing gum, while the choking cigarette smoke hung like a large cloud throughout the theatre.

Life wasn't the same at the Garcías' or in my house after my *madrina Fela* eloped. She, like her father, had an enormously cheerful personality which filled our lives with joy and laughter. Her absence left a big void in my life—she had been like a big sister to me. So when the Garcías moved away, my sadness about their departure reminded me of the day Fela eloped, in more ways than one. For days, I stood watch over the Garcías' house, hoping they would change their minds about moving to Rockport, but they never returned to West Pecan Street, not once.

The Garcías' house didn't sit empty for very long. A newly married, young and attractive looking couple, moved in. The new resident was a salesman in one of the car dealerships in Taft. He wore a suit and tie to work, which made him look prosperous compared with the South Side men, who wore mostly denim clothing to their agricultural and auto mechanic jobs. Right from the start, the man was accused of acting too important among the men on West Pecan Street.

"*Ese pelado se cree muy grande. Cree que es mejor que nosotros*," I heard some of the men on our street say to one another. The couple's pomposity made us feel they didn't want to have much to do with us, so we left them alone.

The young bride was a striking, statuesque girl. Her tight clothes and the manner in which she swished her curvy figure reminded me and the other residents on West Pecan Street of the movie actress Marilyn Monroe. So it wasn't long before the neighbors started calling her "la Marilyn Monroe." I couldn't believe she was a Mexican like me; her complexion was as white as the driven snow. Her light brown hair and tiny, curvy figure stood out among her much darker and very plump neighbors.

The couple couldn't keep their hands off of each other. Every afternoon when he came home from work, she ran to meet him, jumping into their shiny, new car, which was a loaner from the car dealership where he worked. They hugged and kissed until the windows got so fogged that only two large bundles were barely visible. Mornings, when the man left for work, it seemed every living and breathing male on West Pecan Street came outside onto his front lawn. They pretended to be engaged in gardening, while gawking at the young woman, who stood behind the front screen door visibly unclothed, waving to her husband and blowing kisses at him. Her early morning routine made gardeners of even those who had bare dirt for a front yard.

On most Saturday evenings, the couple sat on their front porch sipping drinks. They cooed at each other until the sun disappeared. Afterwards they went inside their house and turned off all the lights.

Life of a different nature began to emerge in the Garcías' house after the young couple moved in. I longed to have a blissful romantic life like that of our new neighbor. I imagined being Brenda Starr, my favorite comic strip character, and dreamed of the day I would fall in love with a man like Basil St. John, Brenda Starr's boyfriend. I realized that Brenda Starr and Basil St. John were only make-believe, while this couple represented a real-life romantic story. But my dreams about them being the perfect romantic couple were shattered. A few months after they moved in, we began hearing cries and screams from the old Garcia house. We knew the beautiful young woman was being hurt by her husband but no one on our street came to her rescue. Some neighbors were heard to say, *"Para qué la ayudamos, ella nunca nos habla. A si es que se chinge, la Marilyn Monroe."*

We saw less and less of the couple hugging and kissing in their car and even less of the young woman standing at the front door waving to husband as he drove off to work. And the two chairs that they had occupied while sipping their drinks sat empty. When we did see the young woman she wore a pair of large, dark sunglasses, while her neatly combed hair was hidden under a bright-colored scarf.

Just about everyone on West Pecan Street had their own theory about why the man beat his beautiful and much younger wife. One of our neighbors told Amagrande, that the day the man started walking to work instead of driving the car dealer's expensive new car was his bride's troubles started. He added that because the man's car sales were low, the dealership owner had taken away the car, then his commission, and finally his job.

One day, the wife's parents showed up. The smartly dressed, middle-aged couple drove their shiny new car, with a small trailer hitched to its rear bumper, to the front of the old García house. The couple helped their daughter load the trailer full of clothes and some furniture. The young woman's bulging stomach was visible, while she struggled to carry items from the house. When they finished loading the trailer, she and her parents drove up West Pecan Street just as the Garcías had done only a year or two before them.

A few months after his wife moved out, her husband packed everything that was left in the house into a beat-up compact car. The Garcías' house became empty one more time. And one more time, I was sad to see its occupants leave. That couple had given me an education about love and hate that I couldn't possibly have learned in a book.

The next occupants of the old García place were a young widow, her three daughters, and a young son; I became friends with the youngest daughter. I wondered why the family had moved from a much larger town to little old Taft. But listening to the girls tell it, their life was turned upside down when their father died suddenly. They came to Taft, like so many people before them, because they had heard its rich land offered many jobs.

The old García home seemed odd and different when I visited the new family. Gone were the laughter and the boisterous personality of Ramón. The house was mostly silent, except when the young widow suffered unexplainable attacks, which occurred at all hours of the day or night. The first time I witnessed the older woman falling down on her bed, I nearly passed out myself with fright.

"Ay Dios mío! Ayúdenme, por favor," the woman cried.

I watched nervously as the three girls took a bottle of rubbing alcohol, using most of it all on their mother's arms and shoulders. The woman lay on her bed in an almost lifeless state, crying and pleading for God's help.

After she fell asleep I ran home to tell Amá what I had witnessed.

"Para mi parece que ella está pasando por el cambio de vida," Amá said.

"Que es *el cambio de vida?"* I asked.

"The change of life is when a woman's body changes," Amá answered in English, in case I didn't understand what she meant in Spanish. "You'll find out more when you get older," Amá continued.

I became more confused than enlightened by Amá's explanation, but I was used to her vague responses. She had a way of leading me down the road and then leaving me in the cold to find my own way out. When I began menstruating at the age of eleven, I became so frightened I left school and ran home to let Amá know, but Amá didn't offer words of encouragement. Instead, she came back with a white sanitary napkin and ordered me to place it between my legs with a tight girdle so it would stay in place. Amá never talked about my monthly discharge again, just as she didn't want to talk further about *el cambio de vida.*

After hearing our neighbor continue to ask for God's help night after night, I stopped going to the old García house.

The next family to occupy it was so poor they couldn't afford to have electricity or running water. Doña Anita was a widow with several children, but only two daughters lived with her. Her oldest daughter, Carmen, lived two houses away in a two-room shack with her four-year-old son, Kiko. Doña Anita had barely set foot in Taft when she became friends with a man from the South side.

This man's family had a reputation for starting fistfights at Don Pancho's dance hall. One Saturday night, one of his younger sons got into a fight with the son of the most prominent gas station owner on the South Side who, because of his business stature, had a little pull with the local policeman, Mr. Johnson. Mr. Johnson was much older than the other policemen in the area, so every time there was a fistfight at Don Pancho's, he'd get knocked over while attempting to stop the altercation. After awhile, the lawman took to cowering under the benches when a fistfight got out of control.

Mr. Johnson was the first Anglo in town to marry a local Mexican-American girl. Yet, interestingly the Anglos didn't run them out of town. Maybe Mr. Johnson's badge had something to do with it. Nonetheless, it was odd to see the old, white-haired man surrounded by his much darker wife and children. Mr. Johnson and his wife lived on the North Side and oddly enough rarely crossed over to the Side South nor did they have much to do with those of us who lived there.

So on this night while the gas station owner's son and Doña Anita's friend's son punched at each other, Mr. Johnson helplessly pleaded with them to stop. But they kept throwing one punch after another until the younger boy threw the final punch, knocking the gas station owner's son flat on the *caliche*-covered street. Mr. Johnson pointed his gun toward the boy while the gas station owner's son managed to raise his head up off of the ground long enough to scream, "Mr. Johnson, *ese bato* was trying to insult my intelligence."

"Hijo de la chingada, que dijo el bato?" someone from the crowd asked.

The boy, who barely understood English, stood with his fists clenched, ready to strike at anyone who moved. He hadn't started the fight, but that didn't seem to matter to Mr. Johnson, who grabbed him by his shirt, throwing him into the backseat of the police car. The boy sat quietly in the backseat, while the gas station owner's son rubbed his hands together boasting to the crowd.

"Ahora si aprendió la lección ese bato, que conmigo no se chinga."

Our new neighbor, Doña Anita, and her friend spent their evenings sitting on the living room floor of the old García home, smoking hand-rolled cigarettes and drinking cheap whiskey. Their silhouettes danced against the bare walls of the house, which was lit with kerosene lamps. Doña Anita told Amagrande that she expected her daughters, Julia and Concha to find husbands in Taft. Both girls were attractive enough, but their skin was as dark as the night is long. On the South Side, many of the boys preferred girls with light-complexion. Still, it didn't take long for the two girls to find love. Julia who was my age was impregnated at the age of fourteen years old by a man who had a wife and several children. After Julia became pregnant her married boyfriend moved his family out of Taft.

When Julia went into labor Doña Anita came to our house to ask Amá to help with the delivery. The old woman promised to pay Amá when Julia got a job. Amá went reluctantly but returned almost immediately, saying she quit after witnessing Doña Anita slapped her daughter across the face several times to get her to hurry and deliver the baby. Julia's baby was born on a small cot in what had been the Garcías' master bedroom.

Amá practiced midwifery, and it seemed there was always some young woman in pain knocking on our front door. They reminded me of *los de la Atayala*—knocking and banging until someone opened the door.

Amá was rarely paid for her services, which were provided on the deliver-now-pay-later credit system. Her deliveries were at times the result of incest and rape and before long, Amá spent more of her time counseling than delivering. She finally gave up the practice—she said it was too all consuming and depressing.

Doña Anita's other daughter Concha finally found a new boyfriend from a good family, but he didn't last long. After the breakup, Doña Anita and her daughters packed up their belongings in a beat-up old pickup and moved to the poorest side of the South Side—*el barrio de la ojelata.*

Before Doña Anita moved away, I became friends with her daughter, Carmen and her son Kiko, visiting them almost every day. Carmen regaled me with stories about her love life. She said her latest boyfriend was kinder than any of her past lovers and was convinced he was going to marry her. But the man, who lived only two blocks away, was married and had a houseful of children.

I spent more time with Carmen and Kiko than I did at my own home and one night when I stayed out too long, Amá sent Enrique to find me. When I arrived, I told Amá a lie. I told her I was with my grandparents. She knew I was lying and took a belt she had used one other time on Enrique also for telling her a lie. Amá didn't believe in striking her children but that night she whipped my body one side up the other with the wide leather belt. She didn't like Carmen or her family and ordered me not to go near any one of them again.

A few days later, I heard loud shrieking wails from Doña Anita's house. I recognized the wailing from my days as a frequent attendant of funerals with my Amagrande. I ran to Dona Anita's house where I found her standing on the front lawn barefoot and wearing nothing but a slinky old dress, telling the neighborhood crowd of Carmen's fate. Apparently Carmen had gone riding with her boyfriend in his new pickup and while drinking beer, the man missed a winding curve, crashing his truck into a ditch. Carmen was killed instantly, but her married boyfriend survived. Carmine's son Kiko was about six years old when he went to live with his grandmother and two aunts. A few months after his mother died, Kiko was taken out of school and spent his time washing and cleaning up after his grandmother and two aunts. When he didn't the job they expected, he was beaten.

After they moved away, it would be another three years before I crossed paths again with Doña Anita and her daughters. My brother's wife, María, prompted the reunion when she came to our house late one evening to ask Amá if she would drive her to the house of Concha, *la puta.*

María said she had heard Concha was flirting with Enrique. My sister-in-law had gotten into catfights with other women she suspected of flirting or having an affair with Enrique. I didn't think much of her complaint, but Amá, who treated her daughter-in-law better than her own daughters, couldn't jump in the car fast enough to drive her to Concha's house. Amá ordered me to ride along. I had a bad feeling about the trip, but I wasn't in any position to question Amá's order or María's suspicion. Our trip to Doña Anita's house took less time than it took us to get into the car. Doña Anita rose from her seat on the front porch as soon as she noticed Amá's green car stop in front of the house.

"*Bienvenidas. Como están ustedes?*" she said warmly.

It struck me that no matter how poor Doña Anita might have been, her gracious manner never seemed to fail her. When the old woman approached the Buick, my sister-in-law, who sat shotgun, asked to see her daughter Concha.

"*Sí, como no,*" Doña Anita said politely.

Concha had barely reached the car when María lunged out of her position in the front seat and grabbed her long, black hair.

"*Que hijo de la chingada quieres con mi esposo, pinche puta?*" María asked angrily.

María took Concha by surprise but not enough to keep her from defending herself. María's long, red fingernails got entwined in Concha's long, messy hair. While María hit Concha with her fists, the young woman tried explaining that she had had nothing to do with Enrique. María, who hadn't witnessed any of what she was accusing Concha of doing, wouldn't listen. She kept calling Concha *puta* while striking her face. Then Concha threw a punch that landed on María's mouth. At that point, María pulled out a small pocket knife and attempted to cut Concha's face but missed. Doña Anita rushed to her daughter's defense, hitting María on the face and head. Amá lunged from her seat hitting at Concha and Doña Anita, who had María pinned down, pummeling her face with their fists. All four women were like cats and dogs, pulling at each other's hair, tugging and tearing at their clothing, while they called each other every Spanish bad name in the book. I shrank down in my seat, embarrassed to see my own Amá behaving like she didn't have a brain in her head.

After it became clear that María was losing the fight, Amá screamed, "*Vámonos de acqui.*" Amá started the car engine and we sped away like a bunch of bank robbers. When we got home, Amá cussed me out for not getting into the fight to help her and María.

I didn't have the nerve to say what I really thought about her and María's behavior so instead I asked indignantly, "How does María know that Concha is guilty of flirting with Enrique?"

"*Cáyate el hocico, pendeja,*" Amá hollered.

I stood between them shaking my head and wondering why María, or any other woman for that matter, would fight over a man. Afraid that kind of craziness would rub off on me, I vowed to myself that night that as soon as I could, I was going to find the first exit out of my mother's house and keep going and not look back.

The García house sat empty for a long time after Doña Anita moved out. Over the years, one poor family after another moved in and moved out, always leaving it in worse condition.

In 1961, Hurricane Carla blew away the old house, leaving only bits of broken glass and weathered lumber pieces lying amidst a field of tall grass infested with mosquitoes and rattlesnakes.

The pecan-bearing trees, along with the fruit trees that gave us pomegranates, peaches, and figs during the summer months, had long been gone. Nothing was left of the old García home except the happy memories I held.

The Garcías were my ideal of the meaning "family," and the memories I shared with them in that small but comfortable and happy home will never die.

Chapter 9

Absent Father

*"A woman has got to love a bad man once or twice to
be thankful for a good one."*
Mae West, 1893-1980
American film actress

Most Saturdays, my sisters María and Jesusa took me to downtown Taft to shop and to visit our Amá at the Johnsons café. One Saturday when I was about six years old both of them took me to the five-and-dime to buy me the baby blue, play telephone for which one week earlier I had rolled over on the floor kicking and screaming. Because I caused such a scene, my sister María hurried me out of the store and I went home without the telephone. When we got home I complained to Amá that María hadn't bought me the telephone.

"Y por que no le compraste el teléfono? Compraselo," Amá ordered.

The telephone was still sitting on the top shelf where I had seen it the week before. The clerk reached up and handed me the telephone. I protected the package as if it were filled with gold. I couldn't wait to get home to use it. On our way home, we walked past Nene's icehouse where there was a large crowd of teenage boys hanging out. Some of the boys waved to my sisters, who cheerfully waved back. But one of the boys left the group and began following us.

"Orale, Putas, pa donde van?" the boy asked angrily.

"Chela, No mires para atrás," my sisters ordered frantically.

They held my hands in a tight grip, picking up the pace.

"Ustedes son puras putas junto con su madre," the boy continued.

All I could think about was my telephone, which María had grabbed away and pressed against her chest along with other packages. I was afraid she was going to crush my telephone or, worse yet, drop it on the road. The faster we ran, the faster the boy ran after us, while the *caliche* on the street jumped wildly from the pounding of our feet. When we reached our front yard, the boy caught up with us and threw a fist up in the air. He got so close to us that I thought his pumping fist was going to strike one or all three of us. His face was sweaty and flushed with redness, yet his handsome looks and neat appearance came through. He wore his jet black hair in a pompadour that resembled Elvis Presley's. He wore neatly pressed pants, while his short-sleeved shirt exposed a set of well-formed biceps.

My sisters and I competed to get through the front door. María got in first, trailed by Jesusa and then me. Our clothes were so wet that they clung to our bodies like fly paper. We rushed to the living room window but the boy was nowhere to be seen. While my sisters stared into the empty street, I searched for my baby blue play telephone and found it intact in its container. I lost myself talking into the telephone while my sisters' chatter echoed in the background.

After that incident, the boy seemed to appear everywhere. I saw him on the school yard. I saw him at Don Pancho's dance hall. But where I saw him the most was at Nene's icehouse and began to notice that when Amá and I drove by, the boy threw his middle finger at us. When I pointed that out to Amá, she said matter-of-factly, *"No le hagas caso a ese pendejo."*

Later, I discovered the boy wasn't the only one to direct hate toward our family. His aunt worked behind the counter of the Taft Drug Store and was known as *la double lip* because she applied her lipstick above her lip line to make her lips look plump. After school I stopped at the drug store along with other classmates to order ice cream cones but *la double lip* waited on everyone except me. *La double lip* ignored me so many times that I ended up having to ask my friends to order a banana nut ice cream cone without her knowing it was for me. One day, I told Amá what *la double lip* did and asked if she knew the woman, but Amá ignored me, as she often did when she didn't want to address an issue or thought I didn't deserve an answer. A few days later, Amá made me wish I'd never asked about *la double lip* or complained about the boy that chased my sisters and me. It was late in the day and the somber gray skies hovered over Taft, bringing with them damp and cold air. As Amá drove her green and white Buick down Green Avenue, we came upon *la double lip* and her husband riding in their car. As the cars met, Amá stepped on the brake. She rolled down the window and yelled to the couple, *"Quien se creen que son ustedes?*

La double lip's husband stepped on the accelerator, jerking himself and his wife against the car seat. While the couple's car sped up Green Avenue, Amá made a U-turn in the middle of the busy downtown street and gave chase. We caught up with the frightened couple in front of the Leland Theatre, where Amá rammed her car toward theirs, forcing them to stop. With her car idling, Amá jumped out and rushed toward the driver's side of the couple's car. *"Abaja la ventana, pendejo,"* she yelled angrily.

"Cálmate Cata, por favor," the man pleaded patiently. But Amá wouldn't calm down. She was angrier than I'd ever seen her. The veins on the side of her forehead pulsed as if they were going to burst, and her face was flushed with redness. With most of Taft's business district as her witnesses, Amá accused the couple of being everything from whores to dirty Mexicans. I slumped down in the front seat of our car, hoping no one recognized me while Amá unloaded on the surprised and frightened couple.

Afterward, Amá drove to Nene's icehouse, where she found the boy that had chased my sisters and me. Amá jumped out of the car, walked briskly toward him, and pushed her face up against his.

"Dime a mí lo que quieras pero a mis hijas no les digas nada," Amá said angrily. The boy stared up in the air without responding to Amá's ranting and raving.

The owner of Nene's icehouse, *Nene el Hielero* as he was known, delivered a block of ice to our house twice a week. He was a short, muscular, handsome man who sported a thick, black moustache. Nene dressed to the nines; his expensive-looking clothes and shiny Stacy Adams shoes made him appear as though he should be working in an office instead of delivering ice. On one of his routine deliveries, I saw Amá and Nene share a gentle kiss after he used a metal pick to place a large block of ice inside the top portion of the icebox. Afterward, they walked out of our house gently brushing their shoulders against each other while they spoke in a dull whisper. After that day, I began seeing more and more of Nene.

On most Friday nights, I'd find Nene and Amá snuggled together on our red vinyl sofa, sipping Jax beer and puffing on one Camel cigarette after another while intently watching Friday night boxing on our black and white television set. After two or three rounds of boxing, I became bored and found myself more interested in the Gillette razor commercials.

On most Sunday evenings, Nene drove Amá and me in his new Mercury either to the Melba Theatre or the Buccaneer Drive-In Theatre in Corpus Christi. I preferred going to the Buccaneer Drive-in Theatre, where the movies were most often in English and in Technicolor. At the Melba, the black and white films were in Spanish that starred Mexican actors I had never heard of. They were dull romantic movies—it was like watching grass grow. But the audience made up for the movies. The men and women got physically and emotionally involved in the movies. Since most movies were filled with sadness and melodrama, the women sobbed uncontrollably, wiping tears from their eyes with wads of Kleenex tissues, blowing their nose so hard that they sounded like a concert of French horns. They talked and screamed back at the actors, especially when a man struck a woman. "*No te dejes! Pégale al desgraciado,*" the women shouted excitedly.

The men weren't any better at containing their feelings. During a fight scene, the men raised their fists in the air while making ducking movements in their seats as if they were in the fight scene. Pedro Infante, who at the time was Mexico's top actor and singer, starred in many movies shown at the Melba. When he got into an altercation, the audience went wild. "*Orale, Pedro, no te dejes, pégale a ese pelado,*" the men shouted excitedly. Pedro Infante was killed in a plane crash in 1953, and it seemed just about every woman in Latin America cried their eyes out, including my Amá, who insisted on seeing every movie the famous movie star ever made. Then of course, I was stuck with having to watch Pedro Infante's movies again and again with Amá.

I enjoyed Catinflas movies the most. Before Catinflas said one word, I, along with the rest of the audience, laughed hysterically at his costume, which consisted of a tattered white t-shirt tucked inside a pair of raggedy, low-waist, black pants. To me, he was funnier than Tin Tan or Fernando Soto *"Mantequilla,"* whom Amá and Nene favored. But it was the audience at the Melba that was more entertaining than the movie itself.

Sometimes Nene took us to see English speaking movies at the Center Theater in downtown Corpus. One of my favorites was *Summer Place,* which starred Sandra Dee and Troy Donahue. I shed tears when Sandra and Troy declared their love for each other. I worried for days after seeing the movie about whether they actually lived happily ever after. I especially liked *Around the World in 80 Days* which practically every Mexican in the Corpus area went to see because Catinflas was one of the stars. Amá and Nene complained that the role Cantinflas played was too demeaning, because he seemed to suck up to David Niven too much.

The three of us liked John Wayne, so Nene took us to see *The Alamo.* The movie was sold out for days and when we finally got there, we stood in a line on Chaparral Street that snaked for several blocks. The day we went, the audience was mostly Mexican. We clapped and whistled when the Mexican soldiers, led by General Santa Anna, were killed, and we cried when Davy Crockett and Jim Bowie lost the battle at the Alamo to the Mexicans. I couldn't understand crying for *los Bolillos*; to me they represented the same *Bolillos* in south Texas that kept us Mexicans out of their lives. Amá and Nene tried to explain that other Mexicans fought alongside Davy Crockett and Jim Bowie. They explained that the men inside the Alamo were fighting for Texas's independence from Mexico. I asked what would have happened to Texas, and to us, if Texas had stayed under Mexican rule. They didn't have answers to my many questions, but both reminded me they were happy to be living in the United States and that I should be too.

Nene took us to the bullfights in Nuevo Laredo, Mexico. I loved going to Nuevo Laredo, even though Amagrande said it wasn't a good example of real life in Mexico, because it was only a border town. *"Tienes que ir adentro de Mexico para encontrar la mera vida del país,"* Amagrande said.

But to me, Nuevo Laredo was as representative of Mexican life as I was prepared to accept at the time. My heart skipped a beat when the lively mariachi music welcomed us into Mexico as we made our way toward the bullring. We eagerly joined the hundreds of people lined up to watch the bullfight. I was fascinated at the grace by which the matador approached the bull to insert the *banderoles* on each side of his neck.

"*Olé! Olé!*" We shouted along with the rest of the audience as the matador teased the bull with his cape.

After the bullfights, Nene drove us to the famous Cadillac Bar. It was an exciting place to be but most interesting to me was watching the beautiful Mexican women walk in with their equally handsome escorts. Their beauty stood out—they looked like movie stars in their tight-fitting dresses and pointed-toe, high heel shoes. Their long, wavy, dark hair, along with their smooth skin and bright red lips, added to their beauty. They were more beautiful than *las Bolillas* from Taft, yet I wondered if their beauty would stand up in Taft as it did in Nuevo Laredo.

Nene was a quiet and reserved man who kept his innermost thoughts and private life to himself. Yet, I managed to learn that our frequent houseguest had been born in Austin, Texas, and was two years younger than Amá. Nene said his mother had died when he was very young and that when his father remarried, Nene moved to be close to relatives in Taft. However, during all that revelation about his personal life, Nene never mentioned that his house sat one block over from ours, where his three teenage boys lived with him and his wife.

Nene gave me a weekly allowance of five dollars. Sometimes when he handed me the five dollar bill, he'd scratch my palm with one of his fingers. I asked a friend what that meant. "You'd better watch out, Graciela, that man wants to have sex with you. That's what he's trying to tell you every time he scratches your palm," she advised cautiously.

The next time that Nene tried to scratch my palm, I jerked my hand away. I kept repeating the same gesture until he stopped scratching my palm altogether. Even though Nene didn't make any other type of supposed sexual advance I remained cautious, always making a point of not being alone with him.

I was about eight years old when I learned that Nene was married. The information came to me through the same channel through which I learned everything else about life on the South Side: Amagrande.

"No sabes que Manuel el hielero es el novio de tu amá y además de todo, está casado?" Amagrande asked sarcastically.

I stayed quiet under the bedcovers in the queen-size bed we shared while she continued talking and talking about my Amá's affair. Amagrande provided unsolicited details of Amá's love affair with *Nene el hielero* that made me cry in shame. I learned about Nene's three sons; one of them was the boy who had shouted obscenities at Amá, my sisters, and me. He was in the same class as my brother, Enrique, and hung out with the same crowd, but I didn't remember him ever yelling at my brother as he did at my sisters and me.

I wished Amagrande hadn't told me the truth about Nene. I could have kept on dreaming that one day Nene would become my father. Instead, I cried myself to sleep realizing but hating the idea that I could never call Nene, Dad.

When I was ten years old Nene separated from his wife. His wife moved with their three teenage sons to a house three blocks from our house, yet Amá continued to sneak Nene into our house just as she had before he became separated. But sometimes she'd drive to his house to entertain Nene while having me wait inside her car. It seemed I waited for hours for Amá to come out, but the wait wasn't for naught—I used the time to learn to spell. I'd spell one word and then another as if I was competing in a spelling bee.

Even though Nene and Amá never got married, Nene and I managed to forge a father-daughter relationship that lasted for almost twenty-five years. He became the father figure that I thought I'd never have and who generously provided for Amá and me. In 1980, when Nene passed away, he took a small but important part of me with him.

I dreamed of calling someone Dad or Papi, or at the least have a father-daughter relationship like the one my cousin Miné had with her father, Tío Mike. It became bittersweet for me to watch the two of them enjoy each other's company. Every day after school, Miné and I stopped at Medina's gas station. And every day, Tío Mike walked from their house, one block away, to meet us. Miné ran ahead of me to greet her father. "Papá, Papá!" Miné called happily. Tío Mike swept Miné up off the ground, snuggling her close to his chest. He pecked kisses on her checks and forehead before placing her on top of his shoulders. I followed alongside while they chatted and laughed. Tío Mike was a good-natured man who did anything and everything he could for his family and at times even for me. Many times he sensed my loneliness and made a point of picking me up and carrying me along with Miné.

Tío Mike served as an army soldier during World War II and spent most of his tour of duty in France. There was talk that Tío Mike had a French girlfriend, but whether or not he did, Tío Mike returned to his family after the war. At first, he worked as a checker at a couple of grocery stores, before ending up as a mechanic in the local John Deere Company.

When I was nine years old, a rooster appeared out of nowhere in our backyard. Amá tried chasing the bird with the bright red beak off of our property, but he kept returning. After Amá gave up chasing the rooster, he came around to our front door and crowed three times. *"Se va a morir alguién en nuestra familia,"* Amá announced anxiously.

The tone of Amá's voice sent chills up and down my spine. I worried that maybe it was she who was going to die. In the Bible, John chapter 13, verse 18, Jesus tells his disciple Simon Peter, "Before the cock crows twice, you will disown me three times." The prediction by Jesus before he was taken away and crucified by Pontius Pilate's soldiers may have been the root of Amá's premonition.

Amá's alarming statement was nothing new. She was always making predictions based on purely superstitious notions none of which ever came true; so I didn't pay her any mind when she brought up the rooster's crowing. In our family, our lives were based on superstitions and predictions from fortune-tellers that Amá visited. She didn't allow my sisters and me to sweep the dust out of our house at night for fear we'd sweep our good fortune away. If we stepped over a sewing needle, Amá said somebody was going to die. Amá never allowed yellow roses inside our house for fear someone would get seriously ill or die. Her superstitions and her visits to fortune—tellers and *curanderos* drove me crazy. Amá visited fortune tellers more often than she visited her own mother, but maybe the fortune tellers gave Amá something to hope for, while her mother gave nothing but severe criticism.

"Vámos para que me leen las cartas," she said often. Amá had a list of fortune-tellers she visited at least once a week. She'd compare

what one fortune-teller told her one week with what another one told her the following week. Whether we went to Taft or nearby Robstown or Sinton, the scene was always the same. The street in front of the fortune-teller's house was lined with cars of all sizes and makes. I hated sitting on some stranger's floppy stuffed sofa for endless hours while Amá had her fortune read. The waiting area was always filled to capacity; all sorts of people sat squeezed in on worn out sofas and rickety old chairs while they anxiously waited for their turn to hear news about their futures.

There always seemed to be some woman with fair-complexion out to get Amá. She'd sit me down to help identify every one of her friends with fair-complexion and sometimes even relatives. And by her own process of elimination, Amá would come up with the person's name. The person could be as innocent as a baby, but it didn't matter; Amá dropped the person from her life; the change was immediate and permanent.

There were times Amá came out of the fortune-teller's house frantic. She'd tell me that at her reading, the fortune-teller threw up her hands and cautioned, *"Hay alguién que te quiere hacer un mal. Asi es que tú tienes que poner mucho cuidado."*

When she learned someone was trying to put a curse on her, Amá drove straight to the house of *el curandero* that the fortune-teller recommended. I told Amá about my suspicion that the fortune-teller got her cut for any referrals she made to *el curandero,* and told Amá. I didn't expect her to agree with me but the intensity of her anger was shocking as she screamed, *"Eres una pendeja. Espero que Dios ne te castige por lo que has dicho."*

Amá relied on healing treatments from *curanderos* instead of visiting one of the local doctors. She took me to a *curandero* to cure me of my constant coughing spells. They were environmental allergies but Amá was convinced someone had put a curse on me. *El curandero* lived in a large old house tucked back into a wooded area surrounded by large leafy trees. It reminded me of a haunted house. While she drove the car up the long driveway, Amá warned that I had to be a believer if *el curandero's* healing was going to work on me. *El curandero* met us at the front door and hugged Amá as if they were long lost friends. I hesitated to walk inside the stuffy, dark living room but Amá pushed me inside.

"Espere usted aquí," el curandero told Amá. The short, stocky, silver-haired man led me into another equally dark room, which he called *el cuarto de los espíritus santos.*

"Quédate parada y cierra los ojos," el curandero ordered.

I kept my eyes half shut to watch what the old man was going to do to me. He took two brown eggs from a woven basket that sat on a nearby wooden table. While he chanted some kind of prayer, the old man took one egg and slid it up and down the front of my body and then took the second one and slid it up and down the entire backside of my body. He placed the eggs on a table nearby and began walking around me while he spat at the space between us.

After spraying my body with enough spit to last a life time, *el curandero* brought out a dead chicken, flinging it up and around my body. Then suddenly, the room went silent. I became anxious and opened my eyes and nearly jumped of my skin when I saw that I was face-to-face with *el curandero,* who looked crazed. His dark eyes bulged while buckets full of sweat ran down his face. I became frightened and started to walk out the door but he grabbed one of my hands, leading me out of the darkened room. *"Ven conmigo,"* he ordered sternly.

El curandero led me out the back door where he placed the two eggs in a shallow hole behind his house. He covered them with freshly dug dirt. But before we went inside, he spat at the covered mound several times and then at my torso area several times too. He told me that the treatment would work immediately but if in two weeks I didn't feel better I should come back for a more intense treatment. From then on I worked very hard at containing my coughing and sneezing spells.

When she wasn't visiting fortune tellers and *curanderos,* Amá trekked to San Juan, Texas about 100 or so miles away to pray to the *Virgen de Guadalupe.* One Sunday after she got out of work Amá insisted I accompany her to San Juan to pay *una promesa a la Virgen de Guadalupe.* After an exhausting three hour trip we arrived late in the afternoon and found the church grounds filled with people in wheel chairs, on crutches, while others were walking on their knees from the entrance all the way inside to the altar where a large shrine of the Virgin welcomed the worshipers. Amá wasn't religious and hardly a Catholic since she couldn't take communion after her divorce. Yet, she walked on her knees like all the others, taking her remorseful self all the way to the Virgin's shrine. She said the Virgin appeared in San Juan and that's why we were there to worship her. Amá confused San Juan de los Lagos located in the Mexican southern state of Jalisco where the Virgin Mary was said to have interceded in saving the life of a daughter of Indian peasants in 1623. Amá believed what she believed and no one least of all me was going to argue about the difference between San Juan, Texas, San Juan de los Lagos, or *el cerro Tepeyac* outside Mexico City, the place where the Virgin appeared to a poor Indian named, Juan Diego in 1531.

After appearing to Juan Diego people all over the world claimed to have seen an apparition of the Virgin but there was no place where the reports were more prevalent than in south Texas. It seemed that we heard daily, news of the Virgin appearing in some unsuspecting cotton field, kitchen window and even on food. When I was 16 years old, a family in a small rural town in south Texas claimed they saw the image of the Virgin Mary in water swirling inside a large tub outside their house. Thousands of Mexican-Americans flocked to the house including my Amá, my Amagrande and me. The line of cars stretched for miles before we finally reached the family's home where we had to pay a fee to park. All kinds of people, young, old, the sick, the dying pointed to the water and swore they saw a blue image they said represented the Virgin Mary. Amá said she saw it too and after much coaxing from her I convinced myself that I too saw the blue image.

The morning after the rooster crowed in front of our house, I was sound asleep when Amá shook me awake to say that Tio Mike had died. *"Que te dije ayer? Te dije que alguién se iba a morir. Tu Tío Mike se murió anoche,"* Amá said anxiously.

My heart began to race. It wasn't that I loved Tío Mike as a father, but he did represent the type of father I wished to have. He could be strict with his children, but his gentleness was a trait that I didn't find in any other member of my family except in Buelito. I found myself unable to stop crying until Amá told me to be quiet and get ready for school. My mind shifted to the Polio vaccines that my cousin Miné and I were supposed to get that day. As afraid of the shots as I was, they were much easier to concentrate on than was Tío Mike's sudden death.

"*Y Miné, va a ir conmigo a tomar los polio shots?*" I asked nervously.

"*Que pregunta tan necia. Todavía miras la tempestad y no te incas. Ojalá que Dios no te oiga!*" Amá admonished.

Amá drove me to school, but on the way she stopped at Tía Lina's. The large, white house that had once been filled with so much joy seemed to have taken on a look of sadness and gloom. I thought back to the good times I enjoyed in that house. I thought about the giant circus tent that had been pitched on the front lawn only a few months earlier. The circus belonged to an Italian family, los Martinellis. The entire Martinelli family performed in the circus. They had a daughter about my age that looked dashing in her tight leotard outfit. She did mini-trapeze acts that I found myself imitating on large tree limbs only to hurt myself in the process. Tío Jesús performed with the Martinelli circus. I screamed along with the rest of the audience when Tío Jesús placed a stick covered with flames into his mouth. After we returned home Tío Jesús showed my sisters and me how he ate fire without burning his mouth: He placed a liquid in and around his mouth that insulated the skin from the fire.

When Amá and I entered Tía Lina's house, Miné approached me.

"*Papá se murió,*" she said sadly.

I wanted to put my arms around Miné, but thought better of it. I recalled Amagrande's words that hugging and kissing were *puro mitote*. Tía Lina walked slowly behind Miné. Her eyes were red and swollen as if from crying all night. Tía Lina said that Tío Mike had died of a heart attack during the night. She kept repeating that she had slept with a dead man. "If I had woken up in the middle of the night, I might have saved him," she said weeping.

Tía Lina had the wake for Tío Mike in the living room of their house. When the casket arrived, my cousin Mike Jr. sobbed uncontrollably calling out for his, Papá. Mike Jr.'s emotional outburst made everyone else in the house sob, including the one person who rarely displayed any kind of emotion, Amagrande.

Tío Mike was well-liked on both the South and North Sides, so a stream a visitors came all day and all night to view his body.

But, it seemed that just about every person who came to offer their condolences asked Tía Lina how it felt to have slept all night with a dead person. The question was at the center of Tío Mike's wake and of his funeral. Tío Mike came to be remembered not for his service to his country, or for being a good and decent man, but for ending up dead in bed next to his sleeping wife.

Miné looked lost for many days after Tío Mike was buried. I thought of the special bond that existed between them, and how much I had wished for a father like Tío Mike. But on the day Tío Mike was buried, I realized that not having a father wasn't so bad after all. In my life, I would be spared Miné's kind of pain as I eagerly followed the path of my fatherless life.

Chapter 10

Buelito

It is said that bad things are suppose to happen on Friday, the 13th, but for me that day in April, 1962, started as happy as I'd ever known. A boy that had moved to Taft a couple of years earlier from Corpus asked if I would meet him at the school's annual hayride. I developed a crush on Bobby Cáceres the moment I met him on the school yard; he was in the eleventh grade and I was in the seventh. I had made a habit of developing crushes from an early age but Bobby was different. He and his family brought a bundle of new energy to the South Side. His father was the new minister of the Ebenezer Presbyterian Church on the South Side, prompting my Amá to call Bobby, *el hijo del precha.* Bobby quickly became known in Taft for his piano playing and singing ability, talents which he used to form a rock singing group of Taft high school boys called "The 4 Royals." His singing group became the main entertainment attraction at Taft dances. Every time he sang, *In the Still of the Night,* I wanted to believe he was singing the song especially for me. So when he asked me to meet him at the hayride nothing or anyone was going to stop me.

At fifteen years old I was crazy about Bobby, even more than I had been for other boys. He was a welcoming departure from my latest interest Alejandro the cotton picker.

I met Alejandro at Don Pancho's dance hall when I was thirteen years old and he was fifteen. His green eyes, long, light brown hair and his thin wavy lips captured my heart. But he came to Taft with his family only during the summer cotton harvest. I waited breathlessly for his arrival. He'd signal his presence by driving past my house several times in a beat up old Chevy that his older brother drove and that was filled with his cronies, other cotton pickers. During two consecutive summers we sneaked behind the old Rialto Theater located near Don Pancho's. We'd kiss under the big, bright moon and talked about getting married and having lots of children. But when Amá learned about Alejandro, she forbade me from ever seeing him again, while at the same time warning me not to get involved with someone poorer than me. Her advice, unfortunately for me, eliminated not only Alejandro but about ninety percent of all the Mexican-American boys in Taft and surrounding towns.

As I prepared to dress for the hayride, Amá walked into my bedroom with the same pained look she had on her face when she lost her handbag in the Kress store in Corpus a few weeks earlier. She sat down on the bed and began weeping—something I wasn't used to seeing her do. "*Papá esta muy malo*," she said softy. I couldn't hide the look of disappointment at the possibility of missing the hayride. Lucky for me Amá thought the look had to do with hearing that her father was ill. I became angry with Buelito for becoming ill on such an important day for me. But later that afternoon when I learned Buelito was near death I forgot about the hayride and about Bobby.

I found Buelito lying on his rustic, old metal-frame bed, barely able to speak or to breathe. I sat down next to him, taking his cold, trembling hands into mine. His ashen face with several days of beard growth made him look ghost-like. I stayed by his side until sundown when family members from Karnes City, Robstown, and Corpus Christi began to fill up the tiny house. But not a single member of Buelito's relatives from Mexico arrived, because Amagrande refused to allow any of her three remaining daughters to call them.

As Buelito lay grasping for air, Amá, along with her two sisters, urged Amagrande to call a doctor but she refused.

"*Su padre no necesita ningún médico. Cállense la boca*," she bellowed.

As the evening wore on, Buelito's gasps for air got worse yet, Amagrande refused to allow anyone to call a doctor. Much later in the night when Buelito began to slip away, Amagrande reluctantly asked Ama to call the town's other doctor rather than her personal physician, Dr. Jenkins. The room went silent when the doctor walked through the front door. He carried a small, black bag which he placed on the floor next to Buelito's bed. After examining Buelito, the doctor gently opened the black bag, removing a long needle from it. When the doctor began to press the needle into Buelito's emaciated, leathery, wrinkled arm, I ran out of the room toward our house. My shoes had barely hit the entrance to our house when the loud wailing of my relatives traveled throughout our property. At that same moment I felt a rush of wind enter our darkened house that was so strong it banged shut the door to my mother's room. It was unusual for wind to blow that hard since the night was still, not windy. As the wind rushed by me, I sensed it was Buelito's spirit saying good-bye as it rocketed off into outer space to another world and to another life. I bowed my head and prayed that wherever God was taking him it would be a better place than the life he saw in south Texas.

I went back to my grandparents' house to see and to touch Buelito one more time before his body was taken away. Buelito's lifeless body laid spread across his bed still dressed in his usual khaki pants, white t-shirt, and white socks. His face looked peaceful, at last. There were so many people sobbing and wailing loudly in the tiny three-room house that my nerves jangled.

When the ambulance arrived everyone in the room began sobbing again, except Amagrande. She sat on the edge of the living room sofa expressionless and dry-eyed. Buelito's ashen white face and frail body was all that was left of his life for us to take into our memory bank.

Before Buelito's body was taken away, someone in our family called Father Joe to administer the last rites but he refused to do that or to even preside at his memorial service. Father Joe reasoned that he had never seen Buelito in his parish and because of that hadn't earned God's blessings. My Amá suggested that Amagrande donate a few dollars to Father's Joe church. But, Amagrande countered by screaming, "*Yo no le doy ni un centavo.*"

The Mexican standoff between Father Joe and Amagrande gave way for Buelito who was baptized a Catholic in Mexico, to have his body taken to the South Side's Ebenezer Presbyterian Church where Bobby's father, *El Ministro Ezequiel Cáceres* eulogized Buelito's life and blessed his soul.

At the burial site I tearfully sprinkled dirt on top of Buelito's coffin. Staring down at the coffin, I recalled the happy times we spent together and thanked him for doing his best to fill in for my absent father.

During the cold wintry mornings Buelito cooked the most delicious cream of wheat for us to share. He favored the thick cream that settled on top of the cereal and Buelito served it to me always. Buelito was our family's *curandero*, he prepared warm teas made from fresh herbs and spices, which he said would cure anything from a stomach ache to a runny nose. Buelito's folk healing methods might have been relevant to him but they were strange to me. I remembered waking up in the middle of the night crying from a scary dream only to find Buelito standing over me with a bouquet of broom bristles wrapped together with a piece of cloth. His tone of voice frightened me as he said sternly, *"Te voy a curar de susto."* As part of his healing process, Bueltio asked that I lie face up on the bed. Then he took the bristles and brushed my body with them. I tried lying as still as possible but the bristles tickled me, making me giggle while Buelito ordered, *"Graciela! Vente! No te quedes!"*

Every time Buelito called my name, I instinctively sat up in the bed, asking nervously,

"Que, Buelito?" Buelito laughed out loud when I sat up and answered him instead of lying quietly in a "coma-like state."

Buelito blamed everything bad that happened to us on some person casting the evil eye on us. I remembered the many times Buelito slid a raw, brown egg up and down my body, while I stood at attention listening to him recite the Lord's Prayer and other select psalms in the darkened bedroom to cure me of *el mal de ojo*. After praying, he'd crack the same raw egg and pour it onto a small bowl. He placed the bowl under my side of the bed that I shared with Amagrande. According to Buelito, the bowl had to remain under the bed all night in order for me get cured from the evil eye. In the morning Buelito removed the bowl from under the bed and gently swirled the egg several times. If the egg was cooked to his satisfaction, he'd happily yell, *"El huevo esta cocido, ya no tienes mal de ojo!"* Buelito said that if the egg coddled overnight it meant the evil spirits had been chased away. Interestingly, the result was almost always a coddled egg, which I suspect had more to do with the south Texas hot temperatures than with some strange evil spirit dancing about our house. The few times the raw egg didn't coddle probably happened during the cold season. Even so, Buelito warned that if the egg didn't coddle it meant the evil spirits were in the house and that he'd have to repeat the egg remedy which thankfully, he didn't do often.

Sometimes Buelito's body had a sour smell—a bitter reminder that his life was anything but comfortable. Amagrande didn't allow him to do much of anything including taking a bath. Every time she left the house, Buelito hurried to boil water in a small tin pail which he used to wash his leathery, wrinkled white skin while he sat inside a large, round tin tub. He used a large wooden ladle to pour water from the smaller pail until it dried up. The aromatic sweetness of the soap gave him such a refreshing smell, giving me a great sense of comfort and protection.

Buelito's last days were agonizing for me to watch; especially difficult was the way Amagrande treated him. Buelito, who had taken verbal abuse from Amagrande for as long as I knew them, finally fought back a few days before he passed away. Their argument started in the kitchen, where I found Amagrande shouting obscenities at Buelito while he kept his head down. Amagrande said things to him about being deaf, lazy and good for nothing. After keeping his head down and remaining quiet for longer than any good person should do, Buelito suddenly lunged toward Amagrande pushing her against the kitchen wall. He could barely raise his voice but managed to say, "Ya me cansastes, basta mujer! In all the years I'd known my grandparents, I hadn't witnessed so much anger between them. I stood awkwardly between them turning my head left and then right as if I was watching a tennis match, while they hurled insults at one another. Amá heard the commotion from way inside our house. She rushed in looking like a wild cat ready for a fight. Amagrande looked for sympathy from Amá, complaining that Buelito called her trash and a whole host of other nasty things.

Amá's face reddened and turned to Buelito, shoving him so hard out of the kitchen that he stumbled in to his bedroom, falling flat on the bed. I followed him and when I began to help him sit up on the bed, the two most important women in my life screamed, *"Ni si quiera te atrevas ayudarlo."*

The last thing I needed in my sweet young life was to get on the bad side of those two temperamental, hard-assed women. I moved away from Buelito leaving him lying on the bed as he wiped tears from his eyes. After that day, Amagrande went out of her way to inflict as much mental pain on Buelito as she had the power to do. She threw things at him, hid food from him and ran him out of the kitchen when she'd find him trying to prepare a meal. She called him bad names I'd never heard and I thought I'd heard them all in their house. When I'd see Amagrande leave their house, I'd run in and sneak food to Buelito, kissing his forehead and hugging him tight as he had done to me only a few years earlier. A few days after their fight in the kitchen, Buelito's health began to decline rapidly so when Amá told me he was seriously ill I wasn't surprised. I just didn't want him dying on the day I was going to have my first high school date.

Buelito slept alone in an old, rusty metal bed that sat in a corner of his room, which was adjacent to Amagrande's bedroom. The house seemed to be the only thing my grandparents shared. The breezes from the Gulf of Mexico missed his room, so it was always stuffy and hotter than a sauna. I didn't know how long my grandparents had slept apart but it seemed odd that a husband and a wife didn't share the same bed. As they got older they rarely spoke. Who knows what things happened between them. All I know is that at the end of both of their lives, they were miserable together but my love toward both of them was equal and unconditional.

Buelito was buried next to his son Victor. That night I slept in his bed and did for many months afterward. The scent of Buelito's life wrapped in the two raggedy blankets he used gave me a feeling of protection just as it had when I sat on his lap ten years earlier. I missed Buelito. He was after all the most important man in my early life.

One thing his death taught me was the manner in which a person's whole life can be so dismissed and so forsaken. I came away shocked at the treatment he received from Amagrande and Father Joe; it was as if Buelito was nothing but mere flesh with bones, absent of life, soul and spirit.

I never again felt the same way about my Catholic faith. As for Amagrande I came to see her through a much different prism than before. My life would go on. Yet, I was convinced that Buelito's protective spirit would follow me always . . . .

Chapter 11

The Enemy Within

"The enemies of freedom do not argue;
they shout and they shoot."
William R. Inge, 1860-1954
English author

There were many stories of Anglos coming into the South Side and doing what they wanted when they wanted without fear of punishment or repercussions. In 1938, Juan and Juventino Mendéz were killed by the town's Anglo policeman, while they lay asleep in their beds. As the story went, the police officer lost his hat at a bar on the South Side, and while he searched all over creation for it, some in the Mexican-American crowd speculated that perhaps Juan and Juventino might have taken it as a prank. It was late into the night when the police officer charged into the Mendéz house and demanded to see Juan and Juventino. Their mother pointed to the room where the teenagers were sleeping. The policeman shoved her aside and before the boys had a chance to sit up and defend themselves, they were both fatally shot in their beds. The lawman then shot the boys' younger brother Paul in the cheek when he tried to protect his brothers, and when their grandmother screamed at the officer to leave her family alone, she too got shot, but she survived along with Paul. The policeman wasn't charged with a crime. The Mendéz killings left many on the South Side quaking in their boots. If the law didn't protect them, who would? For years after the killings, in the vernacular, when the Anglos said jump, we asked how high.

This kind of attitude and acceptance allowed the Anglos to come into the South Side anytime they pleased. But that sort of freedom wasn't shared by us Mexicans: The police routinely stopped any of us driving through the North Side after the downtown businesses shut down, and if we were found walking there, the Anglos called the police who'd chase us back across the tracks. Mexicans and Anglos didn't socialize past regular routine interactions, which included school, shopping, and working.

When I was eight years old I overheard a conversation among several of my Anglo classmates that two boys from Hollywood were going to spend the summer in Taft to visit their grandmother. Hollywood? Wow! I wanted to meet the boys in the worst way. They were from the place movies were made and I somehow felt that if I met them some part of Hollywood life would rub off on me. But because of the unwritten rule of no social contact between Anglos and Mexicans, I didn't get to meet Stacy and James Keach that summer or any of the other summers they stayed in Taft. (I met Stacy Keach in 1992 while he was appearing at the Shakespeare Theatre in Washington, D.C. After his performance we had a conversation about Taft. For a summer visitor, he surprised me with his recall of the difficult times Mexican-Americans faced in Taft.)

The older Anglo women came to the South Side to pick up and drop off their domestic help. The tiny heads of the Mexican women bobbed up and down in the backseats of the shiny Cadillacs and Lincoln Continentals. After dropping off their help, the Anglo women sped out as if they were in some sort of car chase. They barely missed hitting the children that played tag along the road while they pressed down on the accelerator—leaving clouds of white dust dancing along the road to remind us *las Bolillas* had been in the South Side.

The teenage Anglo boys crossed the tracks primarily to look for Mexican girls to "go riding." Sometimes we'd find them gawking from the street at the goings-on at Don Panchos and Los Galindos dance halls, and on Halloween nights we could always count on them to knock over our outhouses. The first time Amá and I saw a carload of mixed Anglo boys and Mexican girls, Ama said, "*Si sus padres saben lo que andan haciendo sus hijos les van a dar unos golpes.*" As the car passed us on Davis Road, the laughter of the crowd prompted Amá to add, "*Solamente las putas se suben en los carros con los pelados, y peor si son Bolillos. Si algo mal les pasa á*

esas muchachas, te aceburo que nada les va a pasar a los Bolillos."
I was too young to climb in a car with *los Bolillos,* so my Amá's
proclamation, fell on deaf ears. But one warm sunny fall day, I came
to realize that while too young to climb in a car full of Anglo boys,
I wasn't too young to be pursued.

On this day I was accompanied by a fourth grade classmate.
While Josie and I chatted about our new classroom, we noticed a
deep green car following us. At first we thought the elderly Anglo
man was driving slow to avoid hitting us. But, after we made a right
turn from Davis Road toward our home, Josie whispered, "Graciela,
don't look back but I think that car is following us." Without looking
back we both picked up the pace but so did the car. Halfway down
the road, Josie left me to walk toward her house half a block away,
but as she veered off she pointed toward the car, signaling that it was
following me. I started running toward my grandparents' house and
made a big sigh of relief after I crossed over the wide, deep ditch
located only a few feet from their house thinking I was out of the
car's reach.

When I began the final approach toward my grandparents' house
the green car was still trailing me. I turned to take a quick peek at the
man inside the car, ignoring Amagrande's past warning, "*No mires
a un hombre mucho porque va a crer que quieres algo más con
él.*" I recognized the driver as the gray-haired, bespectacled older
man I'd seen often driving on Davis Road, to take his blond haired
daughter—one of the most popular girls in town—to school. There
were other times I saw the old man accompanied by his frail, elderly
wife, who used a wheelchair to get around. But I also recognized
him as the man handing out coins to young girls on the South Side,
which he did freely without interruption from anyone. It may have
been because South Side residents thought the old man's actions
harmless that they did not try to stop him, or it may have been
because they were afraid of him because he was an Anglo.

As the green car followed, I worried about what I might have
done to make the Anglo man follow me—I hadn't taken coins from
him; I hadn't as much as even smiled at him. When I reached the
front door of my grandparents' house, I anxiously yanked the handle
so hard that I practically knocked the flimsy door off its hinges.
Amagrande was gently rocking in her chair, sewing design patches

onto a quilt. She raised her head slightly when I ran inside the house and passed Buelito's bedroom, where he lay asleep across the bed, snoring quietly. I ran through the kitchen and flew out the back door, landing on the grassy courtyard that separated my grandparents' house from ours. From there I heard the sound of a car door slamming shut, causing me to look toward the front of the house, where I saw the old man's green car parked. Frightened, I ran to the rear of our house and looked around the corner where I saw the old Anglo hurrying up to the front porch.

The old man let himself inside my grandparents' house without knocking. I peeked into the house and saw Amagrande glance up at the stranger but continued sewing while he made his way through the house. When Amagrande didn't make an effort to stop the old man, I knew I was on my own and frightened beyond anything I had experienced.

I scrambled frantically to find a place to hide and ended up slipping into the crawl space under our house. From my place I saw the old man's shoes hit the back door steps. While I lay still under the house, he paced back and forth between my grandparents' house and our house. My heart pounded hard against my chest; it pounded even harder when the old man walked toward our house, opened the front door, and walked in. His footfalls traveled from one end of the house to the other—at one point stopping directly over the space where I lay. I heard ruffling sounds that made me think he was ransacking the beds in his attempt to find me. While I gasped for air in the stifling, claustrophobic space, my thoughts raced about the possibility that he might find me and drag me out or that a rattlesnake might slither toward me. My heart pounded so fast I thought for sure it was going to burst inside my chest. Suddenly I heard the man's shoes hit the steps leading out the door, where he began walking slowly toward his car. I began to crawl out from under the house as the car sped away, but when I heard the car's loud engine make its way around the back of our house, I slipped under the house once again. The man drove around our block a few more times before finally disappearing toward Davis Road.

I didn't tell anyone what happened, because I was afraid that my famiies tendency would have been to accuse me of tempting the old man. I remembered vividly a few years earlier when a young female relative was molested and nothing happened to her attacker. Given their history, I convinced myself to keep quiet because I knew my family wasn't going to take on the Anglo, no matter that some on the South Side called him white trash. An Anglo, no matter how poor, pathetic, and criminal he or she was, had the upper hand in Taft. My word against his probably wouldn't have stood with my family, much less with the Anglo ruling class of Taft. Although my relative and the South Side teenage girl who was gang raped by several Mexican boys from a nearby town (the rapists only served a short time) weren't victimized by Anglos, our cultural tradition of keeping things quiet allowed the police to look the other way.

When violence and death occurred on the South Side, the police rarely reacted in the same way they did when it occurred on the North Side. Had an Anglo girl been a victim of a gang rape by Mexican boys, the boys would probably have been shot on the spot. A common statement from police in South Texas was "Let the Mexicans kill each other off, there'll be less of them."

On most Saturday nights many of the same teenage Anglo boys that took Mexican girls riding showed up at Don Pancho's dance hall. They milled outside watching us dance to English and Spanish tunes of such south Texas performers as Agapito Zuñiga, Valerio Longoria, and Isidro Lopéz. *Los Bolillos* didn't know the difference between the accordion music of Agapito Zuñiga, and the ranchero music of Valerio Longoria, much less the orchestra music of Isidro Lopéz, yet they tapped their feet and clapped their hands along with the rest of us.

We entertained *los Bolillos* with our polka-type dancing, as did a six year old named Aurora, who performed during intermission. Every Saturday night, tiny Aurora wore the same candy-pink, sequined panties over matching leotards and T-shirt, accentuated by a matching pink ruffle train that ran from her waist to the floor while a glittering tiara sat atop her wavy, light brown hair. She sashayed across the dance floor in pink ballet slippers to Peréz Prado's mambo music. We dropped nickels at Aurora's feet while her plump, dark-haired grandmother hurried to the center of the dance hall to pick up the coins, which she tossed into a large handbag. Little Aurora was the star at Don Pancho's until the day she outgrew her mambo costume.

There were times that the town's constable, Mr. Lee, joined in the dancing. He towered like a skyscraper over all of us and especially over the young Mexican woman he always asked to dance. He danced the *corridos* better than some of us, twirling his dance partner on the creaky wood floor with one hand, while holding down his gun in its holster with the other hand. Mr. Lee kicked and slammed the floor with the thick heels of his cowboy boots, while doing *gritos*. His frequent and only dance partner was a pretty, Mexican woman with fair-complexion whose tight-fitting clothes revealed a large, protruding belly and buttocks the size of big round watermelons. She and her husband had a carload of children, but on Saturday nights her husband was nowhere to be seen, nor was Mr. Lee's wife, whose dark features made her appear more like a Mexican than an Anglo. Some of the older women whispered to each other as the couple took over the dance floor, but the rest of us cheered them as they danced cheek to cheek, clutched together like two peas in a pod.

There were always rumbles at Don Pancho's, and when they happened, *los Bolillos* ran off faster than any of us from the South Side. The summer when I turned twelve, a small group of teenage boys from San Antonio came to pick cotton and, like all the other out-of-town cotton pickers during the 1950s, frequented Don Pancho's. The San Antonio boys stood out among the Taft teenagers, who traditionally wore denim jeans and simple, plain, cotton shirts; the San Antonio boys were dressed in typical *pachuco* dress. Their wide-leg, khaki pants, black shirts buttoned all the way up to their necks, and shiny, pointy-toed, tangerine shoes made them look like poster boys for a zoot suit ad. All four wore small crosses tattooed on their foreheads, a dead giveaway that they weren't anyone to mess with, even if their tattoos were religious symbols—tattoos were tattoos and associated with the bad crowd, *pachucos*.

On this Saturday night, the four San Antonio boys stepped out of a small black car and headed toward Don Pancho's when a local boy yelled, *"Que quieren? Vayánse a la chingada."* That was a typical command from groups of local boys to out-of-towners when they showed up at Don Pancho's. But this time, the local boy was acting alone. While he shouted obscenities, the boys from San Antonio stood silent, staring at the crowd that had gathered. Suddenly, someone's voice in the crowd rang out, *"Son chingones."* Those of us in the crowd believed the warning and yelled at the local boy to stop, but he kept on. As a larger crowd gathered, the local boy got even more wound up, showing off his local muscle with delight. "*Orale putos, vayánse a la chingada de acqui,*" he ordered smartly. One of the out-of-town boys stepped forward and said sternly, "*No queremos pedo.*" But the local boy pressed both hands on the other boy's chest, almost knocking him down on the ground. Within an instant, another of the San Antonio boys pulled out a small gun and pumped two bullets into the Taft boy. Then another of the boys pulled out a gun too and started shooting at the crowd, followed by yet another, who didn't fire his pistol but pointed it at the crowd, while the fourth boy jumped behind the wheel of the car and started the engine. Pandemonium ensued. An older woman standing next to me yelled, "*Ay Dios de la vida! Esos pachuco nos van a matar a todos!*" The crowd of young and old screamed and ran for cover while the three boys jumped into the waiting car, firing their guns into the air. The car sped up Davis Road toward Highway 181 while gunshots rang from every direction. I hid underneath a large truck, praying that its owner wouldn't drive off as so many of the dance hall patrons were beginning to do.

When the police arrived, they found a hysterical crowd and the local boy lying in fetal position, moaning and groaning. After the screaming ambulance drove off, I stood with a large crowd that gathered to assess what we had witnessed. Mostly we criticized the local boy for starting the fight. One person in the crowd said what we were all thinking: "*Se lo chingaron por pendejo.*" There we were, criticizing the local boy, and for all we knew he might be dead.

But he didn't die. And the San Antonio boys were never caught by our local police. A few days after he was released from the hospital, the Taft boy sauntered up and down Davis Road with one arm in a sling, bragging to anyone that would stop and listen, "*Me los chinge a los batos de San Anto.*"

It was a long time after that incident before we saw *Bolillos* again on the South Side. Had we known they scared off that easy, we might have fought against our enemy long before that night.

Los Bolillos came to help us observe *Cinco de Mayo* at *Los Galindos,* a dance hall that became popular when my generation took over the social scene in the 1960s. During intermission, an older leading citizen who was known as having participated in the Mexican Revolution spoke about the significance of the Mexican holiday. The older man explained that on May 5, 1862, the French army, with the loss of several hundred men, was pushed back by the Mexicans in the small town of Orizaba in Vera Cruz. He emphasized the courage and leadership of the Mexican army commander, Ignacio Zaragoza, for whom *Los Galindos* dance hall was officially named. But during his talk, the crowd, made up of mostly teenagers, became bored and restless with the old man's endless lecture.

"Ya cayese el hocico, Viejo pendejo," one teenage boy after another shouted. I didn't think the old man deserved such disrespect, but to be fair the boys were there to dance and chase girls not to be educated about the Mexican revolution.

One October day in 1954, a group of South Side students gathered on the elementary school playground, announcing they were going to the North Side for Halloween. *"Los Gabachos* give lots of candy,"* one in the crowd said, excitedly. *"Si,* I went last year and they filled my bag with all kinds of candy, not the penny junk we get *en el barrio,"* someone else added.

"You mean we can go to *el barrio de los Americanos* on Halloween?" I asked surprised.

"Yes, but only on Halloween, my friend Delia García said cautiously. "Do you want to go with me and my sister?" she asked excitedly.

I couldn't run home fast enough to ask Amá if I could go. Surprisingly, she didn't dampen my spirits by asking a hundred questions. She only wanted to know the type of costume I was going to wear. The García sisters, Delia and Dominga, who were both about my age, came with their mother Lupe to pick me up. When we arrived on the North Side the streets were filled with large crowds of trick-or-treaters running from one house to another. We eagerly jumped out of the car to join them. The excitement of being in *el barrio de los Americanos* on Halloween night helped me to forget my fear of *los Bolillos.*

Los Bolillos were more generous than we expected, handing out Baby Ruth, Milky Way, and Butterfinger candy bars. Some even gave us fresh-baked cookies wrapped in special packages. But we noticed that as soon as *los Bolillos* saw the three of us walking toward their front door, they hurried out to meet us before we had a chance to ring the doorbell. After dropping candy into our paper sacks, they'd wave us off to hurry along.

After stopping at several houses we found one resident that treated us differently. Mr. Copeland, the new high school principal, not only allowed us to walk all the way up to his front door, he invited us inside his spacious, warm, and cozy home. His daughter Maureen was in my second grade class and when she saw me at the front door, she yelled, "Daddy, that's Graciela. She's in my class."

"Invite her in," her father said eagerly.

I stood still—too embarrassed to walk inside—but Maureen reached for my hand and led me inside while the García sisters followed sheepishly. The living room was filled with laughing children while Mr. Copeland and his wife sat side by side on a long sofa. My bare feet sank into the fluffy, cream-colored carpet, which spread over the entire room. I was afraid to take one more step for fear my dirty feet would smudge the carpet. The principal and his wife rose from their seats and cheerfully greeted us, each holding a tall crystal glass filled with some kind of beverage. Maureen and her younger siblings, dressed in Halloween costumes, gathered around the fireplace inspecting their Halloween treats, which they offered to the García sisters and me.

I felt out of place without a Halloween costume, which I hadn't taken time to put on for fear the Garcías would leave without me. Instead, I wore the same coffee-colored, short-sleeved cotton dress I'd worn to school that day. Although I did take time to paint my forehead and cheeks with my Amá's red lipstick to make me look like the Indians in western movies.

While I took bites of the candy, Mr. Copeland asked me many questions. He wanted to know the names of my parents. He wanted to know if I had any brothers or sisters. And he wanted to know if I liked school. It was the first time any one person had taken so much interest in me. On our way home one of the García sisters asked, "Why do you think the principal was so nice to us, Graciela?"

"He's from New York. He hasn't lived in Taft long enough to hate Mexicans," I answered matter-of-factly.

"New York! And just how do you know he's from New York?" one of the sisters asked.

Well, the truth is that I had made an assumption based upon a mistaken identity. I thought I had met Mr. Copeland's mother when in actuality I met Mr. Copeland's mother in-law. This happened when she spoke to our second grade class and I mistook her for his mother. The principal's mother in-law looked elegant in her two-piece matching suit when she spoke to us about New York City, her home. This is where I made an assumption that was wrong, but it got worse. Our class took turns asking questions about life in New York City, a place that enchanted me when I saw its cluster of skyscrapers in books and magazines. I wanted to know so much about New York that I was one of the first to raise my hand, only to end up asking the dumbest question of all.

"Do you have the same kind of money in New York that we have in Taft?"

Mr. Copeland's mother in-law stared up at the ceiling for a moment and politely answered, "Why of course we do."

Everyone in the room laughed, including my teacher. I felt the blood rush to my face and was too embarrassed to ask any more questions, even though I wanted to learn more about New York City.

After that Halloween night, I spent a good deal of time with the García sisters. They had shown me that the North Side wasn't as unfriendly as I thought, yet I continued to believe that the Anglos didn't like us any better on Halloween night than on any other night. I chose to see more and more of Delia and Dominga because of the adventure they had offered into uncharted territory. What else was there for me to learn from them?

I'd walk the three blocks to their house so I could ride to school with them and their two older brothers. I made it a point to arrive early so their mother would offer me breakfast. Their dining table was always topped with platters filled with pancakes, fried eggs, meats, toast, orange juice, and milk.

After school, I usually stayed to play with Delia and Dominga. Their favorite game was seeing how long they could last under their parents' roll top desk. They took turns showing me how long they lasted with the roll top down and expected me to do the same. But as much as I came to like them, I didn't trust them to lift up the roll. The way they spoke about the intense heat they experienced every time they lay under the tightly closed roll top unnerved me. For all I knew they could turn the key that was inserted on the side of the desk and leave me there.

Unfortunately, my friendship with both sisters changed only a couple of years after that Halloween night. One summer day I went to their house to play but found only one of their brothers inside. The tall, skinny brother held open the door but before I had the chance to ask for his sisters, he said, "*Te dejas.*"

Is Delia or Dominga home," I asked nervously.

He shrugged his shoulders as if to suggest he didn't know. I started to walk away but he grabbed my hand and started to drag me inside. I jerked away but his strength overpowered me. He pulled me toward his chest and again asked, "*Te Dejas?*" Without answering, I made such a quick jerk to free myself from his hold that I stumbled down the porch steps, falling on the grassy lawn, where I picked myself up and began running as fast as my legs could carry me home.

I didn't see much of the García sisters after my incident with their brother. And, three years later, when Dominga turned fourteen, she got married. Her parents forced her to marry her boyfriend after they had stayed out all night after a dance. Dominga's parents worried what people might say about her staying out all night with a man that wasn't her husband.

Dominga's parents' worry about what other people might say was typical of the way we conducted so much of our lives on the South Side. Dominga's mother was particularly unforgiving, while her easygoing father was willing to let things go. In the end, the feisty woman, who routinely beat her children with a wide leather belt won out.

I wasn't surprised given Lupe's character and her way of thinking that she forced her daughter Dominga to get married at such an early age. Her explosive temper was evident every day, even when her daughters tried to have fun with her. One time the García sisters and I offered to play a game with their mother that we had learned in school. In this game, one person would hand another person an envelope that contained a large button twisted around with a rubber band, which would pop out when the envelope was torn open. At first, the girls' mother giggled when the button popped out, and the three of us giggled along, but when the button struck her forehead, Lupe's face turned red, while her deep dark eyes practically jumped out at us. She grabbed the wide, black leather belt hanging from a nail on the wall next to the kitchen; striking her daughters on every part of their bodies with such force I thought she'd gone mad. I stood stunned and frightened, not knowing what to do, so I did what any person in my situation would do: I darted out the front door while the girls' cries rang throughout the house.

I missed the García sisters and even their temperamental mother, who had been gutsy enough to drive us to *el barrio de los Americanos* on Halloween night, which few on the South Side dared do. They unknowingly showed me the road to beginning to think about being unafraid to go into the North Side. The Anglos weren't my people—I didn't like them and didn't trust them, because I knew they didn't like me or any other Mexican—yet I knew that soon enough we'd have to coexist in a much closer and more trusting environment. One thing was for certain: The growing numbers of our Mexican-American population were going to force the Anglos to look at us differently, and thanks to the Copeland family and the García sisters, I was well on my road to doing my part to see the new relationship form.

Chapter 12

The End of the Reign

"This is the beginning of the end."
Charles Maurice de Talleyrand-Perigod, 1754-1838
Diplomat and Prime Minister of France
(July 9-September 26, 1815)

The beginning of the end of Anglo dominance in Taft showed, to the Anglos at least, its ugly head in the fall of 1960. I was in my eighth grade math class waiting for the lunch bell to ring when an unusually loud commotion erupted from the junior high school's courtyard. The noise prompted my classmates including our teacher to press our faces against the tall glass windows to get a closer look. The courtyard was filled with a large crowd of Anglo high school students some of whom were crying and leaning on each other's shoulder while others, mostly boys, were cursing and pumping their fists up in the air. As soon as the lunch bell rang, I ran along with other members of my class toward the disruptive crowd.

"I can't believe what is happening," one girl cried.

"We can't allow this to happen," another girl screamed.

The numbers in the courtyard grew larger when many junior high students, some of whom were my classmates, joined in. Before long the courtyard was filled with Anglos crying their hearts out. As I studied their emotionally drawn faces, my attention turned to the large crowd of joyous Mexican-Americans running toward the courtyard.

"Nos echamos a los gabachos!" one freshman with very dark complexion hollered while pounding his chest. Our crowd of Mexican-Americans began jumping up and down with joy because

161

we learned that for the first time in Taft High School's history, the majority of the freshman class favorites elections had been won by Mexican-Americans. My body was covered with goose bumps as the same boy excitedly explained how he and his classmates were able to win eight out of the ten class favorites for Mexican-Americans. He went on to say that even though their majority was about five percent they were able to defeat the Anglos by voting in a bloc. He added they would have been victorious in all ten class favorite categories had they been smart enough to woo the Blacks away from voting with the Anglos. The voting event created by the Mexican-American students of the Class of 1964 signified the beginning of the end of Anglo dominance in school and in our town. It was the beginning of a new era in Taft, and that was something the Anglos were unprepared for and unwilling to accept.

The following year when I became a ninth grader, we Mexican-Americans outnumbered the Anglos by an even larger margin than the class before us. Our margin of 30 percent over the Anglo freshmen was the largest since the first Taft school opened its doors in 1907. We could have nominated a candidate in every category and probably won them all. But it wasn't in our nature. For one thing, we lacked the confidence to put one of our own forward in such categories as "Most Beautiful" or "Most Likely to Succeed." In addition, after spending our entire lives at the bottom of the cultural heap there in Taft, we knew what it felt like and were hard-wired to be empathetic, yes, even to the Anglos who had kept us down all those years. Instead of using our majority to shut them out of all the categories, our deep-rooted inclination was to "play nice." So, in those categories where we were shy about nominating one of our own, we didn't, and voted for the Anglo candidates, hoping it would inspire them to help us in our elections. It didn't. In those categories where we had nominees, they voted against us. Of course, because of our majority it didn't matter, and we elected Mexican-Americans to just about every favorite category.

Our victory proved so overwhelming that the Anglos began crying foul and asked our class sponsors to stop the election. One of the sponsors became so worked up he started screaming at the top of his lungs saying there would be no more elections that day. But we remained adamant and unified, demanding the elections continue.

We won that battle. In one instance we joined the five Blacks to elect a member of their group to a class favorite category. Our support paid off later during my junior year when we needed the Blacks to vote with us. By that year 1963, so many of our fellow Mexican-Americans students had dropped out that our numbers plunged from sixty-one to thirty-two. The total number of Blacks had risen to six, while the Anglos clung to a slim majority of thirty-seven. I couldn't believe how quickly our numbers shrank—we would have been a significant majority had not so many of our Mexican-Americans dropped out of school. But they did drop out, as so many others did before them for a variety of reasons; some got married, others went to work to help support their families, while others simply gave up, allowing the school system to defeat them and push them out.

I came close to becoming a dropout statistic during my senior year when my civics teacher, whom we called Auntie Gladys, tried to expel me from her class only a few weeks before graduation.

That day a small group of Anglo girls sitting in the back of the room were disrupting the class with their chatter while Auntie Gladys was trying to review class material in preparation for our finals. I was lost in my civics book surrounded by the chatty girls when suddenly Auntie Gladys' sour breath hit one side of my face. She bent down and whispered, "Let me see you outside." I followed her toward the hallway. She turned around and pressed her finger against my chest and said angrily, "I am expelling you from my class for talking." I wasn't the one making noise in her classroom but I figured that Auntie Gladys had made up her mind and was determined to blame me and only me. The thought of not being able to graduate with my fellow classmates frightened me to no end. But the more I remained silent the more Auntie Gladys kept poking at my chest while ordering me to get my books and leave her class.

It struck me that if I didn't say something to defend myself I'd end up allowing the school system to mess up one more Mexican. Suddenly, I jerked Auntie Gladys' finger off of chest, looked into her small round tired eyes and said emphatically, "You know who was talking and you know damn good and well, it wasn't me."

"I don't care what you say. You cannot come back to my class," she insisted.

"You are doing this to me because it's a lot easier for you to expel a Mexican than it is to expel an Anglo. I won't let you get away with accusing me of something I didn't do. In fact, I am going to the principal's office and tell him what you are doing to me," I said tearfully.

As I started to walk away, Auntie Gladys nervously offered, "Now Grace, you know I am not prejudiced. Come back into my class and let's forget what happened today."

I didn't like accusing Auntie Gladys of being prejudiced. She didn't need it at her maturing age, and I didn't like hiding behind my ethnicity to defend myself, but I had witnessed Auntie Gladys and other Anglo teachers favoring Anglos over us Mexicans one time too many. It seemed so long ago that I spat in the redheaded girl's face and now I was faced with having to defend myself against an Anglo one more time. I came into the Taft school system defending my rightful place in school and society, and I would leave the same way. This made it painfully clear that in twelve years not much had changed at Taft High School or in the town of Taft, itself even if we Mexican-Americans were fast becoming the majority.

My hometown's social calendar was very much driven by our school's activities. Mostly it was centered on football, but there was one event that stopped the town in its tracks and that was the crowning of the king and queen of Taft High School and the presentation of their royal court which consisted of Dukes and Duchesses, pages and even court jesters. During the coronation ceremony, the Best-all around, Most Popular, Most Beautiful, and Most Handsome boys and girls of the high school were also introduced. Those lucky enough to be elected king and queen found their pictures on the front page of our town newspaper and themselves the talk of the town for days. The king wore an enormous bejeweled crown along with a long, dark satin cape that draped regally over his shiny new suit, while the queen wore an equally sparkling crown and dressed in expensive ballroom attire indicative of her parents' wealth.

The pomp and circumstance of the Taft High School coronation reminded me of the South Texas festivals where the affluent presented their daughters to society. In nearby Corpus we celebrated Buccaneer Days. For an entire week there were a series of luncheons and teas honoring the debutantes, followed by a grand ball where they made their debut in elaborate, majestic gowns that took months to make mostly by hand. A fiesta queen was selected among the debutantes and it was she that reigned over the week's activities along with a prominent member of the community as her king. We ordinary folks rode the carnival rides and during the Saturday night parade we made loud gasping sounds at the sight of the enormously beautiful gowns that graced the daughters of Corpus Christi's wealthiest families. Similar festivals were held all over South Texas cities: Laredo held its George Washington Birthday Celebration, Brownsville had Charro Days and San Antonio had the biggest of all fiestas, called Fiesta Week. The coronation of the Taft king and queen was nothing in magnitude compared to the other South Texas festivals, but its importance to the town's pride and joy was a close match.

The manner in which the election and coronation of the king and queen were carried out by school officials was right up there with the Academy Awards. The names of the king and queen were kept secret up until the day of the coronation. In 1960 I stood in line along with every excited Taft resident eager to shake the hands of the new king and queen. I was overjoyed to press the queen's hand not because she was one of the richest girls in town, but more so because she was the queen of Taft High. For years, the king and queen, like the fiesta queens, came from some of the wealthiest families in town. Every once in awhile one of the poorer Anglos slipped in and when their names were announced the disappointing gasps of the wealthier Anglos could be heard throughout the auditorium. But those gasps were nothing in comparison to those heard when Eliseo Torres was announced as the king of Taft High School in 1962. Eliseo was in my sophomore class. Never in the history of the coronation had a sophomore been elected king—the honor traditionally went to a senior—nor had a Mexican-American been elected to such heights.

There was always tremendous anticipation about who would be crowned king and that year, the Anglos expected the son of the town's two main physicians to be the one elected. But when the name of Eliseo Torres was announced, the reaction from the Anglos, upon hearing that a plumber's son of Mexican parentage was the new king, sent a wave of anger and resentment throughout the auditorium. I wasn't surprised at their reaction, having seen my share of Anglo prejudice toward Mexicans. Yet, those of us in the audience didn't get the full brunt of the Anglos anger as Eliseo did.

After the coronation, it was customary for the king and queen to stand in a receiving line to be congratulated by the townspeople. But that night the majority of the Anglos only congratulated the queen, who was an Anglo, passing up shaking Eliseo's hand while whispering loud enough for him to hear, "dirty Meskin." That night Eliseo ended up weeping instead of celebrating his historical coronation.

But it didn't matter what the Anglos said or did, the time for Mexican-American dominance in Taft had finally arrived. In 1963 the number of Mexican-Americans elected to school favorites and cheerleaders surpassed previous years. I was elated, not so much because we Mexican-Americans had defeated the Anglos in school elections, but more because it gave me a tremendous sense of pride to hear names like Rodriguez, García, and Torres announced at the coronation. Our victory made me proud for the first time of who I was, and it gave me a sense of hope for what I could become. The wheels of change were in motion; we Mexican-Americans were beginning to move together to solidify our strength in school and in town, and I couldn't have been prouder to be a part of that change.

When election time came during my junior year, a few of us Mexican-Americans formed a small group to plan how we would defeat the Anglos, who outnumbered us by only 5 votes. We came away from our first meeting convinced that the only way we could defeat the Anglos was by forming a Brown-Black coalition with our six Black classmates which would give us the very slim margin of one. There were previous times when one or two Anglos from the poorer north side of town voted with us, but while a couple of Anglos voted with us, some of our own Mexicans, whom we called *lambiache,* voted with the Anglos. We knew who the *lambiaches* were and there seemed to be nothing we could do to bring them along. This time I suggested that we nominate one of the *lambiaches* to a class favorite spot so their vote would be guaranteed, but the majority of the group turned thumbs down on my idea with one boy saying, "*Que se chingen.* They let us down in the past, and we can't trust them. If the same two or three *lambiaches* vote with the Anglos, their vote won't make a difference if *los Mayates* (a commonly used term on the South Side to refer to Blacks) vote with us."

After much deliberation our group voted to approach the Black students.

"Send Grace, she gets along with *los Mayates*," one of the group members advised.

"Yeah, but send someone with her so she doesn't give away the store," another laughingly said.

"I'll go with her," volunteered one of my classmates. As we proceeded to walk out of the room, I cautioned our group, "Remember, *Los Mayates* aren't going to go along with us for nothing. They're going to want something in return."

"What would you offer them?" someone in the group asked.

"I would let *los Mayas* (slang for *Mayate*) nominate one of their own to any favorite category they want," I answered.

"How can we be sure all of *los Mayates* will vote with us after they get their nominee in?" another member asked.

"It's a chance we have to take," I answered abruptly.

My classmate and I met with the Black students and made our offer. I began by saying that if all six of them voted with us; they could nominate whomever they wanted from their group to the class favorite category of their choosing. They were hesitant and suspicious at first.

"What do you mean we can nominate anyone we want to any category?" One of the Blacks asked.

"Look, we mean what we say, nominate who you want and we'll support your candidate if you support ours," I said.

"What if we want to nominate Leroy Pleasant?" one of the Black students asked challengingly.

"That's okay," I answered immediately.

"Well, we want to nominate him for most handsome," another one taunted.

The idea was to nominate someone from our class that could be elected the most handsome of the entire school, not just the junior class. I, for one, couldn't see the rest of the high school classes electing Leroy as most handsome of all of Taft High School. He was good looking enough, but never in the history of Taft had a Black student been nominated for any major class favorite category, much less as most handsome of the entire high school. I warned how difficult that was going to be, but the Blacks weren't moved.

"Leroy is our candidate. Either you want our help in beating Anglos or you don't," someone from their side shouted.

"We'll discuss your proposal with the other members of our group and get back to you," I said.

When my classmate and I told our group of the demand made by the Blacks, they broke out in loud laughter.

"Leroy doesn't stand a chance to get elected school wide," someone shouted.

"Why should we care? Our aim is to get our people elected and if we can get *los Mayates* to help we should give them what they want," I said.

Sensing that our idea to form a Black-Brown coalition was about to go down, I reacted immediately. "Well, if you don't want to go along with the choice of *Los Mayas*, do any of you have a candidate you want to nominate as most handsome? I asked sarcastically.

The silence was deafening.

"Okay then, let's give *los Mayas* what they want. In the meantime, we can all sit back and watch the shock on the Anglos' faces when Leroy is nominated," I chuckled.

I thought the Anglos were going to fall out of their seats when Leroy's name came up for nomination to most handsome of the junior class. By the end of the day, history had once again been made in the class favorite election process. Leroy was elected most handsome of the junior class and so were all of the candidates on our slate, including this author, who was voted Best-all around girl.

A new day was born in Taft. The first Black-Brown coalition had been formed and was successful in everything it set out to do. Yet, our group was keenly aware that that same type of coalition might not succeed after our Class of 1965 graduated. Still, we felt satisfied that our class was leaving a voting process in place for future classes to consider.

Although our triumph in class favorite elections brought joy to the Mexican-American community, it also allowed the prejudice of our fellow Anglo students to surface to a level that surprised me. The slights and insults from school officials and residents of the North Side were difficult to ignore. When the 1964 king and queen were elected, both of whom were Mexican, the school officials didn't provide the school owned sparkling crowns and fancy capes to the winners as they had done in the past. And the numbers of Mexican-American students dwindled even more during my senior year to the point that not even a coalition with the Black students would help elect any one of us to any of the favorite categories. The Anglos for their part showed us who was boss with their slim but overriding majority—they chose not "to play nice" as we had done with them during our Freshman year—a lesson learned indeed.

Year after year the Anglos tried everything in their power to change the outcome of the school elections. The class of 1966, which had an even larger Mexican-American student population than classes before it, was told that those students who didn't pay their class dues couldn't vote. The Anglos knew that many of the Mexican-Americans in that class came from poor families who couldn't afford to pay their class dues. But the students wouldn't be deterred; they raised money to pay their class dues with the assistance of the South Side Lions Club.

The way we selected cheerleaders was changed too. The school officials brought in Anglo judges to select cheerleaders rather than having them elected through popular vote as had been done for years. Their reasoning was that since cheerleading was such an important part of the school's football team spirit only the best talent should be cheering. Surprisingly, a year after the change, the judges chose Mexican-American girls to lead the cheers not just Anglos. This defeated the purpose of the school officials intent to keep Mexican girls out of competition so the "judge thing," was terminated a few years later.

Our rapidly growing numbers may have given us the voice we had sought for so many years, but in the end the Anglos controlled the school system, and they found a way to take that voice away from us. A few years after I graduated, the election of class favorites along with the coronation of the king and queen was terminated.

I had been all too happy and proud to be a part of a new dawn in my school and in my town. Yet the ingrained timidity of many Mexican Americans, brought on by years of suffering hard prejudice at the hands of Anglos, surfaced all too often in situations when the urge should have been to fight. That timidity left me wondering how prepared Mexican-Americans were to take even those meager reins of power. No doubt, what lay ahead for Taft's Mexican-American community was going to continue to be rocky. Nonetheless, the footprints of my class and the one before us were going to lead the new school and town leaders toward a more aggressive and powerful direction . . . .

Downtown Taft, circa 1900s

President Taft's visit to Taft, 1909 (Charles P. Taft is left with white beard)

Tia Nicha in typical cotton picking garb, circa 1940's

Tia Lina and Tio Mike, far left, at Don Pancho dancehall, circa 1947

My Family, early 1950s left to right: Enrique, Delfina, Amá, Jesusa, Maria and me (below Jesusa)

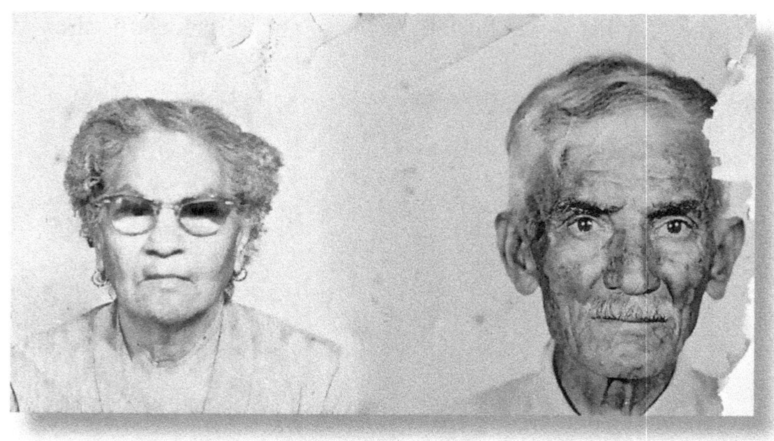

Amagrande   Buelito

With Secretary Joe Califano at a Christmas staff party on December 1978

Harley's three star pinning ceremony, 1985. Gen. Charles Gabriel is at the far left, Harley in the center, and me.

President Reagan announcing his intent to nominate me as the next Director of Community Relations Service in the White House Rose Garden. From left to right: Vice President George H.W. Bush; President Ronald W. Reagan; U.S Treasurer, Katherine Ortega; Manuel Casanova; Rebecca Runge; Rudy Beserra and me, September 1987.

Chapter 13

Time to Leave

*"We feel free when we escape—even if it be but from
the frying pan into the fire."*
Eric Hofer, 1902-1983
American Philosopher

A blast of excitement and change had started my high school life. But while the end of Anglo dominance was all good and well, I had three things on my mind after my freshman year: graduating from high school, moving away, and having a boyfriend. Let's start with the easy part, the boyfriend. All through high school I dreamed of having a boyfriend that would hold my hand while carrying my books to class as other girls' boyfriends did for them. But in my case, there was no boyfriend to hold my hand or to carry my books or do much of anything else for me or with me. I wasn't one of those girls blessed with long, willowy legs and a mass of long, shiny, dark hair. My legs were skinnier than the chickens in my grandparents' coop, my hair was a total mass of unruly curls, my derriere was flatter than a pancake, and the size of my bosom was nothing to write home about. Needless to say, I didn't get much attention from boys.

By contrast, my best friend was such a popular girl that all she had to do was wave her pinky and she'd have most of the teenage boys on the South Side lapping after her. But Tommie wasn't one of those girls whose beauty would light up a room. No, her popularity came, for all practical reasons, from having been elected the first Mexican-American cheerleader in junior high school and later in high school. It seemed every boy wanted to be a part of that historical action.

Aside from developing crushes on movie and television stars I'd never know, I had at least a couple of experiences worth mentioning. Jesse was my first big crush. He and I met when I was fourteen years old and he was a seventeen year old junior at a Corpus high school. I instantly took to Jesse when I saw him surrounded by his parents and other family members at a table covered with liquor bottles wrapped in brown paper bags at a dance in the Memorial Coliseum in Corpus. The Coliseum and another place called the Exposition Hall were popular dance halls with Mexican-Americans. Jesse's dark, bushy eyebrows and dreamy bedroom eyes reminded me of the actor Tim Considine, who costarred in the movie *Shaggy Dog* and in later years was one of the three brothers in *My Three Sons*, a popular television series in the late 1960s. After glancing back and forth at each other several times, Jesse walked to the table where I was sitting with my sister and her husband and asked me to dance. We danced together the rest of the night.

After that night, we saw each other every time I went to a dance in Corpus, which turned out to be about every Saturday night. During the intermission we'd walk a short distance to the T-heads, a lover's lane area made popular by Corpus teenagers. There we'd sit watching the harbor lights gleam throughout the Corpus Christi Bay. When we were away from each other, Bobby Darin's song, *Beyond the Sea* made me want to see Jesse more.

We'll meet beyond the shores, we'll kiss just as before, happy we'll be beyond the sea . . . .

Everything about Jesse, from his wrapping his arm around my neck, to his kissing my lips, seemed so romantic and so magical.

But one night Jesse offered to take me riding in his car instead of walking to the T-heads. He parked the car in a city park near the Coliseum that was dark and empty. Before the car's engine cooled down, Jesse started taking off his pants. In a matter of seconds he was on top of me, trying mightily to take off my undergarments. I tried to slip out from underneath his body, but his weight was too much for me to push against. Jesse had demonstrated on more than one occasion a lightning bolt temper that I didn't want to test if I rejected his sexual advance, so I gently asked that he turn me loose. He held me down even tighter and lashed out, "What's the matter? Don't you think I can support you if you get pregnant? I have a part-time job as a dishwasher. I'll work full-time to take care of you and the baby and we can live with my parents." A baby? A dishwasher? Live with his parents? Jesse told me he washed dishes on weekends and after school, but I didn't think that was his career goal. I didn't know much but from my experience waiting on tables and washing dishes at the Smart's Café I knew there wouldn't be enough money for a family of three to exist in any kind of creature comfort.

While I wrestled with Jesse in the front seat of his parents' car, Amá's advice not to marry someone poorer than me rang loud in my mind. The more I struggled to free myself, the more Jesse lost his charming Tim Considine looks, appearing more like Chester the Molester, huffing and puffing like an old driven horse. As I fought to keep him from stripping me naked, I remembered what my girlfriends had told me to do in the instance a guy got too fresh: I began weeping and slipped in a few words that would make him stop. "What kind of girl do you think I am?" Within a matter of seconds, Jesse jumped off of me and whipped up his pants. He got behind the wheel, burning rubber as he drove down Shoreline Drive as if he was in a car chase. He didn't speak the entire ten-minute drive back to the dance hall. Jesse let me out in front of the Coliseum and as I hurried out of the car, he said in a gruff manner, "When you're ready to go all the way let me know." The gulf winds were so strong that I almost fell down beside the car. I managed to hold myself up, walking hurriedly into the Coliseum, never looking back to face Jesse. Not since the day I eluded the old man in the green car had I felt such relief.

A couple of years later, Amá and I went grocery shopping in Corpus and there in one of the store aisles I came across Jesse, his new wife, and their baby boy. Jesse looked older than his twenty years. His wife, a slim, tall Mexican girl who didn't look much older than seventeen years old, walked slowly beside him in a simple cotton dress, while their baby, who had a bad case of a runny nose, wore a diaper and a flimsy T-shirt. I looked away from Jesse but looked straight into his wife's sad doe-eyes and thought how lucky I was not to be in her place. Jesse passed by without recognizing me and that was a good thing. After seeing him looking so old when he was so young, I was thankful that I hadn't left my virtue and everything else about my innocent self in the front seat of his parents' car that warm spring night in 1960.

After Jesse, I remained the wallflower I'd always been. But it wasn't as if there was a lot to choose from either; the pickings were slim, as many of the boys I grew up with tended to be more like brothers than lovers, and dating Anglos or Blacks was strictly forbidden by the powers that be in town. Like everything else in our community regarding the Anglos, Mexicans, and Blacks, there weren't any written rules that forbade interracial dating; however, everyone in town understood what could and couldn't be done, and I for one wasn't interested in finding out the consequences of breaking that unwritten rule.

But one couple, an Anglo girl and a Mexican boy, tested the rule and learned firsthand that while the Mexicans were accepting of their relationship, the Anglos were violently opposed. Manuel was in my eleventh grade class when he fell for a tenth grader, Virginia. After months of hiding their relationship, they both approached me, as I had been one of their earliest and strongest supporters, even lending them my 1958 Mercury to meet in after school. They wanted to know what I thought about their going public with their relationship. I thought they were out of their minds but they seemed determined. I offered my two bits anyway. "You are both going to have a tough time, especially you, Manuel," I warned.

The next day, Manuel and Virginia showed up on the school grounds holding hands. The entire student body parted like the Red Sea to make room for them, but mostly to stare, as they made their way inside the high school. I was a few feet away from a group of Anglo girls when I heard one of them, one of the poorest in town, angrily denounce the relationship. "That's so disgusting," she said, pointing at the couple. She wasn't the only one who objected and raised hell; just about every Anglo in school ostracized Virginia, ignoring and taunting her. Virginia's father physically beat her the night he found out about her relationship with Manuel. When he got through with her, the short, stocky, red-faced man marched into the H.E.B. grocery store where Manuel worked and threatened to beat him if he continued seeing his daughter. A group of Anglo high school boys led by a boy who liked Virginia harassed Manuel too, chasing him in their car while Manuel walked home from work.

The boys called him a "dirty Meskin" and threatened to beat him up if he didn't stop seeing Virginia. The same group of Anglo boys followed me one night when I drove home, since it was in my car that they had seen Virginia and Manuel smooching. There was talk about other mixed couples liking each other in earlier years, but it was Manuel and Virginia who were the first in Taft's history to expose their relationship so publicly. Their relationship may not have endured, but the two of them pioneered what was inevitable in south Texas, that sooner or later Mexican-Americans and Anglos and Blacks were going to fall in love and marry and have children.

There wasn't an Anglo or Black I was interested in. But even if there were, I knew my courage would not have come close to that of Virginia and Manuel. Nevermind, that I had a hard enough time to getting a Mexican boy interested in me. My crushes rarely resulted in my having a boyfriend. Yet, I kept plugging away. During my sophomore year I had my eye on a football player from the South Side. He was a senior and one of the best linebackers the Taft Greyhounds had ever seen. After one of our out of town games, I approached the heavyset linebacker to walk him off the field, but he hurriedly waved me away, saying, *"Chale! Chale!"* (*Chale* is slang for No). His rejection was overheard by the entire Friday night football game audience, many of whom broke into laugher. *"Híjo de su, el bato te tiro á loca."* several boys said loudly. I wanted to disappear into thin air. As I made my way to the rear of the band bus, an uncontrollable stream of tears fell down my face while my fellow band members whispered to one another and stared. I didn't think I'd ever recover from the humiliation. Later, I found out that the football player had a girl in mind and didn't want to ruin the potential relationship by allowing me to walk him off the football field. It was just as well. I didn't want the girl inviting me to meet her at *la travesía* where rumbles between girls fighting over boys happened on an almost daily basis.

When a girl from the South Side set her mind on a particular boy, she laid claim to him as if he were her very own personal property. Many times the girls fought over a boy who didn't even know he was the object of the fight, let alone the object of their affection. The rumbles all took place in the same area on the South Side, under the same cluster of mesquite trees that stood in the center of a field adjacent to the railroad tracks. The girls came prepared to guard against exposing their underwear, wearing shorts underneath their dresses, or denim jeans. Some girls even took to filing their fingernails until they were sharp as knives so they'd do some real damage to their opponent's face.

Sometime, during my freshman year, I heard that a rumble was going to happen between two girls that were fighting over a distant cousin of mine. I ran to warn my cousin but he seemed only amused. *"Esas viejas estan pendejas,"* he said laughing. He went to the fight for the entertainment, like all of us. When my cousin Miné and I arrived, the crowd was taunting both girls to get it on. We recognized one of the girls as a loud mouth that had a reputation for hurling insults at anyone that crossed her path. The other girl had moved to town a few weeks earlier and seemed too shy to be caught up in a fight. As it turned out, the loud mouth was accusing the new girl of flirting with my cousin, whom she had a crush on. As the two faced each other, the new girl's long, light hair glistened in the sun. It was the first part of her body the other girl grabbed. The new girl tried to walk away but the crowd pushed her back into the other girl's chest. The two tussled back and forth and fell to the ground. The more aggressive girl held the shy, reticent new girl down on the ground, calling her every bad name in the book. Suddenly, the new girl used her fist to smack the other girl on the mouth, drawing blood. At that point the loud mouth girl, sensing she was losing the fight, released the new girl off of the ground, yelling for all of the South Side to hear, *"Vieja chingada, tienes cara de mi panocha."* Everyone in the crowd let out a loud gasp when the "P" word rang out from under the mesquites. The boys let out bursts of laughter and loud whistles while we girls made a sign of the cross and ran off. That broke up the fight. The new girl lifted herself off of the ground and ran along with the crowd of screaming girls. *"Gallina Culeca!"* the other girl screamed.

I felt sorry for the new girl. She hadn't been in school long enough to find her way around to the bathroom, yet she was accused of flirting with some boy she didn't even know. But that was the way of the South Side; stories got started about a person based on rumor and innuendo and before long, the accused, being guilty or not, was tried by the South Side public court.

But back to my loveless life. During my junior year I couldn't find anyone to take me to the prom, so I ended up inviting a relative of my brother in-law, Don Ramon. The chubby, bespectacled, unassuming fellow would have preferred having a root canal to being my date. But, he went more as a favor to his uncle than to be my escort. I had one other date in all my high school years; it was with a boy we called *Jap Chiquito*. Most of his family, with pronouncedly Asian features, looked as if they had been born in Tokyo and somehow ended up in Taft. But they were Mexican, just like all the rest of us. No single member of that family escaped being called Jap: The father and mother were called *los Japs*; the older brother was known as *el Jap*; and all of the younger siblings were called *las Jap Chiquitas* and *los Jap Chiquitos*. That was the way of the South Side; we handed out nicknames freely. There were *los russos, los savages, el camaron, la black widow, Los F's,* etc. etc. etc., The names went on and on, and everyone answered to their nickname, what choice did they have? That is how we addressed them on the South Side.

I went through one failed crush after another, and finally my friend Tommie took pity on me, suggesting we go to the dances in Corpus. "We'll meet cuter and more interesting guys than anyone we'll ever find in Taft," she said excitedly. She added that most of the guys were the type to go to college, and those were the type we should pursue if we wanted to end up with a good and successful husband.

While the Beatles were the rage all over the world, Tommie and I settled for dances that were emceed by a local star, Domingo Peña, who at times was more entertaining than the entertainment. Domingo made his name by emceeing local radio—and later, television shows. He was Corpus's own Don Imus. His manner could at times be overreaching—he once called a guest performer from Mexico *pendejo* in a kidding south Texas kind of way, only to find himself flat on the floor of the Exposition Hall with a dislocated jaw. Nevertheless, his antics and charisma drew in large crowds to the dances which during the early and mid 1960s were mostly sponsored by boys' and girls' social clubs.

Tommie and I decided that the social club dances in Corpus were the places to see and be seen. We thought we had died and gone to heaven after seeing so many clean cut, good looking boys at the club dances many of whom talked about going to college. Even the names of the social clubs gave an aura of high society, De Novos, De-Lords, Paricutins, to name a few. While the girls had equally prominent rings, Prima Debs, Bella Denise, and Hi Fairnessee. The boys' and girls' social clubs had been formed during the days of school segregation in Corpus. They were meant to give Mexican-American high school students a sorority and fraternity-like atmosphere to help them establish friendships within their own community while raising money for local charities. Tommie and I didn't exactly wear out our shoes at the social club dances, but we managed to meet some new and interesting guys while listening to a variety of English and Spanish music performed by the likes of Little Joe, Sunny and the Sunliners, of San Antonio, and Freddie Martinez from Corpus. Many members of the social clubs had talent of their own. Among them was Pepe Serna, who performed comedy routines during intermission. Pepe eventually landed in Hollywood, appearing in movies and television, just as he had told the dance crowd he would—he was my inspiration to follow my dreams.

Tommie and I spent a good deal of our high school life in Corpus either at the social club dances or at high school football games. We especially had our eye on Inéz Peréz, who, besides being cute, was the tiniest quarterback that ever played 4 A high school football in Texas. He was the rage in south Texas, amassing an unprecedented passing record for a guy who stood barely five feet, three inches tall. Inéz was becoming as important as the game itself, and that spoke volumes about him, especially since there was nothing in Texas that matched the importance of football and as we will learn later, no one person except maybe Jesus Christ could stop a football game.

One Friday in late November 1963, Tommie suggested we go to the playoff game that night between Inez's team—the Roy Miller Buccaneers—and the Kingsville Brahmas. I had to figure how to ask Amá, since as I became older she paid more attention to my schedule than she had when I was younger.

During lunch break, Tommie and I were walking toward our chemistry class, talking over our plans to attend the Miller-Kingsville football game. We were deep in conversation that we almost missed hearing a senior girl walking past us say to her boyfriend, "I just heard that some crazy son-of-a-bitch shot President Kennedy in Dallas." We ignored the girl's emotional outburst and continued walking toward our chemistry class, where we found our teacher, Mrs. Cummings, weeping. Tommie and I took our seats along with the rest of the class when suddenly a click, click noise came over the school's loudspeaker. The school principal's voice was low pitched, barely audible. "I have sad news to report. President Kennedy has died . . . ." Before the principal finished his message, many in our class began to weep but not me. I turned to Tommie and whispered anxiously, "Oh! Shoot! Does that mean the football game is cancelled?"

"I certainly hope not," she shot back.

After hearing that President Kennedy had died Mrs. Cummings wept even more. Her lips quivered while she told us that we were dismissed for the day and asked that we pray for President Kennedy's family. Tommie and I darted out of the building with one thing in mind, the football game in Corpus. On our way toward the student parking lot we came upon a large number of students that were crying loudly, consoling one another, while others looked frightened as they rushed to get into their cars and drive off. Yet, all Tommie and I could talk about was the fate of the Miller High School football game and figuring how long it would take us to drive across the Corpus Christi Harbor Bridge in time for the starting kick-off. I dropped Tommie off at her house. As I sped away, she ran alongside my car, promising to call the moment she found out if the game was still on. I rushed home only to find Amá and Amagrande glued to the television set. Amagrande was wiping tears from her eyes, while she sat, slumped down, in the lounge chair that was usually reserved for Nene, Amá's boyfriend. Amá was staring intently at the television set from her place on our red vinyl sofa where I joined her. In the midst of the cameras rolling, showing earlier shots of the Kennedys waving happily at the Dallas crowd, the phone rang, making all three of us jump out of our seats. It was Tommie.

"The game's on! I am ready to go anytime you are," she said excitedly.

I had to figure out how in the world I was going to ask Amá for permission to attend the football game on such a sad day. Asking Amá for permission could be worse than standing in front of a firing squad. She could be deliberately suspicious, raising the type of questions that only the police might ask of a criminal. I tried being nice, offering her a cup of coffee before bringing up the impossible subject. "Amá, there's a football game in Corpus tonight," I said innocently.

Amá turned toward me and gave me the kind of look that I could only imagine a criminal got from a judge prior to being sentenced to death. Before she said anything further, I nervously went into the kitchen to make myself a bologna and cheese sandwich. Amá followed me into the kitchen, interrupting my first bite of the sandwich while she angrily admonished, "*Que Corazón tan negro tienes! El Presidente de los Estados Unidos está muerto, y lo unico que piensas es ir a un juego de fútbol. No tienes vergüenza.*"

I ate my sandwich slowly, giving her time to vent anger, express her sadness and whatever else she was feeling about the day, before I struck again.

"Well, if you or I had died, do you think President Kennedy would have cancelled his plans for us?" I asked smartly.

"*Como te pones a compararte con el Presidente de los estados unidos, pendeja?*" she screamed angrily.

Amagrande saved the day. "*Déjala que vaya. Ella esta joven. El Presidente Kennedy no va a regresar de la muerte si Graciela se queda en la casa,*" Amagrande advised.

The Miller High football stadium was packed to the rafters and with the crowd's demonstrated excitement, I momentarily forgot that President Kennedy had been killed earlier in the day so it seemed had everyone else in the stadium. During halftime I looked forward to hearing the Miller High Band. Their school spirit song, *In the Mood,* and their fight song, *The Notre Dame Victory March* were as popular with football fans as the game itself. Our marching song, *The Men of Ohio* sent goose bumps every time I took a step on the field, but *In the Mood* especially gave me an extra charge of football spirit. However, during halftime everyone in the stadium was reminded that it was one of the saddest days in America, and the halftime show was cancelled for a moment of silence in honor of President Kennedy. The Miller High Bucs went on to win the playoff game, and Inéz Peréz made more headlines.

The next day, I was forced to face the reality of our nation's tragedy by watching reruns of the assassination. I watched President Kennedy's funeral from beginning to end and I, along with many millions of other Americans, worried about his small children. For some reason I paralleled the death of President Kennedy with that of my Tio Mike eight years earlier. They were both World War II veterans that left behind lonely, frightened young widows and very sad children. When I revealed to a friend about feeling sad for the Kennedy children in almost the same way I felt for my cousins when Tio Mike died, she interrupted, "Those children are rich. They'll be fine."

I didn't think it mattered whether a person had lots of money or no money at all; losing a parent at such a young age is bound to affect a person. I had seen Tío Mike's children go through a period of sadness that never seemed to end. Their lives, like those of the Kennedy children, were turned upside down overnight. In the matter of my cousins I wonder how much their lives would have been different had Tio Mike not died so young. As for the Kennedy children, I was struck in later years when I met both of them by how content they seemed. I credit their mother, their environment, and their friends and relatives for helping them become accomplished human beings, and that kind of support can only help regardless of whether a person is rich or poor.

After President Kennedy was buried I, like everyone else, went on with my life. But my thoughts lingered for months afterward about whether the America I had once known was ever going to be the same again. I was concerned about a country as powerful as the United States finding itself in a position where its leader was gunned down in broad daylight in front of millions of people. And it was disconcerting, to say the least, that the president of the United States was killed in, of all places, my beloved home state of Texas. I struggled even more to understand how ONE man could elude the powerful Secret Service and kill the president all by himself. But rather than become obsessed with figuring out who had REALLY killed President Kennedy, I concentrated on my own shaky future.

As I prepared to graduate from high school I found myself in such an untenable situation that I feared my road out of Taft was blocked forever. During my freshmen year, I had enrolled in what the school called a non-college program. The non-college program was nothing more than a quick method to get Mexican-Americans through and out of school. The school officials sold it as an alternative. An alternative! To what? I remembered a school official saying, "You can always switch to the college program if you change your mind about going to college." But in my junior year a classmate helped me understand what I'd gotten myself into when she warned that I was going to be lucky to land a job mopping floors at the Piggly Wiggly if I remained in the non-college program. "That non-college program is nothing but an attempt to keep Mexican-Americans down," she said. I went in to tell the school counselor that I wanted to switch programs, but he let me know straightaway that it was too late. He ended our conversation by saying, "Besides, your parents probably can't afford to send you to college anyway." His remarks cut through me like a switchblade, slicing up my future into tiny hapless bits.

The counselor's attitude reminded me of the high school librarian who was married to the school superintendent and who had tried to discourage me from checking out a book on colleges a year earlier. "What, might I ask, are you going to do with that book?" She demanded. Before I had a chance to respond, she stood up and added sarcastically, "That book is for our students that are planning to go to college, put it back where you found it so **they** can check it out."

"But I just want to read about colleges," I whispered.

While I stood with the book in my hand, the librarian stroked her deep copper hair, looking off into space. I didn't have any idea whether I was going to graduate from high school, let alone attend college, but her manner only made me want to check out the book that much more, which she allowed me to do, reluctantly. I knew of only two Mexican-Americans that had gone to college. One ended up dropping out after the first year, and the other was expelled for stealing. What I did see was one Mexican-American after another stocking food cans, cleaning vegetables, or bagging groceries at the Piggly Wiggly. Yet, I somehow thought I'd find a way to escape that kind of life.

But the counselor and the librarian weren't the only ones blocking my college door. Members of my own family accused me of trying to be like *una Americana* when I talked about wanting to go to college.

"*El colegio es para los Americanos. Que tantos Mexicanos de Taft conoces que van al colegio?*" they asked laughingly.

Every member of my immediate family had dropped out of school, so talk about graduating from high school, let alone attending college, didn't come up. Amá provided generously for my whims and desires, but she was short in providing the support I needed and so desperately wanted in school. She missed parent-teacher meetings and failed to show up at my school events—she was simply not engaged in my academics. My decision to enroll in the non-college program, and my low grades, weren't going to get me accepted into any college in the state, especially the University of Texas at Austin, which was where I REALLY wanted to go. That wish had as much chance of being fulfilled as my being crowned Miss America. A classmate insisted that I need not apply there. "Only Anglos go to UT. Besides, you don't have the grades. Come along with *la Raza* (slang for Hispanics) to Del Mar Junior College in Corpus," she offered. But Corpus was simply not far enough away for my taste.

I spent the early part of the summer of 1965 attempting to get accepted into south Texas junior colleges, but none of them would take me, not even Laredo Junior College, which was known to take just about any warm body regardless . . . . My dream of going to college and moving away seemed more remote as each day passed. But I was determined to head out of Taft to attend some kind of college. I didn't want to end up like many other local high graduates, selling clothes at some department store, not even if it was an upscale store like Lichtenstein's in Corpus. My determination was made even that much stronger when I'd see *los Americanos* drive back to their colleges after spending weekends with their parents. I watched with awe as the happy-faced students raced out of Taft with college stickers displayed on the back windshields from places such as; the University of Texas, Texas A&I, Texas Tech, and Texas A&M. I dreamed of driving out of town just as they did in a car filled with clothes hanging from a makeshift rack. Their lives seemed so different from any I witnessed on the South Side. And I so wanted to experience their type of life.

I found out about Durham Business College by seeing its building on a side street in downtown Corpus after a day of shopping with Amá. It shouldn't have been called a college, since it was merely a trade school that prepared high school graduates to be secretaries, typists, and bookkeepers. Just the same, I called the school to learn more about its academic requirements. The school's dean (I figured the title was to give the allure of a real college) came to our house the very next day to meet Amá and me. He was a strikingly handsome Anglo who bragged that the school had a reputation for graduating young ladies after one year of training who became secretaries to wealthy, famous men in Corpus Christi.

"The school doesn't have housing for its students, but we have ways to help those who can't afford to live in an apartment," the dean stated. "In fact, I know of one elderly lady that is looking for someone to clean her apartment and cook her meals in exchange for room and board. She lives in the Executive House in Corpus. Have ya'll heard of the building?" He asked.

"I have," I answered quickly.

I'd seen the building, which was located near the dance halls I frequented in Corpus. The building was one of the newer residential buildings in Corpus where mostly older, wealthy, singles lived.

"Well, then you know that only rich people live there. Just think about it, you'll be able to live in that building!" he said excitedly. The bone he was throwing to get me to go to Durham didn't impress Amá, who pointedly said, "My daughter doesn't need to clean for nobody."

"I didn't mean she had to clean, she can just keep the old woman company," the man quickly interrupted.

"I just want to know how much the school will cost," Amá asked.

"It's expensive but we have loan plans," he said nervously.

"I am asking again, what is the cost?" Amá asked impatiently.

The dean gave her a figure close to one thousand dollars to start. Amá walked out of our tiny living room, where the three of us had sat squeezed together on our red vinyl sofa. Moments later, she returned with several wads of bills tied together with thick rubber bands. The size of the stash looked as if it had been taken off a Brink's truck. Amá gently removed the rubber band off of one of the wads and out sprang hundreds upon hundreds of dollar bills. The dean's eyes wandered throughout our tiny house and gave the money a look of stark incredulity, as did I!

"That's some of my daughter's college money. I've been saving every dollar I could ever since the day Grace talked about wanting to go to college," Amá proudly told the dean.

Nobody thought to ask Amá why she kept that large amount of money in her bedroom rather than in the bank, but I thought she was probably like Amagrande, not trusting *los Bolillos* to safeguard her savings. The dean practically jerked the bills away from Amá's hand while he hurriedly filled in a stack of paperwork to enroll me at Durham Business College in Corpus Christi. My mind began spinning. I thought if Amá had saved up that much money maybe I could go to another Durham school outside the area.

"Are there are other Durham schools in Texas?" I asked quickly.

"There are," he answered hesitatingly.

He mentioned several cities, none of which interested me—until he mentioned San Antonio and that is when I made the decision to go there.

It was a hot steamy evening in late August when Tommie and I went to the Corpus Christi beach off Shoreline Drive for the last time. She was in love with a boy from a nearby small town. I was surprised at her choice. She was the one who had taught me to go after big city guys who were college bound, yet her current love didn't represent either of those characteristics but she was in love and no one including me could convince her otherwise.

Of all the friends I had made in Taft, Tommie was my favorite. In a town where we were knocked around and dragged down because of the color of our skin, she had enormous confidence, seeming *bien dans sa peau*. Her bubbly personality brought out the best in me. I shared my innermost thoughts with Tommie, never worried they'd pass her lips. She was my soul mate in the truest sense. At the end of the evening, we embraced and promised to stay in contact. But I somehow felt that our friendship, as strong as it was at the time, was never going to be the same again. We were seemingly headed in two very different directions. I just had a sense that our paths weren't going to cross again and I was right.

The next day, Amá helped pack my clothes into two small suitcases for the almost-three-hour trip to San Antonio. Together, we managed to fit all of my belongings into the trunk of her red and white Buick Skylark. Amagrande told Amá she was going on the trip, and insisted that we take her favorite great-grandchild, Mira, along too.

Mira was my sister María's oldest child, and Amá's oldest grandchild. "Mira" was short for Miroslava. I wondered how in the world my sister María had thought of such a rare and eccentric name. But as it turned out, Amá had chosen her name as she had done for many of her grandchildren. Miroslava was named after some Mexican movie star Amá liked. As a child, Mira spent more time with Amagrande and me than she did with her own family. Our six-year difference allowed Mira and me to grow up more as sisters than as niece and aunt. Thus, sharing the backseat of the car with Mira made for a less tense ride out of Taft.

As the car moved slowly up West Pecan Street, Mira tugged at my dress and asked in a frightened tone, "Will you ever come back?" I couldn't find the words to answer her. Instead, I chose to stare out the window as Amá maneuvered the car left on Davis Road. The car made a bumpy sound as it drove over the railroad tracks that served to separate the Mexicans from the Anglos, and then turned left on Highway 181, heading toward San Antonio. I sighed loudly as we passed the Dairy King that had been a hangout for the Taft High School Anglos until 1960, when we Mexican-Americans became the majority and began infiltrating it. As the car sped out on Highway 181, I turned around and stared at the place that had been my home for the first eighteen years of my life. I thought back to all the times in Taft that were more unpleasant than not. And one particular incident still loomed in my mind that had happened only a few months earlier.

I went to my classmate Maggie's house to rehearse for our junior-senior prom skit. I was thrilled to be going to Maggie's house. I had been fascinated with the split-level brick home with the family's initial on its chimney since I first saw it sometime during my elementary school years. I imagined the house to be a magical place full of colorful walls and comfortable stuffed chairs and sofas. But when I stepped inside, the house was colorless, feeling cold and lifeless. I was the only Mexican in the group and felt somewhat uncomfortable about being there. During our rehearsal, Maggie's boyfriend at the time and several of his friends from a nearby town dropped by. Maggie introduced everyone in the room except me. I was hurt that neither of my other classmates, nor the out of town guests, nor especially our teacher sponsor who was my favorite teacher interrupted to say, "You forgot Grace." The two groups went on to chat with each other, leaving me out of the conversation as if I was a mere stump in the field. I felt so irrelevant and couldn't believe it was happening at this time in my school life. Surely, civil relations between Mexican-Americans and Anglos couldn't be this far off; surely my classmates couldn't be so stupid and cruel, but they were. They acted as if that was the way things were supposed to be. I thought back to the day when the teacher pulled me away from playing on the swing with Maggie and realized that kind of thinking still had a place in Taft in 1965.

Hurt is never good for ones psyche no matter how much one rationalizes the cause. However, this incident did further galvanize my determination to not only leave Taft but to make a success of myself at a level that none of those in the room could ever achieve. Frankly, I didn't have a clue how I was going to do that but in the back of my mind, I knew there was going to have to be some serious ass kicking on my part to make that become a reality; after all these were some of the richest and brightest kids in town.

As my Amá's car rolled further out of Taft, the portrait of white cotton and bluebonnets stuck in my mind as we moved away and Taft receded from sight. The cotton gin, the tallest building in town stood imperially among stacks of cotton bales. The cotton fields were naked of plants; only debris lay scattered about. Cotton season was over, and so was my life in Taft. Holding back tears, I took a long sigh and thanked God that I was able to leave Taft in one piece and with my sanity somewhat still intact.

Chapter 14

A new beginning . . . .

*"You cannot change your destination overnight, but
you can change your direction overnight."*
Jim Rohn, American Entrepreneur, 1930
Author & Motivational Speaker

I embraced San Antonio as if it was a long-lost friend. Its sprawling landscape brought together by asphalt loops and its leafy streets filled with all kinds of vehicles seduced me. The city's history was alive through the old Spanish missions still standing in and around the town—reminding me of my Spanish ancestry that I had learned about from Buelito. It felt welcoming to see so many brown faces in and around the South Side of San Antonio, where I lived with my cousin Gloria and her husband Ernest on Mary Street.

The first Saturday after moving in with Gloria and Ernest, I took the North Flores bus to downtown where I was awestruck by the sea of blue uniforms, representing the thousands of airmen that came to get their basic training at San Antonio's Lackland Air Force Base. The entire downtown was filled with young airmen free for at least a day to discover their new surroundings just as I was doing. I found many shops waiting to take my money, among them a small boutique that stood out among all others: The Vogue on Houston Street sold pretty clothes, many of them imported from Italy and Spain. It was there that I opened my first charge account. Every one of the sales ladies displayed a level of courtesy I hadn't encountered in any other store—unusual to say the least, especially considering that this was the same Vogue where a friend was told to leave and go to the Solo Serve, where "her people" shopped. The Solo Serve was

194

a discount store where much of the Mexican-American community shopped for bargains.

Three months after I moved in with my cousin and her husband, I moved out and into a two bed-room apartment. The apartment was one of three others located in a two-story wood frame house downtown on Augusta Street near the Municipal Auditorium. I had tired of commuting and at the same living with two newlyweds. I wanted to be close to Durham Business College and to the downtown action, so when a couple of classmates posted an ad for two more roommates, I tore it off the school bulletin board before anyone else had a chance to respond. My new roommates came from Eagle Pass, a small border town in the southwest part of the state. The first thing they both announced as I lugged my suitcases inside the spacious apartment was their intent to move out as soon as they graduated from the year and a half program. That left me with less than a year to get to know them and figure where to live next. They made it clear they were planning to move back with their parents and find work in some office in their hometown. My future wasn't pre-planned like theirs, and even though I didn't agree with them returning to their hometown, it struck me that at least they had a goal.

We added a fourth roommate, Marta, on the recommendation from one of our Durham classmates. Marta came from a nearby small town and about the only thing she had in common with the rests of us was that we all had Spanish surnames and could speak Spanish. She had an uncanny resemblance to the singer-actress Liza Minnelli, but that's where their similarities ended. Marta, who worked as a waitress, put so much hairspray on her teased, color-streaked hair that no amount of wind could move one single strand of her bouffant-style do. When she wasn't working, Marta spent most evenings at El Toreo Club, which was frequented mostly by Middle East pilot trainees at Randolph Air Force Base. Oftentimes she'd bring a newfound friend to our apartment after the club shut down. Marta's friends' worlds were far from hers, yet they managed to communicate while sipping the heavy, mud-like dark coffee Marta prepared. Sometimes she'd bring some of the customers where she worked too. But no matter who they were or where they came from, they all seemed to have a much smaller shoe size than any of us in the apartment. Small feet were a trait that Amá, without explaining why, had told me to avoid in a future husband.

Our landlady was an old Anglo born and raised in south Texas. Yet I found her tolerance for us Mexicans surprisingly measured. She spat many orders we should follow as her tenants and bringing boys inside after dark was strictly off limits as if there weren't twenty four hours in a day. The two other Mexican families in our building were always sucking up to our landlady by ratting on us every time they saw a boy in our apartment. But when they saw a Black classmate of mine enter the building they must have made one hell of an emergency call. No sooner had I closed the door to our apartment than I heard loud banging. When I opened the door I found our landlady standing with her hands resting on her hips, dressed in her usual flower print frock and chunky black shoes. Her curly hair, dyed a bluish color, seemed to stand on end while she looked as if she could kill. To say she was hopping mad is an understatement. Fearing the obvious, I stepped through the door, forcing her back and closing it behind me. Before I could speak she shouted, "Did I just see a nigger girl go inside?" "No, you didn't," I said emphatically.

Surprise! Surprise! She didn't believe me. But rather than force her way inside to find out the truth she issued a stern warning. "Well, see that you never bring any of them people here. If you do, I'll throw you and the other girls out. Do you understand me"? She screamed.

Later that day I related to my roommates what happened but only Marta sided with the landlady. I, along with the other two roommates, went to work to get Marta to move out but that was like trying to move Mt. Everest. Time did it for us. A few months later, after graduating from Durham Business College, we all moved out of the apartment on Augusta: The girls from Eagle Pass returned home. I moved in with a friend temporarily until I found my way to Washington, D.C., and Marta moved in with someone else. Our paths were never to cross again.

Durham Business College was located in the downtown area off of one the longest roads in the city, San Pedro. The diverse student population impressed upon me that not all of the students from low-income homes were Mexican, nor were many of the students poor. Among them was a former fiesta queen from Corpus who offered to drop me off in Taft on weekends. At first I couldn't believe I was riding with Helen, who came from one of Corpus's most prominent families, but was an Anglo to boot. She proved to be a kinder and much more thoughtful soul than I had stereotyped her to be.

The majority of students at Durham's were locals while a few like me came from small towns in south Texas. A handful came from Mexico who enrolled to acquire typing and bookkeeping skills that would help them start their own businesses. I hadn't given much thought to starting my own business, but at the same time couldn't see myself taking dictation from some man in a pin stripped suit whether he was black, brown, white or indifferent. When my training ended I had no idea what I'd do with the skills I learned at Durham until I ran into a couple of classmates. "We're going to the Post Office to pick up government forms; want to join us?" They asked excitedly. They were hoping to find work at one of the military bases in the area. I hadn't given much thought to securing a job at a military base since my cousin Gloria had warned me that it could take months, if not years for a vacancy to open up. Nevertheless, I took up my classmates' offer and along we all went to the nearby Post Office to fill in the federal employment forms. But the clerk on duty didn't exactly lighten up our day. While he handed out the forms he warned sternly, "Don't get your hopes up—none of the military bases are doing much hiring these days." The four of us stood staring at each other, not sure what to do next, until I spoke up, "What the hell does he know, let's fill them out anyway?"

I didn't expect to ever hear from any of the military bases, but to my surprise a job offer from Kelly Air Force Base came almost immediately after I had mailed the employment forms. Although the offer of a GS-2 clerk-typist wasn't exactly going to test my mental or for that matter my typing ability, I excitedly took it on the advice from a friend that bigger jobs at the base would follow. In fact, getting the job at Kelly turned out to be an important stepping stone toward my career in public service.

My job at the air material facility consisted of filing two-by-three index cards containing descriptions of small hardware items such as nails, hammers, bolts and screws that came as orders from our military in Viet Nam. As a GS-2, I was at such a low-level in the workplace that even the civilian maintenance crew gave me orders. I ended up doing work no one else wanted to do, including walking from one end of the large barn like building to the other several times a day to drop off and pick up files that didn't make much difference in the scheme of military operations.

One of the first things I learned at Kelly was military protocol especially as it applied to rank. The head of our division was a GS-13. We gave his rank deference by moving out of his way while he arrogantly walked down the hallway. But higher than the GS-13, was an Air Force colonel, a military officer so high up in the chain of command that we rarely had the honor of seeing him. Just about every civilian co-worker warned me never to speak to the colonel unless he spoke first. And heaven forbid I'd ever run into the general, my job was to step out of his way and say even less to him. I didn't expect I'd ever run into the general but I did pass by his house every day on my way to the parking lot. One day I accidently stepped on the general's front lawn, prompting one of my coworkers to yell, "Get off that lawn, the general lives there!" I stared at the famous house and wondered how it might feel to live in such a grand and important place. "You wish you lived in a place like that, don't you? You have to be married to a general and you'll never do that," he said laughing.

It became clear after a few weeks on the job that I was going to have to do some serious soul-searching about whether to continue at Kelly or look for another line of work, or maybe even try getting into a four-year college to become a physical education teacher which was what I really wanted to do. There wasn't much to the job I was doing that a well-adjusted fifth grader couldn't do. And it seemed that the way promotions ran, I was going to be stuck being a GS-2 for a good deal of my adult life. Promotions didn't come easy at Kelly as I learned early on from a coworker, who warned, "Don't expect to move up anytime soon. There are some of us who've been working for more than twenty years, and I for one have only received a few promotions in all that time."

"Will it take that long for me?" I asked naively.

"That depends if your boss likes you. See that girl standing by the door?" the coworker asked. "She was recently promoted to a

GS-3 after only five years. And the only reason she got promoted is because she's in good with a GS-11!" she added.

"A GS-11! I haven't met anyone higher than a GS-7. That means I'll never get promoted," I said anxiously.

"If you want to move up the civil service career ladder I suggest you think about moving to Washington, D.C.," the coworker advised. "I hear in the Pentagon you go in a GS-3 and come out a GS-15 in no time," she teased.

After less than a year of filing index cards, making Xerox copies for low-level civil servants, and eating lunches that I'd purchased from a mobile food van that tasted like year-old leftovers, I decided my future could possibly lie elsewhere. I became even more convinced that I had to leave Kelly after I saw a grown man crying in front of all his coworkers when he learned his promotion to a GS-9 had been approved after he had waited twenty years. I set my sights on Washington, D.C. just like my coworker advised.

My relocation to Washington, D.C. happened much quicker than I anticipated. Back when I first filled in the federal government standard form 171 I playfully checked the Yes column that asked if the applicant wanted to work in Washington, D.C., never thinking that someone would actually see my response and offer me a job. But some person in the Department of the Air Force's personnel office in the Pentagon did notice, calling me within weeks. I didn't have to agonize about taking the Air Force's first offer, a GS-3 secretarial position, because the scores on my civil service exam were so low I considered myself lucky to have gotten the call at all. But the Pentagon always had a big turnover in those low-ranking positions, and, apparently, they were happy to have a warm body, so they hired me.

My decision to leave for the nation's capital was made that much easier by the encouragement I received from my coworkers. Only one coworker predicted I would be back at Kelly's front gates in less than six months.

"You'll never make it in Washington, D.C.—you're too nice a kid to make it on Washington's fast lane. It's a dog-eat-dog world up there. And if you do go, you'd better think about taking a dog along. I bet you never heard President Truman's advice, 'If you want a friend in Washington, bring a dog,'" he said laughingly.

It seemed the entire workforce at Kelly got wind that the Pentagon had offered me a job. I was the talk of the base up until the day I turned in my building pass. I, in turn, played my 15 minutes of fame for all that it was worth, accepting a long list of well wishes, farewell parties and gifts.

At Durham College I had made many friends. I wished that any one of them would accompany me to Washington, D.C. But the controlled world they came from wasn't going to allow them to travel anywhere after graduation except back to their hometowns where most were expected to find work to help support their families. My friends were beautiful and bright women who had the ability to achieve just about anything they set their minds to. But whatever ambition they had was stolen by self serving parents breathing down their necks day and night. They took a bus home every Friday to spend the weekend with their parents in their hometowns of Dilley, Carrizo Springs, Del Río, Eagle Pass, and Crystal City whether they wanted to or not. They were expected to marry a hometown boy so they could live close to their parents and keep the family circle going, not in places of greater opportunity but back in the hometown.

That was one aspect of our Mexican culture I had a difficult time understanding and accepting. Amá never put that kind of demand on me. She didn't order me to get a job to help support her, nor did she insist that I go home every weekend. In fact, it was Amá more than anyone, who encouraged me to move to Washington, D.C.

If some of my Durham classmates gave me a sense of friendliness, the Town Pump, a local San Antonio bar, raised my confidence level. I was greener than summer grass when I took my first step into that smoky and noisy bar where mixing between Anglos and Mexicans was allowed. The young military guys from different parts of the country proved to be gentle souls with no agenda other than to have a good time with the type of girls they'd only seen in movies—they became enchanted with our exotic looks, as many admitted. Yet I realized, as did many of the girls in the Town Pump, that the guys were strangers who more than likely had "a girl back home," not to mention that their short tour in San Antonio wasn't going to allow much time for us to get to know one another. In some cases their military rotating tours brought some of the same soldiers back to San Antonio but that was rare indeed. It seemed Barbara Lewis's

Hello Stranger played two or three times each night on the jukebox. The couples on the dance floor held each other closer when she crooned,

Hello Stranger, it seems so good to see you back again, how long has it been? It seems like a mighty long time.

The song was relevant to how life worked in the Town Pump. Yet, some couples met long enough to fall in love and in many instances marry. I wasn't looking to fall in love and certainly not yet searching for a husband, but my more mature friends urged me to meet OTS (Officer Training School) guys in preparation for a future husband. "They're going to be officers one day and that's the type of guy you want to meet and marry," one of the older girls said.

Another girl piped in, "Stay away from guys heading for Viet Nam. They'll be going to another base after Viet Nam, while some may not even make it out of there alive."

I could have done without that advice since the majority of the guys at the Town Pump were headed for Viet Nam. My first night at the Town Pump was taken up with one young soldier after another asking me to dance. Never had I been so popular on the dance floor. But it was a tall, good looking army draftee from New Jersey that turned me on my heels. He asked me to dance while Johnny Mathis' soft, deep voice took over the noisy bar, singing, *It's Not for Me to Say.*

Oh, but here for the moment I can hold you fast and press your lips to mine and dream that love will last.

When we reached the dance floor, Jack asked, "What do you do?"

When I answered that I was a student, he countered by saying he was a recent Princeton graduate.

"Geez, I couldn't even get into Laredo Junior College, and here I am dancing with a Princeton graduate," I thought.

After the first dance, Jack asked if I'd mind remaining on the dance floor with him. Jack and I danced all evening, oblivious to everyone around us. I was spellbound, ignoring that his 6-foot-3-inch height over my 5 feet and 3 inches made us look more like Mutt and Jeff than a couple smitten with each other, even if only for one night. We spent the evening holding each other tight, Jack often bending down to hear me speak. Sometime in the early evening Jack reached down to kiss me. The kiss seemed to last forever, sending a sensation to the pit of my stomach that I'd never before experienced. Jack was the first Anglo to kiss me. I thought that if all Anglos kissed like him I couldn't' wait to meet more of them. As the night wore on, all Jack could talk about was his next military assignment in Washington, D.C. When Ramsey Lewis's *The In Crowd* played over the jukebox, Jack expressed excitement over the prospect of meeting Lewis, who performed at a D.C. nightclub. His mind had moved on while I was still trying to catch my breath after his warm, tender kisses. After the bar closed, Jack's hand slipped away and I regretfully came face-to-face with the reality of life at the Town Pump, the fast moving rotating assignments made it impossible to establish a lengthy relationship with the military guys.

After Jack, I met other military guys who, like him, were recent-college-graduate draftees. But none of them came close to matching Jack's charming ways, his good looks, and his intellect. The romance of the evening with Jack lingered in my mind for many months afterward. It was that one night with Jack that helped me set the standard for the kind of man I wanted to marry one day.

While the Town Pump held a special place in my life at the time, some of my Durham classmates thought of it as nothing but a bar where girls from good families didn't go. The stigma of meeting guys at bars bothered me but over time I came to learn that most of the girls at the Town Pump were schoolteachers and nurses, while many others were students like me. Sure there were some rough girls that reminded me of those from Taft who fought over guys. In fact, I came very close to getting my face slashed by one girl from the West Side, who became angry when a soldier from Fort Sam she liked asked me to dance instead of her. I didn't go into the bathroom, where she waited for me with a switchblade tucked in her handbag, when a friend who overheard her plan rushed out of the bathroom to warn me to leave the bar altogether; that was the first and the last time I ever had to do that.

Luckily, the West Side girls didn't show up often. And when they did, they'd end up chasing away the handful of Anglo girls that showed up occasionally. Every now and then, a handful of local Mexican-American guys came into the Town Pump, but they didn't stay long, because every girl turned down their dance offers. Once I became friendly with a handsome local college student only to have a friend scold me, "Don't dance with the Mexicans. If you do, you'll never get rid of them. Besides, Mexicans are a dime a dozen in San Antonio—so don't waste your time with them in here."

The Anglo girls might have left with their tails between their legs, but the Mexican-American guys fought back. After the Town Pump closed, they waited in their cars while the Anglos walked us to our cars. They'd hang their heads out the car windows yelling, "*Orale, Se revolvieron los frijoles con el jamón*," a metaphor in which the beans represent Mexicans and ham represents Anglos.

I became convinced the military guys I met at the Town Pump were more interested in who I was, not what I was. Yet, in time I learned that many of the couples that met there and married ended being divorced. Cultural clashes and class differences broke up many marriages. When I heard that a girl from the West Side was marrying one of the best-looking guys at the Town Pump I was happy for her but at the same time worried whether they would make it, since their lives were so different. She had a five year old son from a previous relationship, while her handsome boyfriend hadn't been married. His height almost reached the Town Pump's ceiling, while hers barely reached his waistline. Their wedding took place at her parents' tiny wood frame house on the West Side less than five months after they met. During the wedding, the groom stayed away from his new, Spanish-speaking in-laws, with whom he couldn't communicate, and even from his bride, drinking with his friends in the dirt-filled backyard until he could hardly stand up.

A few weeks after the wedding, the couple moved to Florida. We heard reports later that the handsome sergeant had begun beating not only his wife but also her son. Before long, both of them were back living with her parents on the West Side. Their story made me realize that it was one thing to date a military guy but a whole other story to marry him. Yet, at 19, I became engaged to an Army draftee from Seattle, Washington, six months after we met. My fiancé was of German extraction, with blue eyes as bright as the clear Texas sky. We couldn't have looked more different if we had tried. But in matters of the heart, different appearances don't seem to matter. Richard wanted to return to his hometown of Seattle when he got out of the Army and that I found terribly unappealing. I simply wasn't ready to settle down. So, after a yearlong courtship, we both decided to go our separate ways.

The confidence I gained in San Antonio helped me tackle the next phase of my life. I was prepared to become a civil servant working for *el gobierno*, as my Amagrande referred to the government. In fact, I credit much of my thinking about public service to her and three others. Amagrande always spoke about *el gobierno* as if it was a person.

"El gobierno siempre ayuda a mucha gente," she often declared. How generous of *el gobierno*, I thought. Yet in her next breath, Amagrande expressed concern that *el gobierno* would take her and Buelito back to Mexico because they weren't *cuidadanos*. She didn't explain what *cuidadanos* meant, so I became frightened that *el gobierno* would take me to Mexico too. But Amagrande calmed me, saying, *"Si te portas bien el gobierno no te hace nada."*

My high school civics class tweaked my curiosity of *el gobierno*, but it took three Mexican-American men from Corpus to get me to think about becoming a public servant.

The first two men were members of the Texas State Legislature. They came at different times to speak during Career Day at my high school. The first of the two spoke to our eleventh grade class. The man had a slight Spanish accent, yet he was articulate and engaging. Carlos Truan enthusiastically advised us to think about entering public service either by working in a federal or state agency or through elected office.

The other state representative spoke during my senior year. The first words out of his mouth were, "I don't speak Spanish very well, nor if you notice, I don't have a Spanish accent." Tony Bonilla used several Spanish words to demonstrate his inability to pronounce them, yet I had heard him more than once speak clear Spanish in his campaign ads. The more he talked about his inability to speak Spanish, the more I felt Bonilla was exposing the distinction between himself and us Mexicans in the room. In my world, a person with a Spanish accent was considered a member of the underclass, and Bonilla's remarks implied that we were such and he wasn't, because he didn't have a Spanish accent. It would have been a good start if the representative had urged us to learn English and to speak it without a Spanish accent. But he didn't do that, nor did he advise us to do much after we graduated. It was all about him and his success. Yet, for me to see two Mexican-Americans elected to state office in south Texas during the 1960s was impressive. In each of their own way, they both inspired me to follow the path to public service.

But the person who inspired me the most about becoming a public servant was Dr. Héctor P. García. Dr. Héctor, as he liked to be called, was a physician in Corpus Christi; he was well known more for championing the rights of Mexican-Americans than for his medical work. He was south Texas's own Martin Luther King, Jr. He fought for our civil rights even visiting Taft in 1948, to advise a group of Mexican-American World War II veterans led by Don Pancho Iglesias, owner of Don Pancho's dance hall, to address the problem of school segregation in Taft.

After serving in World War II, Dr. Héctor formed an organization of veterans, called the American GI Forum, to fight for the rights of Hispanic veterans; as other cases of discrimination against Mexican-Americans surfaced, Dr. Héctor expanded the mission. In 1949, Dr. Hector's bravery brought the American GI Forum and Dr. Héctor himself to national attention when he answered the call from the widow of Army Pvt. Felix Longoria. Pvt. Longoria, a native of Three Rivers, a small south Texas town had been on the Island of Luzon, in the Philippines, only a few weeks when he was killed by a Japanese sniper in 1945. It took the United States Army four years to ship his body back to his hometown. But when his body arrived, the owner of the town's only funeral home refused to handle the private's burial.

"The whites won't like it," the Anglo funeral director told Pvt. Longoria's young widow.

The burial was a problem too, as Three Rivers, like Taft and other south Texas towns, had segregated cemeteries. Even in death, it seemed the Anglos wanted no part of Mexicans and Blacks; they couldn't see themselves lined up with minorities on their way to the pearly gates.

The newly organized GI Forum came under fire from Texas Anglos when Dr. Héctor used it to catapult Pvt. Longoria's case to the attention of Senator Lyndon Johnson and the nation. The decision about where to bury Pvt. Longoria took more time than it should have, but in the end Dr. Héctor's leadership helped earn him a burial spot in Arlington Cemetery, the first Mexican-American to be buried there.

A positive result of Pvt. Longoria's burial controversy was the friendship that emerged between Senator Johnson and Dr. Héctor, which lasted until their deaths. And I am convinced that it was their friendship that helped improve the plight of Mexican-Americans in south Texas.

When I was in high school, Dr. Héctor's influence could be felt throughout south Texas. His photo made the Corpus paper many times. He appeared often on Domingo Peña's television show and was heard on local radio stations just as often. His message about fighting for our rightful place in America was generally the same no matter where he spoke.

During the time I lived in Taft, I didn't meet Dr. Héctor, yet he inspired me as no other person did. His sincerity, his compassion, and his demonstrated lack of fear of the Anglos gave me the kind of push I needed to follow my dream of wanting to leave Taft to make something of myself.

The day to leave San Antonio came soon enough. My dream to travel to a place far away from Taft was about to come true. As the Braniff Airlines plane lifted up toward the wide, sunny Texas sky, I felt like thumping my chest and shouting, "Whoopee!" Yet, I was more than aware of the risks that lay ahead. I didn't know anyone in Washington, D.C., and knew even less about the culture and temperament of my new surroundings. Nonetheless, my excitement couldn't be contained. I was ready to start a new life and vowed not to look back.

Chapter 15

The Nation's Capital

*"I learned . . . that one can never go back, that one
should not ever try to go back-that the essence of life is
going forward. Life is really a one-way street."*
Agatha Christie, 1890-1976
English Writer

For a person born and raised in stifling hot and humid weather, Washington, D.C.'s weather was a heck of a shock when I arrived, in the dead of winter. To be fair, it wasn't as if I had a choice. I had a job waiting with the Department of the Air Force and its personnel office wasn't going to accommodate any foolishness I might have had about the weather. I gathered my luggage and scurried out of the airport to find the shuttle that would take me to downtown, Washington, D.C. My light coat and low heel shoes couldn't begin to protect me from the wet, cold chill that went through my dry skin like a sharp knife. That was January 1967 and I was excited about being in Washington, D.C., even if the freezing temperature shook me like a leaf on a bad, windy day. The air was so gripping cold that I could barely move one foot in front of the other.

By the time I climbed into the shuttle my feet were near frostbitten. The passenger sitting next to me offered her fur coat, which I took, anxiously. The warmth of the mink over my shoulders nearly put me to sleep. But its owner kept me awake, talking and asking questions. The smartly dressed, middle-aged woman was a Corpus native who turned out to be the owner of the *Corpus Christi Caller Times*, the city's major newspaper. I couldn't believe I was sitting next to the owner of such an important part of Corpus and believed even less that my tiny, near-frozen body was wrapped in her expensive fur coat. As the shuttle made its way into the Washington, D.C. area, she suddenly yelled excitedly in her high pitched Texas twang, "Look over there, honey. That's where you're going to work."

The Pentagon loomed larger than life, even in the dark of night. The snow-filled ground surrounding the five-sided building reminded me of my first snow experience, when I was twelve years old. The rare and small amount of snow that fell on Taft that day was enough to shut down the town and enough for us to make a few snow balls to throw at each other. But this was another world and trekking through the Washington streets when they were covered with thick snow was a whole different experience. The next day, even though I rode the bus to the Pentagon, my shoes were totally ruined when I walked through the melting snow. Thankfully, the Pentagon operated as a small city and there were shops on the "Concourse." There I was able to buy the first of many snow boots from a store called Woodward & Lothrop.

I reported for work to the Strategic Division within the Office of the Deputy Chief of Staff for Programs in the Department of the Air Force. My new office was located on the fifth floor of the Pentagon—easy to say but it took me most of the morning to find the place. Collectively, all of the corridors that run through the Pentagon are about 17 1/2 miles in length. I must have walked close to that distance, stumbling through the maze of corridors like a drunken sailor. My new boss was sitting in his tiny office when I nervously walked in much later than expected. The other secretary in the office welcomed me in and immediately took me in to meet the branch chief and my new boss, Colonel Howard E. Cody.

"Ice wonerin, where ya war," Colonel Cody said as he stood up to shake my hand. He had seemed larger than life sitting behind his desk, but when he stood up he was barely taller than me. I was surprised to learn later in our conversation that his oldest son played for the New Orleans Saints. "With such a diminutive size father," I thought. Colonel Cody's pronounced southern accent reminded me of the way Taft Anglos spoke. I wanted to run out of the office and find someone else to work for, thinking that like the Anglos back home, he'd probably be prejudiced against me for being Mexican. But after our conversation, the colonel shook my hand firmly once again while looking straight at me and said, warmly, "I am happy to welcome you as part of our team, Grace."

Two years after I arrived in the office, Colonel Cody retired to his home state of Alabama. In those years that I worked under his supervision, Colonel Cody was nothing less than a gentleman, treating me fairly and with the utmost respect. His kindness taught me not to stereotype every Anglo that had a southern accent as being prejudiced.

My duties were simple if I paid attention and did what I was told by the other secretary in the office. Together, she and I worked for a much larger staff than I had expected; two civilian GS-13s, three lieutenant colonels, a couple of majors, and one captain for a total of nine including the full colonel. Back at Kelly, I had worked under the supervision of only two people, neither of them higher than staff sergeant.

My coworker at Kelly AFB was correct in saying that service grades were higher in the Pentagon, as were the ranks of the military personnel. I was astounded to see so many full colonels in one place and asked the other secretary for the reason. "That's because so many of them are biding their time before they retire. A handful of them may make general but not from this office, that's for sure," she said matter-of-factly. She was almost correct. During the two and a half years I worked in the office, only one colonel made general.

In the military community, it's tradition to throw a promotion party for friends and family; the new general threw himself a promotion party, inviting everyone in the office except the enlisted personnel and secretaries. One of the secretaries in the office told me of the party. "Our boss doesn't draw a distinction between the secretaries and the enlisted personnel who aren't allowed to socialize with officers due to a non fraternization policy in the military," she said. There will be other promotion parties and we may be invited, it just depends on the officer," she continued. The non—fraternization policy was one of many policies and unwritten rules that were so foreign to my way of life.

Aside from being uninvited to officer promotion parties, my job in the Air Force was far too routine. The work simply was not of an urgent nature. Nonetheless, on the day after Martin Luther King's assassination on April 5, 1968, I was ordered to stay late and work overtime. That evening, there was rioting throughout downtown Washington, D.C., with many buildings burning. By the time I left the office, I heard that transportation was getting hard to find and the day was getting darker by the minute. But that wasn't all: I was shocked to see a good part of the nation's capital, my new home, in flames and being destroyed. I ran down to the Pentagon bus and taxi area located under the Concourse only to find it empty of vehicles and people. The public transportation in and out Washington, D.C. was virtually shut down. I hurried out of the bus area and onto the Pentagon grounds, hoping to find a taxi, and ran into a worried looking, slightly gray-headed, middle-aged man. "I don't think we are going to have any luck finding transportation," he said, shaking his head. As we continued searching for transportation he asked, "Where do you live?"

"I live in Northwest D.C. near the National Cathedral," I answered anxiously.

The man must have sensed the panic in my voice. He comforted me by placing his arm around my shoulder, saying warmly, "I live in Chevy Chase. Do you want to walk with me toward the State Department where I'll call my son to pick us up?" "Yes, of course," I answered promptly.

We began walking down the road from the Pentagon to Memorial Bridge, which on normal working days would be so busy we couldn't cut across—but today there were only a few cars traveling. The smoke from the burning buildings was even more intense than I had witnessed earlier in the day. I was relieved when we crossed over into D.C., but as we made our way around the Lincoln Memorial the sound of screaming emergency vehicles racing throughout the city reminded me that it wasn't safe to be on the streets. While we waited for the light to change on Constitution Avenue, a carload of young Black men sped by pumping their fists outside the car and yelling, "We're gonna get you whitey!"

We walked hurriedly toward the State Department where the man used a phone booth to call his son. We waited by the State Department, where several more carloads of mostly Black teenagers sped by shouting all kinds of obscenities against white people. I was scared to death and thought that we were both going to be attacked. I didn't think people of my skin color were the target of the Blacks, but so what; I was with a white man and clearly felt these folks were going to become more aggressive and violent as the night wore on. The man used me as a protective shield, staying close behind while we waited for his son. In the nick of time, the son showed up in an old station wagon and before he came to a full stop, his father and I were hurriedly trying to open the doors. We sped off, making our way toward the Northwest section of the city, where rioters weren't as prevalent. By the time we reached Connecticut Avenue near my house, people were walking up and down the busy street as if nothing was going on in the rest of the city. Later that evening the rioting became worse, prompting the National Guard to deliver my cousin, Milli, from her job at the Sheraton Park hotel two blocks away in an armed truck with guns drawn.

After the rioting, looting and burning subsided, a good part of the city looked as if a bomb had fallen on it. Many stores closed. Some went out of business immediately; others reopened in a few days but went out of business later. One of those that closed a few years later was my favorite, Rich's Shoes. The store carried the prettiest shoes, which I collected with great fervor. While a friend and I tried on shoes, we flirted with the owner's son, whom according to the other salesmen was named Frank. We liked to tease and startle the young boy by shaking our foot up and down while trying on shoes. Who would have thought that the shy, unassuming boy would end up being the famous Broadway show critic and New York Times columnist, Frank Rich?

After the riots I returned to my job with the Air Force with a much different view of my co-workers. The question of my safety on the day after Dr. King's assassination didn't come up—it seemed to me I was just a body occupying a seat that would be refilled in a second if I didn't return. After that I began to look for another position. I worried too that after spending nearly two years typing endless charts about Air Force B-52 sorties over Viet Nam, I'd be stuck doing that for the rest of my life.

I had spent my first week in Washington, D.C., at the YWCA, moving afterward to Hartnett Hall, a residential hall located on the Northwest part of the city close to Dupont Circle. The main building was a rather stately brownstone but the rest of Hartnett Hall where my room was located was a gray, depressing structure built at the beginning of the twentieth century. It had the feeling of a college dorm; women lived on one side of the building and men on the other.

Our meals, which were served three times a day, were included in our rent. The food was nothing to write home about but the Black women that worked in the dining room are worth noting. Back in Texas the Blacks I knew were much friendlier than the Black women that served food at Hartnett Hall. The women seemed tougher than nails. They appeared to be the kind that would smack anyone that crossed them and ask questions later. During mealtime, any one of them would think nothing of knocking off someone's elbows found resting on the table. Every utensil and dish was in its proper place and they expected the diners to keep them that way. If we moved a cereal bowl or salad plate to another place on the table, we'd find ourselves being lectured about table manners. I must have been the most relaxed at the table, because the same woman stood over me every morning and every evening correcting my every movement. I couldn't imagine any one of those tough women putting up with discrimination from "white people," as I quickly learned they were called in Washington, but in 1967 I found racism still held a place in Washington even though Blacks were the majority.

After six weeks of Hartnett Hall living, a friend from Texas called saying her sister lived in Washington, D.C., and knew of someone in her building looking for a roommate. I immediately called her sister, who just as quickly arranged for me to meet Sandy from Pennsylvania. My friend's sister and her three other roommates occupied the first floor and basement of the brick row house while Sandy occupied the top floor. Sandy and I hit it off; she asked if I wanted to be her roommate. I accepted and moved in the next day. I was anxious to leave Hartnett Hall, but I was going to miss the Black women in the dining hall. While they seemed gruff and unfriendly, they tried to instill something in me that was apparently lacking and I was that much better for it.

I had so few belongings that I made the move in one cab ride. When I gave the cab driver the address, he shouted excitedly, "Oh, you're moving to Cleveland Park, with the rich and important folks." I was too new to know the difference between Cleveland Park, Woodley Park, or Rock Creek Park, which I learned soon enough were names of affluent neighborhoods in Washington, D.C. My new home was located on Cathedral Avenue, which was named after the National Cathedral, located only three blocks up the street. The narrow, snow covered, street was filled with people dressed in long overcoats, tall rubber boots, and heavy wool scarves draped around their necks. I had never seen so much clothing piled up on one human being. But one thing was certain that if I was going to survive the unusual cold climate of my new surroundings I'd have to dress that same way.

Shortly after moving in, our landlady stopped by the house to see if any repairs were needed. Nicole d'Amecourt was a strikingly attractive woman that seemed only a few years older than those of us living in her building, yet she appeared more mature. There was an aura about Nicole that made her seem different from other people I'd met. Maybe it was her poise or the graceful manner in which she moved and spoke. Her voice was soft yet her words were precise. After she left, one of my roommates mentioned that Nicole was a descendant of French royalty. Nicole's pedigree wasn't a surprise. Her manner was so uniquely proper and distinct. I only wished that one day I would be able to emulate such impeccable manners.

As I moved about the neighborhood, I remembered the cab driver's words about the sort of people that lived in Cleveland Park. On most mornings, I'd see Senator William Proxmire, a Democrat from Wisconsin proudly showing off his toothpick-thin, white legs while he jogged down Rock Creek Park toward his office on Capitol Hill. Senator Eugene McCarthy from Minnesota lived close enough to my residence to be a member of my parish, St. Thomas Apostle on Woodley Road. The first time I sat next to him at Sunday Mass I couldn't believe I was sitting next to such a notable person. The last notable I had sat next to in church was a teenage boy from Taft's South Side we called, *El Wino*.

There were embassies and ambassadors' private residences all around me. The embassy of Switzerland was one block away and across from our house was a small, wood frame bungalow that was the embassy of a tiny West African country. One evening after work I saw a small crowd of people assembled in a large open area of the building. I walked closer to take a better look and saw several people in native costumes milling in front of a table covered with large food trays. I walked up to the door to get an even closer look and before I knew it a large man in a colorful native costume came toward the door, inviting me to come in. "Oh, no! I live across the street and only wanted to take a look inside," I explained nervously. But the man insisted I come in, taking my hand and leading me inside. The man introduced himself as the ambassador and in turn introduced me to the handful of guests as if I was some important person. From seeing the near empty room, he was probably happy to see someone other than his staff fill it up, and I was more than ready to claim I attended my first embassy party.

A year after I arrived in Washington, D.C. I went home for Christmas and ran into my cousin and childhood friend, Miné. By now my cousin had changed her real name from Minerva to Milli and who could blame her. On the South Side, girls were given mostly names symbolic of our religious affiliation; María and Guadalupe were common names. Even if the name Minerva came from the ancient Roman goddess of wisdom, that name seemed odd on the South Side. I found Milli wasting away her talents and her good looks in the tiny seaside town of Portland where she was living with her mother and two younger siblings. I needed someone to pal around with in D.C. and my cousin needed to be saved. So before my holiday vacation was over, I talked Milli into leaving Portland and coming to D.C. to live with me.

By this time, I was living on the first floor of the spectacular row house which I shared with three roommates. My roommates were quiet and retiring young Anglo women who spent most evenings rubbing their feet with a cream lotion called pretty feet and rolling their hair with plastic foam rollers. I sensed they weren't in Washington, D.C. to become career girls as much as they wanted to find a man to marry them. They entertained young aspiring men from the Pentagon, Washington law firms and Capitol Hill with Saturday dinners; cooking specialty meals that were found in only the best restaurants. My culinary and entertaining skills were no match for those girls who spent hours poring over recipes, table settings and invitation lists. For me it was much easier to hit the singles bar scene than to do all that prep work just to meet guys, so having Milli to go out with was nirvana.

At first we frequented two clubs, the Crazy Horse and the Tombs but found mostly college kids from Georgetown University asking us to dance. We wanted to meet older, more mature career minded men. We found them at a supper club called the Bastille located on the upper Northwest part of town on Wisconsin Avenue. The club became known for its delicious food but more for the talented live band that played everything from the group Classics IV to old Sinatra tunes. It was a mix of singles and married couples that filled the club each weekend. The married couples sat in the dining area while we singles took over the bar area. Milli and I made the Bastille our home for a few months until we befriended the only two Blacks that broke up the all white club crowd. The neatly dressed, tall, good looking men who wore large Afros stood all alone among the crowd of mostly blond-heads. They reminded me of the old story of Blacks being able to finally integrate the local swimming pool and when they jumped in all the whites in the pool jumped out. That was similar to the way Jimmy and Harvey were treated; when they entered the bar all the whites parted company as if they were diseased. The first time they asked Millie and me to dance we gladly accepted. I danced with Jimmy while Milli danced with Harvey. The crowd stopped to stare and when they sat down at our table the crowd stared even more.

Milli and I met Jimmy and Harvey two other times at the Bastille. But on our third meeting, the club's Maitre d', who was from Morocco, asked Milli and I to see him before we left the club. We suspected what he was going to tell us but we didn't expect his words to be so explicit and degrading. The first words out of his mouth were, "You are nice girls but I am warning you if you continue talking to those two guys I may not let you in the club. Don't you understand, the more you talk to them, the more you're encouraging them to return, and before I know it my club is going to be filled with their people, which the patrons don't want." By the time the Maitre d' got through lecturing about who we should be talking with, we felt like two common criminals. We returned to the Bastille a couple times afterward—but the atmosphere just didn't feel right, forcing us to find another place to show off our dancing skills. As for the Bastille, well it closed its doors a few months after we left it.

Milli and I joined a singles' organization called JOPA-Junior Officers and Professional Association that held dances at various spots throughout town. The organization was comprised of young military officers and young professionals. JOPA was started by Michael O'Haro, a naval officer who became more popular than the organization he built. The men were mostly Marines stationed in and around D.C., one of which was Charles Robb who later married President Johnson's eldest daughter Lynda Bird. Every once in awhile we met some goofy guys and to keep them from bothering us, we gave them wrong phone numbers and silly Spanish names.

On Saturday afternoons, Milli and I strolled up and down Connecticut Avenue where we shopped in small boutiques that carried names such as, Joe's Place and Up Against the Wall. We were in another world far from the South Side of Taft but adjusting quite nicely to our new surroundings. Though, I am convinced that I wouldn't have enjoyed my new surroundings and might not have survived the nation's capital had it not been for my cousin being by my side.

The Viet Nam War was at its peak during the early 1970s and my next Pentagon job couldn't have been at a busier place in all of the federal government. My new job, as a GS-6 Secretary was located in the East Asia and Pacific Region Office within the Office of the Assistant Secretary for National Security Affairs in the Office of the Secretary of Defense. When I entered my new office, the personnel officer's earlier description of it being, "busier than a whorehouse on a Saturday night," was accurate. There was a flurry of activity; two young, pretty secretaries sat in the main office typing madly while the phones rang off the hook. Several men were standing around the secretaries' desks, hurrying the two young women to finish typing the documents in their typewriters. Before I had a chance to get acquainted with my typewriter, the four men I was assigned to help piled around my desk with typing assignments that all had to be done before close of business. My Amá's investment in Durham Business College seemed to be finally paying off.

The assistant secretary of our organization was a former University of Virginia professor, Warren J. Nutter. After only a few weeks on the job, I came to realize that Mr. Nutter was exceptional. He held one of the toughest positions in the defense department yet he did it with charm and grace, unlike the other men I worked for who lost their tempers at the drop of a hat. The government would be a far better place if we had more political appointees with his skills and demeanor. I spent the spring of 1970 typing top secret briefing reports about overnight incidents in Viet Nam for President Nixon's National Security Council (NSC) Advisor, Dr. Henry Kissinger. The initial draft reports were handed to me in barely legible handwritten notes prepared by Army, Navy, Air Force officers, as well as high-ranking civil servants. My job was to transpose their chicken scratches into a legible, typed document in a matter of seconds while five or six anxious action officers hovered over me. Dr. Kissinger's temper was well-known throughout the Pentagon. There were many stories about his legendary shouting at whoever was close by if he didn't receive his daily Department of Defense report briefings on time and without typographical errors.

I spent just about every waking hour at the Pentagon and didn't so much as have a thought that anyone noticed the long hours I worked, never mind the enormous stress I endured. But Dennis Doolin, the deputy assistant secretary for international security affairs, did notice and it was he and his wife Kathy that helped push my public service career in a completely different direction from the one I was following at Defense. I was a grade GS-7 when Dennis stopped me in the hallway of our fourth floor office. He mentioned that Kathy, a high-level civil servant at the Department of Health, Education, and Welfare (HEW), was looking to fill a vacancy in an office under her supervision that dealt with Spanish-surnamed Americans and thought I would be a good candidate.

"Are you interested?" Dennis asked excitedly.

I had no idea what Dennis was talking about but answered in the affirmative just the same. A few days later I found myself sitting in front of Kathy's desk in her third floor office in HEW's north building, or as it was called, "HEW North." I recognized Kathy as the slim, young blond-headed woman who rode in the same city bus I took from Washington, D.C. to the Pentagon a year earlier. At the time I was impressed with the demure, bespectacled woman, one of a few women to hold a high-level position in the Pentagon, and couldn't be more thrilled to be able to work and learn from her as the new deputy of the Office of Special Concerns. Over lunch,

Kathy emphasized that my duties as administrative staff assistant in the Office of Surnamed Americans were not strictly secretarial. The Office of Spanish Surnamed Americans was a subdivision of the Office of Special Concerns, located within the prestigious, think-tank-type Office of the Assistant Secretary for Planning & Evaluation (ASPE). As Kathy led me out the door she mentioned that if I took the position, I'd have the opportunity to earn my undergraduate degree through the Upward Mobility Program, which could help me move up the civil service career ladder. Her offer was too good to be true. I was being offered a position that would help me get out of the secretarial field, plus the opportunity to earn a college degree while I worked during the day. Only a fool would turn down Kathy's offer.

The Office of Spanish Surnamed Americans, along with the Offices of Asian Americans, Blacks, Native Americans and Women, made up the Office of Special Concerns, which was created during the early Nixon Administration. The Spanish office consisted of a director, a deputy, a management intern, a secretary and an administrative staff assistant. As administrative staff assistant, one of my major roles was to serve as advisor to both the director and deputy on policy issues directly impacting the Hispanic population. But instead of allowing me to advise them on any one issue they treated me as if I was their personal butler, ordering me to fetch them and our office guests, coffee and food. I felt it was difficult for me establish a professional and trusting relationship with Manny Carrillo, because he hired me at Kathy's recommendation even though he didn't know me.

Elliot Richardson, who was the HEW Secretary at the time, enthusiastically supported the Office of Special Concerns. The office was established to advocate policy development in the areas of health, education and welfare on behalf of minorities and women. During Richardson's short time at HEW, the Office of Special Concerns had a voice in just about every key policy developed in the department. But when Richardson left to become the Secretary of Defense, the Office of Special Concerns began losing much of its support and its clout within the department. Richardson had been the force that allowed us to go after much-needed policy reviews for minorities and women, much to the consternation of the nonminority policy staff. He was one of those powerful intellects who had the ability to do many things at once and do them exceptionally well. That ability left a lasting impression on me. One afternoon, during a briefing by the minority office directors on current and future office activities, I noticed Richardson doodling on a long white pad rather than look up at the briefer. From all the doodling he was doing it seemed to me that he wasn't paying attention to what was being said, that is—until he'd pop a question, and then another, and another, startling the more-than-relaxed speaker with his intense questioning.

A few months after he left, Richardson won the respect of many around the country when he resigned rather than fire Archibald Cox, the Solicitor General of the Justice Department, as he'd been ordered to do by President Nixon. I learned much from him that day and during the brief period I worked under his leadership at HEW. Years later I sat next to him at a dinner at Harvard University where I was a student and he was our guest speaker. After the dinner I walked away feeling lucky that I had the opportunity to know such a modest yet enormously talented man during a crucial time in my public service career.

After a few months in the Spanish Surnamed Office it became crystal clear that my assigned duties once again weren't exactly going to test my intellectual ability. Most of my day was spent answering letters from Hispanic organizations and individuals that been shoe-boxed for months on end. The rest of my time I sat at my desk listening patiently to irate Mexican-Americans, Puerto Ricans and Cuban-Americans rant and rave about everything from their inability to receive federal funds for pet community projects to complaining about Anglos violating their civil rights. For some reason they came in with the distinct impression that our office could fix any problem they faced, and when we came up short to meet their expectations, I especially was accused of being *una vendida*. While I patiently listened to their accusations and insults, Manny and Phil were always conveniently absent.

Manny was a larger-than-life Mexican-American whose bombastic personality and ability to express himself in both English and Spanish earned him celebrity status with the Hispanic community and the powers that be in the department. He spent a great deal of his day attending interagency meetings with high-level officials, which he preferred, leaving the less important meetings to his deputy. After his high-level meetings Manny developed the habit of bringing some of the noteworthy attendees, without warning, to introduce to his staff.

One time he brought in a small, frightened-looking man dressed in a simple, rumpled, earth tone color suit that looked as if it had been bought at Goodwill. I looked up at the quiet, reserved man who looked like he might have been one of Manny's old buddies from his teaching days in the Mexican-American community in Denver. I continued my work. Manny cleared his throat loudly, a sign for me to stop what I was doing. He ushered the unassuming man toward my desk and announced, proudly, "Grace I'd like for you to meet, the deputy secretary of the department, Frank Carlucci." "Holy shit," I thought, almost falling out of my chair. I'd seen Carlucci a few times walking the hallway but on this day he looked tiny and lost standing next to the much taller and bigger Manny.

After that day I prepared myself to meet the president of the United States, since Manny might invite him into the office if he could. In this way I came to know many famous and not-so-famous Americans. But most impressive was meeting the great-grandson of President William H. Taft, William H. Taft IV. I expected Will, as he was called, to be rotund like his presidential ancestor but he was tall and wiry with a complexion so white it made him look almost ghostly. Will was a political appointee, serving as Executive Assistant to the Secretary of Health, Education and Welfare. His pregnant wife Julia, who also worked in the department, was at his side. They both appeared genuine and friendly. I was thrilled to meet a person that was a relative of Charles P. Taft, for whom my hometown was named.

I went home for Christmas in 1971 and spent most of my one week's vacation with Amagrande who had fallen ill. The day after Christmas I walked into her bedroom to say good-bye only to find her sewing patches on a small quilt from her rocking chair. When I bent down to kiss her forehead, Amagrande wrapped her arms around me in a warmer and more affectionate embrace than she'd done in the past. I returned the embrace, holding her tight and far longer than I'd done at any other time. Without speaking, I slipped my arms away and began to walk away. When I turned around to wave good-bye I caught Amagrande wiping tears from her eyes. It was rare to see Amagrande weep. As she waved back, Amagrande said, "A*diós*," a word she had taught me never to use when departing. She was superstitious; fearing that a person using the word *adiós* instead of *hasta luego* meant their death was imminent.

Eight months later Amagrande passed away. Amagrande suffered mightily those eight months, barely able to breathe. At the end, not even the machines she was hooked up to helped release much needed oxygen from her lungs. During one of her most painful nights, Amagrande told everyone in the hospital room that no one leaves earth without paying for their sins. She confessed that it was her turn to pay for everything bad she had done to her husband and everyone else. I remembered the many times she told me about her belief that heaven and hell were lived on Earth, and not anywhere else. After we buried Amagrande next to her son Victor and Buelito, I went to see her rocking chair one last time. My lasting memory was seeing her weeping in the chair and saying *adiós* to me that cold December day in 1971.

The woman, who routinely embarrassed me, was the single most influential person in my early years. Her coarse behavior gave me pause many times, yet she was the one person who taught me to mind my manners, to always address elderly people with the title of *señor* and *señora*. I took it she meant the same thing in English so the words sir and ma'am weren't far from my vocabulary. She taught me to be courteous and kind to other people and urged me to graduate from high school. She warned me never to lie, and above all, to respect the American government.

"*Con el gobierno Americano no se juega,*" she said more times than I wanted to remember.

Amagrande had been a much greater part of my life than I realized and my only regret was never telling her how much I loved her.

Interestingly, the day we buried Amagrande is also the day I came face-to-face with my father. We came together through a cousin who invited me to her house to meet my father who was visiting. Adan Flores greeted me warmly yet he came across as boisterous and full of himself. Our time together was short, but long enough for Adan to say he was sorry he hadn't been a part of my life and was proud that I carried his name. I was elated that the father I missed having, existed after all. Yet, I felt that the many years we were apart made strangers out of us. I didn't hold much hope in establishing a loving father-daughter relationship with Adan especially since we lived so far apart but I was thankful just the same for having met him.

In 1973, a draft departmental report on the education status of Hispanics and Native Americans was presented at a meeting between federal officials and representatives from those communities. The purpose of the meeting was for the Hispanic and Native American community representatives to review the document and provide feedback to the federal officials on the findings prior to finalizing the report and releasing it to the public. But during the meeting, all the attendees could talk about was the terms used in the report to refer to their respective populations. The Hispanics became angry at being called, "Chicanos," "Mexicans," and "Spanish speakers." The Native Americans complained of being referred to as Indians. Their complaints became so heated that the meeting had to close, while nothing came of the recommendations made in the report that could have positively affected millions of Hispanic and Native American schoolchildren.

After hearing about the complaints, Secretary Weinberger directed that an inter agency committee be formed to examine and identify racial/ethnic terminology to be used in all department forms and reports to identify every person that received social services and everyone that was employed by the department. Manny Carrillo attended the first meeting, but when he noticed the room filled with mostly mid-level civil servants, he sent Phil, his deputy, to all future meetings and instructed that I go along to listen and take notes, but not to speak. A few weeks after Phil and I attended our first meeting together, Phil left our office to take a position in another federal agency. Manny allowed me to attend the committee's future meetings in his place, but only because and I quote, "They take up too much of my time," while cautioning me not to say anymore than I absolutely had to.

The Ad Hoc Committee on Racial and Ethnic Definitions was split into subcommittees, which included civil servants from throughout the federal government that were representative of the major groups affected: Whites, Blacks, Hispanics, Asians and Native Americans. The Hispanic subcommittee meetings were contentious, at best. We argued fiercely over the government adopting terms such as: "Spanish-speaking," "Spanish surname," "Chicano," "Latino," and "Hispanic." Spanish-speaking and Spanish surname were eliminated from the get go after most of us in the group made the case that any person could learn to speak Spanish and could obtain a Spanish surname through marriage. Chicano had been a regional term that was identified with the Mexican-American population so it wasn't going to do anything to help identify the other Hispanic subgroups such as Puerto Ricans, Cubans and other Central and South Americans. Our group discussed at length, recommending the term, "Latino." But we found the term was masculine in nature and would include peoples of Italy and other Europeans with Latin roots. As our discussions reached a certain level, I became convinced that "Hispanic" was the term that best identified those persons with Spanish surnames that claimed their origin was Spanish. In 1975, our subcommittee recommended that term to Secretary Weinberger which he accepted. The final decision to have the rest of the federal government adopt "Hispanic," as well as the other racial/ethnic definitions developed by the other subcommittees came about during President Ford's administration not President Nixon's as has been widely misreported.

In early 1974, Manny left the office to pursue another civil service position in HEW and I became the acting director. During the time I served as acting director, a number of explosive policy issues came to my desk, which at the age of 28 and at a GS-9 level, I didn't feel confident or prepared enough to address. Illegal immigration became a major issue that came under media scrutiny after the American public began to complain that there were too many "Spanish people," especially from Mexico, entering the country illegally to work. But mostly they complained that the illegals were taking advantage of free medical and social services.

One particularly hot and humid summer day, I received a call from one of Secretary Weinberger's assistants requesting that I attend a meeting at the Department of Justice on behalf of the secretary. He mentioned off-handedly that the meeting would be attended by high-level career civil servants and political appointees. When I arrived, the Attorney General Edward (Ed) H. Levi was sitting at the head of a long, shiny rectangular conference table surrounded by a group of young fresh-faced men. The rest of the room was filled with intense-looking older men, all of them Anglo except for one young Black man that sat at the other end of the table. He was the only one to pop a smile at me. When the attorney general called the meeting to order, everyone scrambled to find a seat around the conference table, leaving me to grab one of the remaining chairs that leaned against the wall. The main topic of discussion was whether the United States government should develop a national identification card. Everyone around the table chimed in, but the attorney general stopped the conversation, saying he wanted to know what Cap Weinberger thought about the card and whether illegal aliens (as he called them) should receive health, education and welfare services. The moment I heard the attorney general ask who was representing Cap Weinberger, my heart began pounding while sweat build up under my armpits.

I hadn't expected to do anything at the meeting other than take notes as I had done in so many other meetings. I kept my head down, hoping that someone else from HEW was in the room to rescue me. But I was it, the one and only representative from my department. The attorney general searched around the room and asked again, this time in a much louder tone, "Is there a representative from HEW?" I reluctantly raised my hand and with that all heads in the room turned toward me. The room went silent while every person waited for my response. I am convinced that a live, nude Marilyn Monroe wouldn't have received as much attention. As I struggled to spill a few words, the attorney general asked, impatiently, "Well, what's Cap's position? Should we be providing social services to illegal aliens?"

"Oh, Mary, Mother of God," I thought. Sweat was building up on my face and under my armpits, while my stomach made gurgling sounds. I was either going to have a serious bathroom accident or pass out of sheer fright and embarrassment. Words were forming in my brain, but none would come out of my mouth. "It's all right. Take your time," the lone Black man in the room said.

I murmured something or other that the Department wasn't in favor of adopting a universal ID card, but it became clear to everyone in the room that I was petrified beyond help. I added in some form of babble, that we in the Department didn't have proof that illegals were using social services nor were we going to do the job of the Immigration and Naturalization Service by checking applicants for their residency. The policy positions weren't what anyone at the Department told me to say. They were my positions which I firmly believed and supported. The friendly Black man, who someone said later, was Richard Parsons, an aide to Vice President Rockefeller, didn't falter; he continued to smile, while encouraging me to continue my response. I swear, if that man hadn't shown his strong support, I probably would've passed out and been face down on the floor. The valuable lesson I learned that day was that preparation is a must no matter who is in the audience.

Shortly after my disastrous performance at the Justice Department, a new director was hired in the Spanish-Surnamed office. I was more than happy to see Víctor Vásquez take over. I needed to get back to studying the policies issues before me so I could be in a position to articulate them in a convincing and clear manner. And the person most responsible for helping me through that process was a young Michigan State professor I helped recruit. Harry Pachon was as bright as they come but his familiarity with the bureaucracy was slim at best. I helped him find his way through the bureaucratic maze while he helped me to conduct research, write and articulate department policies. Harry was just the person we needed to challenge the Anglo policy wonks who seemed to resent those of us in the minority offices meddling in their policy work. But, Harry was successful in neutralizing their resentment with his charm, intellect and academic credentials.

When I went to work in HEW in 1972, I moved from Northwest D.C., to an apartment located within walking distance to my new office. I lived alone in a ninth floor apartment that oversaw the Southwest part of the nations' capital. I was happy to be on my own and comfortable in my new surroundings, although I was aware that the crime rate in Southwest D.C. was much higher than in Cleveland Park. Muggings, stabbings and shootings were the norm on any given night. I was mugged soon after I moved into the area but after having survived the violence of my childhood, I wasn't going to be frightened away.

One night in 1973, the phone rang. Amá was on the other end crying loudly. She tried speaking but the only word that spilled out was, Delfina. My heart sank; I wondered if my eldest sister had passed away. The thirteen years between Delfina and me kept us from becoming close. Still, our bloodlines connected through our Amá, were enough to bring us together emotionally, at least to some extent. Once Amá got control of her emotions, she revealed angrily that Delfina had run off with another man, abandoning her husband and seven young children. I felt my heart sink even lower. At first, I felt shame, then anger. I could understand leaving her husband, who was old enough to be her father, but abandoning all of her children as if they didn't matter was hard for me to grasp. Her irresponsibility and self-serving behavior created a family crisis of monumental proportions. Surely scandals weren't new to our family but never before had any one gone as far as abandoning their own children.

No one in our family could say what drove Delfina to leave her husband and children.

We could only speculate that perhaps she was tired of her old husband or perhaps she was so in love she didn't want anyone interfering with her new love life. Years later, Amá told me that Delfina had placed much of the blame on her for leaving. Delfina faced some rough times as a young woman and her relationship with our Amá could be distant and at times competitive. Yet, there were issues in my sister's life that I couldn't possibly comprehend and didn't make an effort to even try. Admittedly, my siblings and I should have made an effort to reach out to Delfina. Instead we kept her out of our lives like a bad penny and rarely saw or spoke to her before she died in 1998.

Interestingly, the man Delfina ran off with ended up leaving her for another much younger woman. If ever there was any truth to Amagrande's declaration that we pay for our sins, here on earth, Delfina's story certainly gives it some credence.

Yet, it wasn't as if Delfina was the first on Taft's South Side to abandon her children. Years earlier, other women had abandoned their young children in a similar fashion. In 1973, my family wasn't any more prepared to handle my sister's decision to abandon her children than the families before us. At first Amá chose to hang her head in shame, worried more about what *la gente* would say than about jump starting the lives of Delfina's children. However, to Amá's credit it was she who ended up parenting them.

When Jimmy Carter was elected President in 1976, change in policy direction and in personnel came to the entire federal government, as it always does when a new administration comes to town. President Carter named Joseph A. Califano HEW's new Secretary. Califano was well known in Washington as a prominent lawyer, but mostly he was known as President Lyndon B. Johnson's domestic policy advisor. He brought a new wave of energy and excitement that had been lacking in the department. And he brought with him a floor full of high-ranking women and minorities, such as I had never before seen in my years in government. Previous secretaries were pushed into the limelight by emerging policy issues; Califano pushed himself into the limelight by the issues he pursued. Immediately after he arrived, Califano pushed many of the the social service buttons from welfare reform to abortion to education to non smoking. Before long, there was any number of groups protesting in front of his home and at the department.

While I admired Califano's enthusiasm to change things in the department, I disagreed with his anti-smoking campaign. I felt strongly that as long as smoking is legal, no one should tamper with that right. Califano became so obsessed with his anti-smoking campaign that he'd stop HEW employees in the hallways and elevators, asking them to stop smoking. One of the secretaries in our office rode the elevator with Califano with a cigarette in her hand. During the ride, Califano essentially told her to stop smoking and our secretary essentially told him to mind his business, not really knowing who she was talking to. Afterward, the secretary came running into our office saying excitedly, "I think I just told the man off when he asked me to stop smoking." A group of us gathered and confirmed to her that indeed it was Califano she had tangled with over her smoking. The secretary, who grew up in one of the roughest neighborhoods in Northeast D.C., was scared to death Califano would find where she worked and fire her for having talked back to him. For days afterward, she took the stairs rather than risk meeting Califano again in the elevator. In the meantime, Califano stood his ground about nonsmoking and before long the tobacco growers began to complain to the White House. In my opinion, this began his downfall as President Carter's cabinet member.

While Joe Califano brought excitement to the department, I didn't think that in my mid-level position I'd be affected by his presence. But to my surprise, my experience and knowledge of the Hispanic community was once again sought, this time by the Democrats. A few months after he arrived, Joseph A. Califano called a meeting of some of his political and career civil servants to discuss how to help *Chicanos*, as he called Hispanics. I received a call from Jerry Bennett, one of the key assistants in the assistant secretary's office, to attend the meeting with him. Califano walked into his conference room looking exceedingly happy, putting everyone around the table at ease. But Califano had a reputation from his days as domestic policy advisor to President Johnson for being high strung and temperamental. And I for one didn't want to do anything that would cause me and the rest of the others in the room to find out just how hot a temper he had, so I sat quietly staring at the bare wall directly in front of me.

During the meeting, I clung to his every word which was *Chicano* this and *Chicano* that. His message wanting to help *Chicanos* made me want to jump out of my seat and yell, "*Viva la raza!*" Yet, his continued usage of *Chicano* reminded me that *Chicano* was one of the terms that had driven the education report advisors to leave their meeting, prompting the formation of the racial/ethnic definitions committee. I turned to Jerry and whispered, "We need to remind Califano that *Chicano* isn't an all-inclusive term to describe Hispanics. Besides, there are many Mexican-Americans that don't like to be called *Chicano.*"

Jerry whispered back, "He'll have you for lunch if you try to correct him."

"Well, if we are going to develop a program for all Hispanics, we should tell him," I argued forcibly.

"Then go ahead and tell him," Jerry urged. After pausing for a split second, he looked me in the eye, and declared, "But don't look for me to save your ass after he chews you out in front of the crowd."

Not one to set herself up for a dressing down in a roomful of career civil servants and political appointees, I kept quiet at the meeting. However, I spoke to Califano through his White House Fellow, Fernando Torres-Gil about the importance of using *Hispanic* instead of *Chicano*. A few days after my conversation with Fernando, Joe Califano established an interdepartmental task force called the Hispanic Initiative. The task force was comprised of mostly career civil servants and led by Fernando. But, the two highest ranking Hispanic political appointees in the department, Arabella Martinez and Blandina "Bambi" Cárdenas were the task force's key advisers, and it was they who would ultimately review our findings and make their final recommendations to Califano.

The biggest challenge of our task force on the Hispanic Initiative was to figure out how to establish a process within the department to address helping Hispanics, without offending other minority groups or amending programs that Congress had mandated to help minorities in general. I became a member of the task force after that first meeting in Califano's conference room.

After spending almost a year developing the Hispanic Initiative, our task force presented its results to Arabella Martinez, the assistant secretary for human resources. A few days later Arabella called a meeting of the task force to present her revision of our work. To my surprise she made so many changes that what was left couldn't possibly be implemented expeditiously, which was necessary in order not get bogged down in the bureaucracy. The wheels began to come off the Hispanic Initiative. In my opinion, Arabella had shown a less-than-complete understanding of how federal programs were planned, developed and implemented when she made the changes. While our group tried to educate her and Bambi about the federal bureaucracy's procedures, only Bambi took the time to listen. The task force's Hispanic Initiative was the product of staff effort based on many collective years of federal experience. But because Arabella was the highest-ranking Hispanic in the department and the one Califano looked to for advice, hers was the final voice on the matter.

In the summer of 1979 I left the department to work on my master's degree at the Kennedy School of Government at Harvard University. Two years earlier I had graduated from the University of the District Columbia where I had earned a Bachelor of Arts degree in Psychology through the Upward Mobility Program. While UDC may not have been nearly as prestigious as the alma maters of my colleagues in the Office of the Assistant Secretary for Planning and Evaluation (ASPE), I learned much about the African-American community and their significant contributions made to America.

The Harvard masters program for which I was selected was primarily designed for up and coming mid and high-level civil servants throughout the federal government.

In previous years all those selected for the masters program had been Anglos, the majority of whom were men. I learned about the masters program through a friend in another department, but when I inquired further, I was met with resistance by the staff in the assistant secretary's office that was responsible for selecting a candidate. The new deputy assistant secretary, Peter Schuck who was a Carter appointee, was the most vocal against my applying.

During a meeting in his office, he asked if I knew the type of people who were selected to attend the prestigious mid-career program. When I admitted my ignorance, he mentioned the name of a young Anglo woman who was a high-level civil servant in the department. "It's a person like her that is accepted," he warned. I didn't allow that conversation to continue to it's logical, to him at least, conclusion. I got the hint but was determined, and sure enough when I put my papers in to be considered for the program, Peter turned me down. However, I kept the idea warm and a few months later Peter left to return to his teaching post at Yale. With this bottleneck gone I applied again. This time, my colleague and friend Jerry, helped process the paperwork and guided it through the system, encouraging the new assistant secretary, Ben Heineman, Jr. to support me. I am not sure how much arm-twisting went on but in the end Ben signed the papers and I didn't give his initial reluctance more than a second of my time. I was headed for Harvard!

Califano left the department shortly after I did when he was fired by President Carter. Some version of the Hispanic Initiative was completed, but its implementation fell to Califano's successor,

Patricia Harris. Secretary Harris did all she could to move the Hispanic Initiative forward, but too much time had passed from the day Califano enthusiastically walked into his conference room declaring he wanted to do something for *"Chicanos."* It was my experience that for a new proposal in the federal government to get traction requires the nurturing and feeding by the same person who started it. Califano saw the big Hispanic elephant in the room and wanted to embrace it more than any other federal official I came to know, and that left a lasting impression on me.

During my participation on the Hispanic Initiative, I became impressed with the level of power enjoyed by the energetic young men and women who were part of Califano's political staff and by their ability to make us civil servants jump on command. These people were political appointees, chosen by Joe Califano but vetted by the White House and served at the pleasure of the president. My association with Califano's political appointees allowed me to understand and to recognize that there is public service and then there is public service.

I continued on my career in public service but with my eye on a possible next move-to become a political appointee.

Chapter 16

Politics

"In politics, if you want something said, ask a man; if you want something done, ask a woman."
Margaret Hilda Thatcher, 1925-
Prime Minister of Great Britain, 1979-1999

The human excitement that filled Harvard yard over having Jackie Kennedy Onassis among the proud relatives of graduating students almost stole the graduation moment for me. Like so many Americans I was fascinated by the widow of President John F. Kennedy. She had emerged as such a powerful American figure after President Kennedy, was assassinated and for a time it seemed the American public couldn't get enough of her. Yet, on June 6, 1980, when I was face-to-face with one of the most famous persons on earth, I was more annoyed than star struck. Mrs. Onassis, who was at Harvard's commencement exercise to see her daughter Caroline graduate from Radcliffe College, seemed like just another parent, casually dressed and unassuming among the excited but reserved crowd. Yet while others in the crowd stared and did anything they could to get Jackie Onassis's attention, I focused on my moment of glory—having fulfilled my dream to graduate from an Ivy League university.

I was going to miss my life at Harvard. The school had played such a pivotal role in my life, both academically and socially. I so enjoyed the school that I decided to get married at the Harvard Chapel as a reminder of my happy times there. Academically, the Kennedy school was certainly at the top of its game. The case studies we were given to solve were complicated and as difficult as anything I had ever done in my life but the work was enjoyable and rewarding. On weekends, I joined my two closest classmates, Sergio Levin and Ken Jaramillo, in discovering the famous campus and its surroundings. We shared beers and burgers at Charlie's, jogged along the Charles River and ventured into Boston to tour the many historical landmarks.

The sunny, warm graduation day seemed to slip by so fast. Yet, the euphoria of graduating from an Ivy League university stayed with me for days—that is, until I returned to Washington, D.C., to resume my civil service career at HEW, which had been renamed the Department of Health and Human Services (HHS). (The E part of HEW had become the Department of Education.) But that wasn't the only thing that had changed in the old HEW department; my old Office of Special Concerns had been all but eliminated by political appointees from the Carter Administration. I came away surprised upon learning that the Democrats, known for leading the fight for the rights of minorities, would do away with the symbolic offices so important to the minority communities. But die the offices did. I learned that I would remain in the Office of the Assistant Secretary for Planning and Evaluation where the unit had been housed, but assigned to the deputy assistant secretary for evaluation.

My new boss was Joe S. Wholey, an evaluation expert and member of President Carter's administration. He, like other political appointees, was trying to make the trains run in the federal government not only to serve the public but also to impress upon them that President Carter deserved to be re-elected. I hadn't heard of Joe S. Wholey until I reported to work in my new office in June of 1980. The buzz around the office was that as Chairman of the Metropolitan Area Transit Authority, Wholey was chiefly responsible for the development of the computerized fare cards used in the newly built subway system in Washington, D.C. When I heard that, I was concerned about how his evaluation plans were going to be received if the metro rail card, which, at best, was receiving mixed reviews, was any indication of his talents.

My first assignment under Wholey's leadership was to conduct an evaluability assessment of selected bilingual education programs throughout the country. An evaluability assessment can be a highly useful tool that, in essence, is a pre-evaluation—an assessment to put things in place before a formal evaluation is undertaken in order to ensure the formal evaluation is accurate and useful. Yet, in my opinion, an evaluability assessment which may or may not lead to an evaluation of a federal program is a process that takes too long to complete in a bureaucracy that can be convoluted and cumbersome, resulting in the public not being served as efficiently and effectively as it should.

Wholey spent most of the day closeted in his office poring over evaluation models, rarely coming out to see or talk with his staff. But when he met with me and another colleague, Jerry Haar about the evaluability assessment he seemed friendlier and much more gregarious than I had thought him to be. He emphasized that our mission wasn't to evaluate the bilingual education program for improvement, but rather to collect information to determine if the program could be evaluated at some point. In my opinion, if there was a program that needed evaluating, it was bilingual education. Here was a federal program designed to help school districts provide equal education opportunities to children with limited English-speaking abilities through a transitional bilingual process, yet those who were responsible for running the programs were virtually exempt from accountability. There were few measures to speak of that helped determine how well the children did in their academic achievement. The program had taken many turns since Congress passed the Bilingual Education Act in 1968. When Jerry and I visited the bilingual education sites we discovered several areas in the programs that needed improvement. In most instances we found the bilingual program directors eager to have us help them improve services.

We heard stories of rampant fraud, waste, and abuse, but in our visits to ten bilingual programs, we found only one such instance. In that particular instance we found the bilingual program poorly managed by a director who was not an academician and who had most of his family on the federal payroll. The more questions we asked, the more uneasy the director and his staff became. It seemed we were uncovering suspicious information that we weren't authorized to examine further so we closed the meeting before we got ourselves in deeper than our assessment responsibilities allowed.

When the president orders a cutback in spending, those of us in government must be prepared to make hard recommendations about which federal programs should be reduced or eliminated altogether. An evaluation process can serve as a catalyst to meet this order. But, in my opinion, Wholey's type of evaluation designs essentially led to doing nothing in the short-term to improve or eliminate programs, but that didn't surprise me. Behind the man's desk hung a large poster that read: "Not to decide, is to decide." I found that government can be its own worst enemy with regard to doing nothing for the public in an efficient and effective manner while at the same time growing and spending itself out of control. This kind of evaluation did not interest me and I was ready to launch my public service career in another direction.

By the end of the summer of 1980, I knew that either Wholey or I or both of us would be gone before the end of year, and I was happy either way. In my case, I was newly married to an Air Force brigadier general and knew he would be reassigned out of the Pentagon sooner rather than later. And as for Wholey, I felt that his days were numbered since it looked more and more as if Governor Reagan of California was going to defeat President Carter in the election.

My goal was to become a political appointee in the Reagan administration. But since I had not worked on Reagan's presidential campaign or done much else to help get him elected other than vote for him, I knew my chances were slim at best. This was the first time I believed in a candidate so strongly that I was willing to quit my safe job and join his administration. Reagan's philosophy of less government, lower taxes, and a strong defense captivated me and made me the staunch Republican I am today.

Shortly after President Reagan was sworn in, I called a friend who was assigned to the new president's transition team to tell him I wanted to join Reagan's administration.

"Your chances of that happening are not good. The White House is looking to place individuals loyal to the president and those that worked hard on his campaign," he said sternly.

I didn't let my friend's discouraging but truthful words dissuade me. I pressed on, telling him that my husband was being transferred to Carswell AFB in Ft. Worth as the 12th Air Force Division commander and asked if there would be a political position in the Dallas-Ft. Worth area for which I could be considered.

A few days later, I received a call from the White House personnel office. The caller wanted to know if I was interested in the Dallas Regional Director position for the Department of Education. I held the desk tightly to keep from falling over with excitement. The White House staffer set up an interview with the person responsible for overseeing the ten regional offices at the Department of Education. We met in his office in Washington, D.C. He opened the meeting by talking about the importance of family and asked me more than once why I didn't have children, whether I was planning to have children, and how many. After a long and rambling discussion on the importance of family, the man got up from his chair to escort me out while saying he was interviewing other candidates. As he rushed me out the door, he said that the candidate that could generate the most political support would get the job.

"Go out and call every prominent person you know that will write or call the White House on your behalf. It can be a major party contributor, an elected official, or someone close to the president," he advised eagerly.

Hearing his advice, I felt encouraged about the possibility of getting hired. I knew many people in the administration, including some key party contributors in Dallas and Ft. Worth, and began calling to ask for letters of support. But while I was busy doing that, I received a call from White House personnel.

"The Department of Education is announcing the name of the new regional director in Dallas," the young woman on the other end of the phone said politely. Before I had a chance to respond, the young woman hurriedly said I am sorry and hung up.

On the South Side of Taft, provoking the wrong person could get you a switchblade stuck in your chest. In politics, I learned that a switchblade doesn't have to be used to inflict pain. It can be done with a deliberate mental stab, which more often lands on your back. It's not until you're left bleeding emotionally on the ground, gasping for that last breath of air, that you realize you've been had. That was my first lesson in Politics 101. The Department of Education official never intended to hire me. I became angry with myself for not having had my antenna up high enough to see past his lies. But even if I had detected a glimpse of deception on the man's part, I probably would have chosen to ignore it because I wanted the regional director job in the worst way. I took away a valuable lesson from my first political interview, but I also learned that being the wife of a general officer wasn't a selling point to a type of man who thought I should be supporting my husband's career, rather than gallivanting through the halls of a federal building trying to advance my political career as he implied during my interview. Never mind that the military also didn't take too kindly to seeing the wife of a high-ranking officer getting involved in politics—something my husband was reminded of by a higher-ranking officer shortly after we arrived at Carswell.

After failing to become a member of Reagan's administration I did what most generals' wives in our command spent their time doing; attending the Officers' Wives' club teas and luncheons, travelling with my husband to the various Strategic Air Command (SAC) bases under his command and entertaining the many dignitaries that visited Carswell Air Force Base. In a quirky kind of way, I looked forward to my new life as wife of the Air Division Commander—it was after all quite a departure from my life in Washington, D.C. as a public servant.

At Carswell, we were assigned a large house near the base's golf course. And yes, it was bigger than the general's house at Kelly AFB. All that meant was that we were literally off the base, far away from other military personnel and very close to the B-52 engine run up area which operated at the wee hours of the morning. On the plus side, the home had a sprawling landscape that hosted all types of animals and all manner of birds that kept me company while my husband flew the "Looking Glass"—the airborne command post, almost every weekend. Military protocol governed our lives but all for the good since it brought order to an otherwise unwieldy system. Needless to say, we didn't have to worry about waiting in line for a tee time or a dining table at the club. And if that wasn't good enough, when we visited a club or restaurant in downtown Ft. Worth, the entire staff treated us grandly.

Even though my husband was the highest ranking military officer at the base, my role in the Carswell Officers' Wives' Club, was more of a figurehead. I was essentially expected to sit quietly and look pretty. The board was made up of young officers' wives' or "gals," which I learned soon enough was the term used among military wives to refer to one another. It was these young wives that were the decision makers, while I, along with the senior colonel wives, served as advisors. Although much to my naïveté, I learned quickly that it was the Wing Commander's wife that really ran the show, and oh boy, what a handful she turned out to be.

The first Air Force Officers' Wives' Club was established in 1923 as a social club to bring the wives of pilots together for friendship and social networking. Although, the first actual military wives' club dates back to the American Revolutionary War, as the clubs grew throughout the Air Force, they became more formalized; office elections were held, welcoming and farewell teas and luncheons were held for the wives of the officers, and volunteer programs on the base and off were developed. The wearing of gloves and hats at club events soon became *de rigueur* for the wives and guests. By the time I came to Carswell much of the formality had been dispensed with. But the traditional teas and luncheons each month were in full swing as were many of the volunteer programs. To keep with the time, today's Wives' Clubs are called Spouses' Clubs and are much smaller, and there are less of them around the world than when I joined in the 1980s.

Soon after I arrived on base, I was invited by the president of the Officers' Wives' Club to give a speech at one of their monthly luncheons. I chose to speak about "working wives," a sore subject with the older military wives but a winning subject with the wives of the lower-ranked officers. After my speech I began hearing from the younger wives about wanting to work but they were afraid that if they did, they'd end up ruining their husbands' careers. I asked the same question to each of the callers and each gave the same answer: the person who told them not to work was the wing commander's wife. As surprised as I was to hear their complaints, I was more surprised at the cavalier attitude of the wing commander's wife. It was as if she, not her husband, was the commander.

A few months later, I raised the issue of "working wives" again by writing an article for the Carswell Officers' Wives' Newsletter. The article, which was a lot more mild-mannered than I would have liked, created hysteria throughout the Strategic Air Command (SAC). There had never been a wife of a general who took a step away from the traditional culture of military life and dared to write about it. I was venturing into uncharted territory, where I was uninvited and unwelcome. At a meeting of commanders' wives, another general's wife approached me and angrily said, "If Peggy Ellis was around, she'd have you and your husband out of the military."

"Who the hell is Peggy Ellis?" I asked, showing my ignorance.

Peggy Ellis was the wife of General Richard Ellis, who had been the SAC commander a few years earlier. Many officers' wives still shook in their boots when they recalled her visits to the bases where their husbands were assigned. According to them, Mrs. Ellis made a lot of demands and supported the belief that officers' wives shouldn't work.

But this was the 1980s and many things were changing in the military, including the attitudes of the younger wives, who were well on their way to becoming the next generation of generals' wives. It was impossible with the ever-changing military assignments of officers and enlisted men, for their wives to develop a career. So for them, it wasn't about going out and forsaking their military lives for their careers; it was more to put their college educations to use and to earn, in many cases, much-needed extra income for their families.

When I wasn't learning the way of military life at Carswell, I spent a lot of my time getting to know the civic and business leaders of Ft. Worth, who staunchly supported our military in the area. They were colorful characters right out of an Edna Ferber novel. There was a lot of old money still filling up the banks in Ft. Worth, and many of the families that had inherited all those millions had one story after another told about them. T. Cullen Davis, who at one time was one of the richest men in America and accused of murder and found not guilty, showed up in my husband's office carrying a bible and talking in riddles. His professed "born again" shtick didn't pass the smell test of credibility with my husband who had more important military things to do than listen to Davis.

So that was my life at Carswell AFB: mixing with the money people in Ft. Worth, attending officers' wives' teas, and putting up with the pushy wing commander's wife.

Less than a year after arriving at Carswell, Harley and I attended a dinner at the Shady Oaks Country Club, which was dominated by the legendary Ben Hogan. After the dinner, which included top Air Force brass and Ft. Worth civic leaders, General Charles (Charlie) Gabriel, the Air Force Chief of Staff took Harley aside and whispered that he was slated for a new assignment. Harley and I were sad to leave Ft. Worth; it offered so much suspense, drama and downright fun. But we quickly turned to our new life and began to speculate about where the new assignment could be, but we had little to go on, since General Gabriel hadn't related any detail at all. A few days later, the mystery was solved when General Bennie Davis, the SAC commander, called Harley and officially told him he was going to be the war planner at SAC headquarters in Omaha, Nebraska.

We left the legendary and exciting Ft. Worth a little less than a year after arriving for the dreary cold Midwestern town of Omaha. When we drove out on Interstate 10 headed west, I thought back to the regional director's position that I so badly wanted and hadn't gotten. As it turned out, it was good that the position didn't materialize since I wouldn't have been in it long enough to find the water fountain, much less to help President Reagan.

When I met Harley he was assigned to the Pentagon replacing another Air Force Major who did business with the men in my office. My heart jumped at the sight of the short guy with dark curly hair from Adair, Oklahoma. His handsome sensual face reminded me of the singer Tom Jones. Although there was immense attraction when first we met nothing came of it until many years later.

When we did talk he often spoke of his Mother as the most important human being in his life. She had influenced him both as a mother and as a teacher and principal of the school and his younger sister Karen attended. However, like any two people with competing lives we drifted apart and only reunited much later. Harley and I eventually were married and he became everything to me; he was the father I longed for, the brother I wished for and the husband I dreamed about.

After I became Harley's wife, I knew if I wanted to work in politics, I had to keep that part of my life off the front page, so to speak, since members of the military aren't allowed to get involved in politics. Although military spouses aren't governed by the same policy, I had to walk a tight rope so as not to draw unnecessary attention to my husband's career. Thus, I was low key when I signed up as a volunteer on the campaign of Congressman Hal Daub from Omaha. But my assignment there consisted mostly of: making copies of campaign literature, addressing envelopes, and making calls to voters in Nebraska's second district. Yet, I felt this was my chance to get involved politically which was something I longed to do since the day I slipped on a T-shirt with AU H_2O decorated on the back and the front in support of Barry Goldwater during the 1964 presidential campaign.

When I wasn't volunteering in the congressman's office or teaching, I was attending social events with the other generals' wives who were at least a generation older than me. Although we didn't have much in common in generational terms, I got along with the generals' wives and was thrilled to be living among them on Generals Row at Offutt AFB. Our military quarters were in the form of red brick homes that had been built between 1894 and 1898, and on weekends many of the younger military officers and enlisted personnel drove by with their families to view the historic homes we were lucky to live in. I didn't get to be friends with many of the generals' wives since I spent most of my time working on Daub's campaign and teaching at two local universities. But those that I came to know I found to be upstanding citizens, although there were some that would push their mother **and** their grandmother over the Memorial Bridge—if it meant another star for their husbands. Most of them had college degrees but hadn't worked outside the home, since being married to a military man is not exactly the easiest way to form a career.

At first it was difficult getting used to talking and socializing with the generals' wives; their conversation mostly centered on sharing food recipes, finding bargains at the local Omaha department stores and wanting "grandbabies." The difference between them and the women I knew in Washington, D.C. both as co-workers and associates was enormous. Many of the Washington, D.C. women I came to know were hard-core feminists and lesbians who wouldn't dream of leaving their careers for any man or woman. At one time I became part of a group of Washington, D.C. area women that met monthly to discuss policy issues affecting our gender. At one meeting, Gloria Steinman came to speak. I sat in the room along with the other women totally mesmerized by the pencil thin, glamorous-looking woman, taking in each word that spilled out of her mouth as if it was truest in form. At that same meeting a future senator came in with her partner. I thought how brave and bold she was to be so, "out." But looking back, her "closeted life" was protected from further public exposure by our group and that is the way it should have been. In my own family we had one particular member who closeted himself until his recent death. I witnessed the dilemma he experienced in wanting to expose his real life. It was painful to watch him suffer, but in order to survive in our family and in our hometown he did what he thought best.

While I learned much from my feminist associates and friends, I didn't get caught up in the feminist movement for two reasons. I saw the movement as being led by well to do Anglo women whose lives had been based more on privilege than poverty. They could reach their goals as Anglo women a lot easier than those of us still struggling with our ethnic heritage. Add to that our class status and we faced a serious challenge making our way up America's ladder of success. Never mind there were some issues the feminist movement presented that could be over reaching. That, plus their cherry picking in favor of certain women to defend and protect didn't sit well with me. If we are going to say we support every woman's right then that's exactly what we should do, regardless of faith, color or political persuasion.

At the Strategic Air Command, I became a close friend of General Bennie Davis's wife, Pat. She was one of those rare generals' wives of her generation who didn't make an issue of military wives working. She liked the article I had written on working wives so much that she had it printed and disseminated at every commander's conference during the time her husband was the Strategic Air Commander. I credit Pat Davis for beginning to change the way the military overall viewed working wives. I might have written the article, but it was her place in the military hierarchy that allowed my message to be heard and to take hold. And none of that would have happened if it weren't for the forward thinking and vision of her husband, General Bennie Davis.

After Nebraska, Harley's next assignment was at the Pentagon. We moved to Washington in the summer of 1984. At that time, there was a lack of military housing at Bolling AFB, where Air Force generals were housed. We had no choice but to rent a friend's house in McLean, Virginia, while we waited for housing to become available. The townhouse on Brentfield Drive became the focus of the next exciting chapter of my political life. It turned out that our next door neighbors were Wyoming Senator Alan Simpson and his wife, Anne. Our landlords told us not to expect the Simpsons to have much to do with us. They were a private and quiet couple who spent a great deal of time with their family and their constituents in Wyoming. But a few days after we moved in, Anne brought us a welcome gift. We found the Simpsons a lot friendlier than our landlords had suggested. Before long, we exchanged keys to our homes so that either couple could look after the other's premises and often times, Senator Simpson regaled us over dinner with hilarious anecdotes about his youth in Wyoming.

Soon after Harley reported to his new job at the Pentagon, as the deputy to the deputy chief of staff for plans and operations, I got busy once again figuring how to get back into politics by either working in the Reagan Administration or in the Reagan/Bush re-election campaign. But after several attempts, I wasn't having much luck. My first rejection was from Bob Tuttle, the director of White House personnel. A friend in the White House arranged a meeting with him.

Bob seemed friendly enough, but after hearing me talk about my wanting to serve in the Reagan administration he cut me off. "There aren't any vacancies and I understand the campaign doesn't have any jobs either. Thank you for your time," he said as he hurriedly ushered me out of his office.

I walked to Lafayette Park, across the street from the White House, and took a seat on a bench that was shaded by large trees. The bench became my refuge for the day while I pondered Tuttle's declaration that there weren't any jobs to be had in the president's administration or in his re-election campaign. Not one to give up, I called the congressman I had helped in Omaha. I knew that help could come to those who work on a politician's campaign. Although Congressman Daub didn't return my call, his chief of staff, Jack Horner, did almost immediately. Jack didn't hesitate to offer to call someone in the campaign after I told him I wanted to work as a volunteer. A few days later, Jack called and asked that I report to the Reagan/Bush campaign headquarters.

At the headquarters, the receptionist asked me a hundred questions before allowing me to get inside to meet with the head of volunteers for the campaign. The tall, serious-looking man didn't seem all that interested in taking advantage of my free services. After listening to me explain my reason for wanting to help Reagan-Bush get reelected, he pushed back his chair and stood up, stroking his thick dark moustache, ready to escort me out the door while announcing that he didn't have anything for me to do. I refused to move from the chair.

"But I was recommended by Congressman Hal Daub's office," I insisted.

The man shook his head and repeated again that he didn't have any work for me to do. I felt that if I didn't convince the boss of all of the volunteers then I couldn't convince anyone to allow me to work in the campaign. I refused to take no for an answer.

"I'll work anywhere," I insisted.

"Now that I think about it, you could work in the Spanish office," he said matter-of-fact.

"I don't want to be pigeonholed in an office simply because it's representative of my ethnic heritage. I have policy experience, perhaps I can work with the policy staff," I suggested. The man began walking toward me and said forcefully. "It's the Spanish office or nothing. Take it or leave it."

If I truly wanted to work on the re-election campaign I felt I had no choice but to take his offer. "Where's the office?" I asked resignedly.

"It's around the corner. You can't miss it. The words Spanish Office are pinned in the front of the cubicle. Just go in there and start answering the phones. There's rarely anyone in that office, so you might as well act as if you own the place," he said sarcastically.

The head of the volunteers was correct; there wasn't a soul in the office. As I made my way into the tiny cubicle, the phones on top of two old metal desks were ringing off the hook. After a few hours of answering calls about everything from press interviews to briefing requests from the staff of Ed Rollins, the campaign director, I eagerly took over what I thought to be a rudderless ship. But just as I was getting comfortable, the ship's captain stomped in. "Who are you and what are you doing here?" she asked angrily.

"The head of the volunteers sent me to help out," I answered.

"I don't need any help!" she snapped.

"Well, he told me this office needed help, so here I am. Oh, by the way, my name is Grace Flores-Hughes, what's yours?" I asked firmly.

"My name is Lyvier Conns. I know my name doesn't sound Spanish, but I am a Mexican-American from Arizona," she said proudly.

No doubt, I was suspicious about her true ethnic identity, but I'd come to learn that people don't necessarily have to have a Spanish surname to be of Hispanic heritage. Back in 1974, this particular topic had been one of the most contentious arguments of our racial/ethnic ad hoc committee in deciding which ethnic term to recommend to Secretary Weinberger.

Lyvier ran the office because its director, Bob Estrada, worked from Texas a good deal of the time. I knew Bob and called him about my wanting to work in the Spanish office after I sensed Lyvier's uneasiness with me. I didn't blame her. She didn't know me from the man in the moon and knowing campaign culture as I'd come to know it, she could be replaced by me or any of the other volunteers in a New York minute. That's the quirky side of politics; a campaign worker or for that matter a volunteer, can be dismissed for no particular reason other than someone didn't like you or didn't like the way you smelled. A two weeks' termination notice doesn't apply in campaigns. When you're let go, you're lucky if you have one day to clear your desk. And with a dismissal, there usually comes a permanent banishment from that campaign or any other campaign. Of course, that doesn't apply to the relatives of the powerful and wealthy campaign contributors. Liz Pickens, the daughter of T. Boone Pickens comes to mind. She, not only didn't have to worry about rubbing someone the wrong way, her office was one of largest in the campaign and with fewer people in it than ours. We had to get by with only two desks taking turns sitting down while as many as eight of us volunteers squeezed into the tiny cubicle. But I am certain that had any one of our parents had as much money as T. Boone, we would've had just as big an office as his daughter Liz.

Thankfully, a few days after I started working in the Spanish office, Bob Estrada came to the campaign headquarters and asked me to stay as long as I wanted. In time, Bob became my friend and supporter and without him I wouldn't have survived the campaign, or for that matter, my presence in the Reagan and Bush Administrations.

Shortly after my arrival several other volunteers joined our office, and I became close friends with one of them. What brought us together was the security guard at the main entrance. The guard was a tall Anglo girl with boxy shoulders dressed in knee-high black leather boots. We took to calling her "the Nazi" because of her dress attire, rough manner and over the top scrutinizing of our presence in the campaign. She asked us the same hostile but stupid question every morning:

"And just where do you think you're both going?" She asked suspiciously.

And every morning we responded wearingly to her same stupid question, "To work in the Spanish Office."

The Nazi made us sign in even after we got our campaign badges. We noticed that she didn't scrutinize other campaign workers as she did us, which led us to suspect she was giving us a hard time because we were Hispanic. It became such a waste of our time to outrun and outfox the Nazi every day, but there wasn't anyone other than Bob Estrada, who was rarely in the office, to complain to about her.

As if it wasn't bad enough trying to avoid the Nazi once we made our way inside the campaign headquarters, my fellow volunteer and I had our work cut out for us. She and I did everything from answering phones to editing press releases to working with the Spanish media. On any one day I could spend much of my time photocopying campaign literature to be mailed to Hispanic voters. It seemed that everywhere I went to work in politics, I couldn't stay away from the photocopy machine. But I didn't complain. I figured the campaign was about re-electing the president not about me. Besides, I decided that if I copied enough papers, someone in the upper echelons of the campaign might notice. That was a naïve thought on my part. It was rare for our campaign director, Ed Rollins or his deputy, Lee Atwater, to show up on our floor. We had to go up to their offices if we wanted to be seen, and even then, we had better have a damn good reason for showing up there. Their staff that consisted of mostly pretty, blond, young women guarded them closer than probably the Secret Service guarded President Reagan.

Lee Atwater was more visible than Ed Rollins—allowing us to know him a tiny bit better. No doubt he was as interesting an individual as he was a political operative. While his reputation preceded him as a ruthless person who would do anything to get his candidate elected, I instead concentrated on his quick wit and his efforts to create "a big tent" atmosphere within the otherwise Anglo-dominated Republican Party. A few months before his deadly brain tumor was discovered, a girlfriend and I ran into Atwater at a political fundraiser. A friend from the White House staff who stood with us stopped Lee as he walked past us to introduce him to my friend and me.

"Do you all know Lee Atwater?" my friend asked.

Lee didn't wait for us to answer. He took one curious look at my girlfriend and me and said loudly, "Am I going to have fun tonight!"

The four of us chatted but mostly we laughed at Lee's entertaining stories. Lee was engaging but a gentleman the entire time. In the end, Lee suffered mightily from his brain tumor both mentally and physically. I'd much rather choose to remember Lee Atwater for the breakthroughs he made with the Republican Party to court more minorities, especially Hispanics, than for anything he did against any one political candidate.

Ed Rollins and Lee Atwater may not have stopped by our office, but President Reagan did. Sometime before the election, the president showed up to the campaign headquarters, and stopped by every cubicle to personally thank us for our work. Though President Reagan's Secret Service entourage followed his every move, he still took time to speak to each one of us individually in the office and shake our hand.

But as thrilled as I was to meet him, President Reagan wasn't the first U.S. president I met in person. After President Nixon's first inaugural parade, Nixon stopped to shake my hand while he walked on Pennsylvania Avenue in front of the White House. On another occasion, I was walking out of a building in downtown Washington, D.C., where I found President Ford getting out of his limousine. I ran toward him and grabbed his hand to shake it. He smiled from ear to ear but when I hollered over the noisy crowd, "Mr. President, when are you going to hire more Hispanics?" his smile disappeared and a look of puzzlement came over him. I suspected he didn't know what "Hispanic" meant. This was, after all, the same man who, on a campaign trip to San Antonio, tried to eat a *tamale* with its husk still on. Maybe that is why I was so bent on being a Republican, even if the party wasn't exactly welcoming me with open arms: so I could teach Anglo Republicans how to eat tamales?

I learned many things when I worked on President Reagan's re-election campaign. But none served me better than observing so many of the campaign workers do the unthinkable and unpredictable to get a political position after the election. I was all too aware that people who choose to work on campaigns do it to get some sort of political appointment. But at the risk of sounding naïve; I must admit I was struck by the degree of blatant sucking up and backstabbing that went on. Many of the men, especially, were guilty of sitting at their desks while the rest of us women did "shit work," as we called copying documents and making deliveries. Yet those same men were chomping at the bit to get important posts with the administration even if it meant sacrificing common sense and their personal pride. There was enough campaign literature to be copied to last a lifetime, but many of the men stayed away from a copy machine as if it was a rabid dog. Ed Rollins must have gotten wind of them, because he issued a memo calling for everyone on the campaign staff to do their part in getting the president reelected, even if it meant making copies all day long.

A few days after President Reagan was re-elected, I heard from staff of other ethnic offices that the "upstairs" had asked for campaign workers to send their resumes. But to my surprise and that of the other volunteers in the Hispanic office, we learned that Lyvier had sent her resume without asking the rest of us to do the same. Her story was that only the paid staff was asked to submit their resumes. That was another lesson in Politics 101: Don't depend on others in the campaign to talk you up to the powers that be and don't expect help from anyone to forward your resume—you have to keep your ear to the ground, eye on the ball and help yourself.

After the election, some of us who didn't end up with political appointments were asked to serve on the President's Inaugural Committee. I couldn't resist taking one more nonpaying job, because I figured the Inaugural Committee was going to be my last shot at getting a political appointment. At least that's what I was led to believe by others on the committee. Besides, I imagined I'd rub shoulders with movie stars, wealthy contributors, and other important friends of the president. Actually, I did end up, quite by accident, sitting next to a daughter of one of the richest Texas oil tycoons. His daughter sat next to me during a re-election fundraiser for President Reagan and Vice President Bush. I immediately recognized her and tried to make small talk but when she saw a group of young girls, all of whom were minority, approach the table she looked as if she was having a seizure and asked me, "They aren't going to sit here, are they?" Before I had a chance to respond, her small-size frame, dressed in a two-piece knit suit, raced away from the table. She headed directly toward a table filled with other women that looked more like her. To this day I don't know how it was that she ended up sitting at a table designated for volunteers.

A few months before the presidential 1984 election, I finally met my inspirational leader, Dr. Hector P. Garcia at a reception where he was honored after being awarded the Presidential Medal of Freedom by President Reagan. As a volunteer in the reelection campaign, I had access to some White House events but the event that led me to meet Dr. Garcia was by far my most memorable and meaningful. My heart pounded as I made my way to the table Dr. Garcia was sitting at with his family. When I introduced myself, he admitted he heard about a Mexican girl from Taft that married a general. He quickly asked if my husband was present and when I introduced him, Dr. Garcia seemed so impressed with Harley that he ignored me. I was over the moon having met Dr. Garcia even if he seemed more impressed with my husband than with me.

After the 1984 election President Reagan received the largest number of Hispanic votes of any president, and it seemed that every one of those voters wanted, perhaps I should restate that, DEMANDED, tickets to the inauguration. So instead of rubbing shoulders with some wealthy friend of President Reagan's, I stayed at my desk from dawn to dusk answering calls from irate Hispanics who demanded tickets for themselves, their family members, and just about every friend they ever made. Those that had contributed money to the president's reelection campaign were an even bigger pain in the rear. They demanded tickets that would seat them close to the president, and on top of that they demanded to meet the president.

Then there were those bearing gifts. One person came with a portrait of the president that she had commissioned a Mexican artist to paint. The artist must have wanted to give the president a Hispanic-type profile, because the portrait ended up resembling Ricardo Montalban more than President Reagan. The portrait donor insisted that I arrange for her to personally present the portrait to President Reagan. She wanted him to agree to hang it in the Oval Office. Another contributor brought in a hooked rug almost the size of a football field and insisted that the president place it in the Oval Office. If the campaign provided me with lessons on how to handle petty and scheming human behavior, the inaugural committee allowed me to observe human behavior at its most ridiculous while I used whatever diplomatic skills I possessed to keep from having to scream at someone.

After President Reagan was inaugurated I went to work as a volunteer in the White House Office of Public Liaison. I did everything from drafting presidential messages to helping arrange White House briefings for the head of the Liaison's Hispanic office, Cathi Villapando. Cathi was a Mexican-American and like me, a native born Texan. I warmed up to her, thinking we were going to get along swimmingly. At first we did, but then I began to see the darker side of her personality. She was short tempered and had an uncanny knack for playing people against each other, most of whom were her biggest supporters.

I may have had managerial experience, but Cathi had me over a barrel when it came to politics. I wasn't exactly the sharpest knife in the political drawer, and she knew it. She had years of political experience in the Republican Party, and was on a first name basis with many powerful figures. I naively thought she would mentor me, make me her protégé. But Cathi didn't teach me the ways of the political world. Instead, she had this lowly volunteer work like a dog day and night, five days a week, and often times on weekends.

Cathi wielded an unusual amount of power—she was an assistant to President Reagan and as a result the White House staff funneled many policy issues and outside groups concerning Hispanics to her. During the almost twelve months I worked for Cathi, she did make an attempt to help me find a job with the administration, but only after much prodding from me. She sent letters—that I drafted—to a couple of cabinet secretaries, but only one responded. I interviewed with one of the assistants to Margaret Heckler, the secretary of the Department of Health and Human Services. He was a young conservative who stressed the need to have conservatives everywhere in government. Before I had a chance to warm the chair he blurted, "What's your position on abortion?"

I was surprised that he would fire such a question right out of the ball park

"My position on abortion is the president's position," I answered nervously.

"You aren't answering my question," he said sharply.

I didn't want to get into a confrontation with him, but sensed he was deliberately leading me in that direction unless I gave him the answer he was looking for.

"I have to, answered your question," I said sternly.

"No, you haven't," he fought back.

"I gave you an answer. It may not be what you want to hear, but that's my answer," I argued.

The young assistant swung his chair away from the desk and walked me out the door.

"Thank you for coming," he said sternly.

I knew I wasn't going to be hired before I stepped out of his office. My pro-choice stance was something I didn't talk about to anyone. I was well aware that the conservatives ruled in the administration and if I wanted to become an appointee in the Reagan Administration, it was in my interest to keep my pro-choice stance to myself. I didn't consider myself a pro-choice activist. I wasn't for abortion as a substitute for birth control and certainly not in favor of abortion on demand. My pro-choice stance was based on what I had seen happen to so many young girls on Taft's South Side and nearby towns who ended up pregnant through rape or incest. But I felt that the conservatives in the Reagan administration were not interested in how a young girl became pregnant.

After that interview, I continued helping Cathi, hoping that I would run into someone in the White House personnel office that would help me find a political post. I felt like walking away many times, but I knew that if I left, my chance of making political connections was gone. Besides, when Cathi was away, I actually enjoyed doing my job. There was something different and exciting happening every day in the White House. I had the opportunity to view many welcoming ceremonies of visiting heads of state, and I had the opportunity to observe how the White House operated under President Reagan and Vice President Bush, whom I saw on many occasions.

In 1989 Cathi became the 39th Treasurer of the United States under President H.W. Bush's administration but resigned three years later when she got in trouble for tax evasion and obstruction of justice. I felt sorry for Cathi. She advanced above her humble south Texas beginnings to be named to a position at the sub cabinet level. The many powerful contacts she had made over the years made her one of the most influential Hispanics in the Republican Party and was a role model to many. Yet, she squandered her place in history for reasons only known to her.

It took me almost an entire year after I interviewed at the Department of Health and Human Services before I received a call from the White House Personnel Office about a possible political appointment. The job was special assistant to the Associate Administrator for Minority Small Business (8(a) program) in the Small Business Administration (SBA). I took the job without knowing much about the 8(a) program, but by that time, I was ready to earn some money, ready to leave Cathi and fed up with seeing other people get hired in the administration that hadn't lifted one finger to get the president elected.

At my new post at the SBA, my new boss, Willie González had once reported to me at the 1984 Inaugural Committee. I found myself taking orders from someone who had once taken orders from me. This was another lesson in Politics 101: In politics, a person can be on top at the campaign or at the inaugural, but can end up at the bottom of the political appointment ladder. So be nice to everyone-you never know who you'll be working with or for.

I was excited about finally reaching my political goal, but also felt that my appointment to the SBA was going to add to the number of Hispanics serving in the Reagan administration. I felt this was an important milestone given the number of calls I had received in the Office of Public Liaison from Hispanic organizations and the media about the Reagan administration not appointing enough Hispanics given the high number of votes he had received from our community. They were right, but I felt that those irate Hispanics should have been calling the White House Office of Personnel instead of me. Mickey Mouse had more clout regarding Hispanic hires in the Reagan administration than I did. But, as I had seen my fellow Hispanics do, they took it out on their own kind rather than complain to the Anglos that made the decisions.

I found the SBA to be an interesting agency, to say the least. The agency had been created in 1953 to provide federal assistance, both training and monetary, to small businesses. The 8(a) program where I was assigned was established to provide federal assistance to small and disadvantaged companies. Congress required the companies to prove they fit into the "small size" category and that they were minority owned. Before I arrived, SBA had been in the headlines after a scandal broke out about a minority owned company's kickbacks to SBA officials. There were other headlines about companies that claimed to be minority owned but were not.

The federal procurement process can be a magnet for scandal, and the 8(a) program became its featured attraction. I wasn't sure I was prepared to walk toward that stick of federal dynamite, but since that was about the only political job available I had no choice but to take it. I found myself working side by side with a team of civil service employees with amazing pasts. One was a former CIA employee and another fellow had even been one of the drafters of the reconstruction of Europe after World War II.

It seemed that as career civil servants became older and deemed "less essential," the government "dumped" them, as we say in government speak, in the most obscure of federal agencies.

I was in my job as special assistant to Willie less than a year when all hell broke loose. One afternoon, our office received a request from the Acting Administrator's office regarding the 8(a) status of a company in West Virginia. The call came to them from the office of Senator Robert Byrd, of West Virginia. I was given the task to find the answer. That was a simple enough task since I had done that type of inquiry several times, but this time the civil service employee that handled the case gave me the wrong information. She said the company from West Virginia had been disapproved for 8(a) status when in fact it had been approved. By the time I gave the correct information to the Acting Administrator's office, Senator Byrd had already called in to the acting administrator's office, ranting and raving.

The acting administrator didn't need this kind of attention especially from someone as powerful as Senator Byrd. Chuck Heatherly had unnecessarily put himself on Congress's radar screen when he fired practically all of SBA's ten regional directors upon his arrival without the authority of one nominated as the next SBA administrator—typically those decisions are left for the person that is nominated by the President and confirmed by the Senate. After calling Willie on the carpet about the false information, Heatherly ordered him to fire me. Willie came into my office and announced nervously, "Chuck wants someone's head to roll because of the wrong information provided to Senator Byrd's office, and yours is on the chopping block. In fact, he wants you to pack up and get out by the end of the day." At first I began to weep and then I became angry with Chuck for firing me outright without hearing an explanation from me. Then I became disappointed with Willie because he didn't stand by me.

Another lesson in Politics 101: Don't get too attached to your political appointment; you can become history at the snap of someone's fingers. And while you are at it, don't expect your fellow political appointees to stand by you in a time of crisis.

I knew full well that if I allowed myself to walk out of the SBA building without first trying to defend myself I could kiss my political career good-bye and I'd never work on another political campaign or in a Republican administration again. In politics, it takes only one firing to have your name permanently removed from any White House appointment list—rarely does anyone who is fired from a political appointment ever make a comeback. I wasn't prepared to become history so early in my political career. Although the job paid well, upholding my reputation meant a lot more to me than holding onto Uncle Sam's money leg. I remembered Buelito's words about Emiliano Zapata's *"Prefiero morir de pied que vivir de rodillas."* I wasn't going to beg Heatherly for my job but I was damned if I was going to let him hurt my career as he had hurt those of the regional directors he fired. They were party faithfuls, working in an administration they believed in, and didn't deserve such treatment.

I called for a meeting with Heatherly's chief of staff, who was a tall, pencil thin, young woman and much more likeable than her boss. While Linda appeared sympathetic to my side of the story, it became clear to me that she was merely following Heatherly's orders when she said, "I know you are one of the hardest working political appointees in the agency, but Chuck is very angry and has made up his mind. I am sorry, but you're going to have to go." Her words fell on me like a ton of rocks, crushing every bit of my soul. Holding back tears I thought about how quickly a whole political career can go down in flames and there is very little a person can do to put out the fire, or is there? While I sat slumped in one of the leather chairs in Linda's office, something came over me that would save my career. I threatened to call Senator Al Simpson. Actually, I didn't think it was a good idea for me to approach Senator Simpson about my situation. Our friendship was just developing.

Besides, the senator struck me as a no-nonsense type of man who wasn't going to stop his important senatorial work to listen to my personal story. Still, I threw out my bluff and left. A few minutes later, while I was packing things in my office, in walked one of Heatherly's assistants, and happily announced that the boss had thought it over and wanted me to stay.

Thankfully, Heatherly left the SBA a few months later. His replacement was former Senator Jim Abdnor, of South Dakota.

When I met with the two key members of the senator's staff, Les Melhalf and John Thune, I was still the walking wounded. But they were comforting and reassuring about wanting to work closely with me and the other political appointees in the agency. John Thune especially was concerned about the spirit within the agency and made every effort to build good relations between Senator Abdnor's political staff and the agency's career civil servants. It didn't surprise me that John later became a congressman and then a senator. He impressed me then, as he does now, as one of those exceptional and rare politicians who do not forget where they started.

Shortly after he arrived at the SBA, Senator Abdnor offered me the Associate Administrator for Minority Small Business (8(a) program) position. I was the first woman named to that post. I felt prepared to take over as I had witnessed Willie handle effectively, calls from the offices of congressmen, senators, and 8(a) applicants. Yet, I was challenged every day.

The 8(a) program, had seen its share of scandal, but I must admit that in the time I served in SBA there wasn't one single company owner or anyone else who tried to bribe me or offer me gifts. However, in terms of harassing me and making my life as miserable as their power would allow, the congressional staffers were another matter. It was heady at first to receive calls from the offices of congressmen and senators that I had read about in the newspapers and seen on television. But after awhile, I began to tense up every time my secretary announced that a staffer for Congressman X or Senator Y was on the telephone. I knew they weren't calling to thank me for the great job I was doing. While they didn't hold a gun to my head to approve a constituent's 8(a) certification or extend their stay in the 8(a) program, I had a very good sense that a metaphorical gun was loaded and cocked and pointing straight at my head in case things didn't go the way they wanted.

One overly exercised legislator was a congressman from a southwestern state. He called me into his office to explain to him and his staff why his constituents, who were also in the room, hadn't had their participation in the 8(a) program extended. His performance could have gotten him an academy award. But after all that, the Congressman's constituents' request to remain in the 8(a) program did not meet the requirements for program extension. I could understand his ranting and raving after all his job is to look after the people who elected him and the exhaustive inquiries sometimes proved essential because second reviews, like second opinions, can prove helpful, but unfortunately that wasn't the case for the southwestern congressman's constituents.

After awhile I learned to take the elected officials emotional displays in stride even if at times they acted godly. But then, who could blame them? I can't count how many times I saw people at Washington receptions literally knocking over chairs and tables to shake a senator's hand or to ask a congressman for an autograph. I chose to view them as workers hired by the people who make this country great. In spite of their fame and their sometimes giant-size egos, the senators and congressmen have problems just like the rest of the American public: they divorce, they bounce checks, and some get so greedy that they end up in prison. There are some former legislators that you wouldn't invite to your house for fear they'd show up naked on the internet, steal your sterling silverware or your husband—and that's just the men.

I somehow knew that the SBA post wasn't going to be my only political appointment, but little did I know what lay in store for me as I followed my political public service career in the Reagan Administration.

Chapter 17

The Presidential Appointment from Hell

"Grace under pressure." (Referring to his wife, when asked what he meant by "guts")
Ernest Hemingway, 1899-1961
American Novelist

In May 1986, I picked up *The Washington Post* where I read that an old friend had passed away. Gil Pompa had been the director of the Community Relations Service (CRS) at the Department of Justice. Gil had served at the Department for several years, first as deputy and later as director of the small conflict resolution agency. The position of CRS director is a four-year-term presidential appointment; the CRS director serves at the pleasure of the president, as do other political appointees. But presidential nominees, unlike "schedule C's," as lower-ranking political appointees are called, are nominated by the president and confirmed by the Senate. Typically, appointees of the president, be they schedule C or presidential, serve as long as the president wants them to. Many that join the administration don't stay the entire four years of the president's term, unless theirs is a term appointment, which can be anywhere from four to six years.

The late Dick Darman, whom I met during the 1970s at HEW, and who taught me at the Kennedy school, said that two years is the most a political appointee should work in an administration, lest they become part of the permanent government. I agreed with Darman on many issues, but this was not one of them. It's my experience that it can take a person at least a year to find their way around the halls of government, never mind that most of that time is spent on personnel issues rather than supporting the mission of the office. In my opinion a person deciding to work for a president should be prepared to commit at least four years of his or her life. This length of time should allow the person to effectively manage their agency, which in turn allows him or her to effectively help the president and serve the American public well.

Political appointments are basically given to people who helped the president get elected. Schedule C's are persons that serve the president in the federal government in capacities ranging from mid-level assistants to high-level deputy assistant secretaries. Presidential appointees serve in sub cabinet level positions and require Senate confirmation; if confirmed, they earn the title "Honorable" for life. That may be about the only perk associated with a presidential appointment; everything else about it is hard fought and can be risky. Even some of the best people will be dragged through the mud—Supreme Court Justice Clarence Thomas is one such example.

So when I learned that Gil had passed away my mind turned to his successor. Gil's body hadn't even made it out of cold storage and all I could think of was how to get named to his post. I was sad that my old friend had died, but at the same time I felt compelled to rush to the head of the line and throw my name in for consideration, knowing that every Hispanic who had ever dropped as little as a dollar into the president's campaign would throw their name in the ring. Of course, others eager to serve would do the same. Presidential appointments are few and not easy to come by.

The director of the Community Relations Service could be highly visible, depending on who held the post and how much support the White House lent the occupant. It had two missions: to resolve conflicts related to race and ethnicity and to resettle Haitians and Cubans fleeing from their countries into this America. Even though I liked my work at the SBA, the mission of CRS intrigued me, plus this was my chance to become a presidential appointee, a level in government I had never thought would be within my reach. A few days after Gil's funeral, I called a friend in the White House personnel office about the CRS position. Over lunch, we further discussed my interest in the post. But as our conversation moved along, my friend insisted that the job required someone with a law enforcement background, since its primary mission was to end riots resulting from racial/ethnic conflicts. But after much deliberation, I convinced her that a person with a lengthy career in management made more sense to be appointed as the next CRS Director and she pressed on with my name to the powers that be in the White House.

I recognized it was a long shot for me to get the post. First, I would have to be interviewed by one or more members of the White House personnel staff. If I made that first cut, the attorney general's top staff would interview me and if I made that cut, then the attorney general himself would interview me. During that interview process the FBI and other investigative agencies would vet me before President Reagan would even think of nominating me for the position. After the vetting, should any embarrassing issues in my background crop up, they could very well derail my nomination. After all the investigations are complete, my name would be sent to the Senate Judiciary Committee for further review and a vote. If the Judiciary Committee voted in the affirmative, my name would be forwarded to the full Senate for a final vote and confirmation.

I knew that all things being equal, I was assured of clearing all those hurdles. I also knew that things in the bare knuckle world of appointment politics were never equal, and that I had about as much chance for the CRS post as I had of being crowned Miss Universe. At the same time I figured that if I had cleared all those hurdles presented to me in Taft, I could clear just about anything Washington hardball politics threw at me. A few days after we had lunch, my friend at the White House called to say that after she introduced my name, the powers in the White House liked the idea of my being considered for the CRS post. Interestingly, one of those was the very Bob Tuttle who a couple of years earlier had spurned my offer to work in the president's administration and reelection campaign. What changed? Me? Him? or The situation? Another lesson in Politics 101: Don't burn your bridges by bad mouthing someone you might run into again, because the next time they could be in a position to seriously impact your career.

A short time later, I received a call from the Justice Department to meet with the deputy attorney general, Arnold (Arnie) Burns.

When I arrived at the main Justice building on Constitution Avenue, I thought back to the day I had stood in the attorney general's conference room so frightened I could barely speak. This time was different. Yet, when I entered Burns' conference room I was surprised at the number of people in the room. I took a seat alongside Burns on a large leather couch while a number of his assistants occupied seats around a conference table while others stood in different places throughout the room. Before I had a chance to catch my breath one question after another popped from every direction in the room. From the manner in which they were questioning me, I felt as though I was up for the most important job in the world. A few days after that rather spirited, hair-raising interview, I was called by a Justice Department secretary to return for yet another interview. This time, the interview was with the Justice Department's number three man, Brad Reynolds. Reynolds was considered one of the most conservative members of the president's administration. I called every conservative friend to prepare for my interview. They all had more or less the same response.

"He's a most intense fellow. Watch out for him. If he smells that you aren't a true conservative, you won't get the job," they warned.

Reynolds occupied what had once been the office of the legendary late FBI Director J. Edgar Hoover. It was an especially well-lighted and spacious office. When I announced myself to one of Reynolds's secretaries, I found John F. Kennedy, Jr., sitting at a small, corner desk, clipping newspaper articles. While I sat waiting for Reynolds to meet with me, one of his secretaries introduced me to the young Kennedy, who was interning during the summer. John was polite and gracious. I couldn't imagine a Kennedy working alongside Reynolds. Those two were as far apart in their political philosophies as Kennedy's father was from Richard Nixon when they ran against each other in 1960. But it struck me that there was much for them to learn from each other and I was more than pleased to see that happening between a Democrat and a Republican in the supposedly non political Department of Justice. It took a long time for Reynolds to break away from his other meeting, allowing me time to observe the late President Kennedy's son at his work. He was tall, but seemed much slimmer than I expected. He was the kind of handsome that took your breath away. His face was almost perfectly chiseled. It did strike me, though, that while his Kennedy relatives had that toothy smile and blond Irish look, he didn't much resemble them. He was, in a category all of his own.

My meeting with Brad Reynolds didn't last long. While he made small talk and asked a question or two about my knowledge of the CRS, he never once cracked a smile. His intensity unnerved me. What if I got the CRS post? Would I be able to survive such an intense and serious man? After ending our meeting, the tall, lanky Reynolds stood up from his desk and walked me out of his office. I thought about all those other interviews where I was ushered out the door before I had a chance to bat an eye and I figured the result of this meeting would be the same.

But to my surprise, a few days later, I received a call from a member of the attorney general's staff to schedule a meeting between Attorney General Ed Meese and me. I had read a lot about Ed Meese in the press. He was in the news as the counselor to President Reagan during his first term. When I interviewed with Meese in the summer of 1987, he was still making news, but that had more to do with his involvement in the Iran-Contra affair and other domestic issues. During his early days in Washington, Ed Meese had made some remarks along the lines of "we've got to be meaner than junkyard dogs." The media seized on his comment and by the time they got through writing about him, it seemed Meese himself was meaner than a junkyard dog and no one else. Yet during my interview, Meese was cordial and nothing like the press played him out to be. It probably didn't hurt that a letter on my behalf from his old California friend, Charles Wick, was sitting on his desk. Our meeting lasted longer than I had expected, yet I left his office not sure he was going to hire me.

A few days later my friend at the White House called and said my name was sitting on the president's desk waiting for his approval. During our conversation I took the chance to suggest that the president announce my nomination during Hispanic Heritage Week.

The White House announced the president's intent to nominate me in the Rose Garden during Hispanic Heritage Week in September 1987. It was <u>intent to nominate</u>, not <u>nominate,</u> because I hadn't been thoroughly vetted in time for the president to make the announcement.

During the Hispanic heritage ceremony, I stood alongside President Reagan and Vice President Bush and some other key members of the administration. As I faced the rolling television cameras and heard President Reagan announce his intent to nominate me, I thought about my days in Taft. I thought about my school friends who had influenced my life and I thought about my friends from West Pecan Street who also influenced my life, in yet another way. But mostly I thought about how proud Amagrande would have been to see me on stage with the head of *el gobierno* of the United States that she so proudly hailed yet feared.

I realized the position to which I was being nominated by President Reagan wasn't the end all of political appointments. But having reached the assistant attorney general level after starting as a GS-2, was for me the pinnacle of success.

A few weeks after the president's announcement, Arnie Burns, the deputy attorney general, called to tell me that Meese had made the decision to hire a deputy that he trusted would keep the CRS running while I awaited Senate confirmation, which in an election year could take months. I knew the deputy. He was an Hispanic male from New Mexico who had worked in Washington for several years as a career civil servant. Since I wasn't yet confirmed by the Senate, I didn't have much to say to Burns about Meese's decision other than thank him for letting me know. I didn't think I had to worry about the deputy making decisions at CRS in my absence, because I figured the Senate would confirm me in a matter of days. But I couldn't have been more wrong!

In most instances, background investigations and eventual Senate confirmation take only a matter of weeks. But in my case, there were delays in conducting my background investigation, and while that was going on, the deputy busied himself hiring new staff. Under normal circumstances hiring is not done until the head of the agency is confirmed. In the meantime, I began to get phone calls from Senate staff that the deputy and two other Hispanic males he had hired were telling anyone in Congress that would listen that I wasn't qualified for the position. This gave fodder to the Democrats, who would rather keep from voting on my nomination until after the 1988 election. Since the CRS position was a four-year appointment (although the president can ask for a person's resignation at any time), it was in the Democrats' interest to leave the post vacant so the next president, presumably the Democratic nominee Michael Dukakis, could name his own person.

Interestingly, Michael Dukakis had been my advisor while I was a graduate student at Harvard's Kennedy School, and as a result we had forged a cordial friendship. However, in many instances politics isn't about forging friendships between people of opposite political parties so they can serve in the same administration. I didn't have any illusions that Dukakis would ask me to stay if the Senate voted me in before the election and he became president, even if we were on friendly terms. For my part, I liked Michael Dukakis as a person, but there were many policy issues on which I disagreed with him. Besides, a new president should be able to choose his or her own team. That means that political appointees from the previous administration should have the common sense to leave the new administration willingly, and not have to be dragged through the exit door kicking and screaming all the way. I say this because during my government career (both as a career civil servant and as a political appointee), I witnessed more than one political appointee make a spectacle of themselves by refusing to leave office, even after being issued a pink slip (dismissal slip) by the new administration.

CRS was becoming the appointment from hell. I was called more than once by the Democratic staff of the Judiciary Committee for interviews about my qualifications. It seemed they were listening to my detractors from CRS. It was becoming clearer and clearer by the day that the deputy at CRS wanted my job and was doing all he could to derail my nomination. But I also felt that some top officials at the Justice Department didn't think I'd ever get confirmed given the timing of my nomination during a presidential election year, so they'd just as soon let my nomination die on the vine and allow their guy, the CRS deputy, to be acting CRS director until they could nominate him or get him into the Dukakis administration as a career civil servant. I figured in their own tacit way they were supporting the deputy and in essence purposely fueling the flames of his acrimonious actions and those of his two cronies against my confirmation.

Things got so out of control that Senator Pete Domenici, of New Mexico, asked me to come to his office to explain why I was making decisions about CRS before I was confirmed. It turned out that one of those Hispanic males hired by the deputy was a constituent of the senator's and had him all worked up about rumors that I had threatened to fire him and the deputy when I got confirmed.

Senator Domenici reminded me of Father Joe. He had the same serious look and sour demeanor. The meeting started on a not-too-friendly basis. I was forced to explain to the senator that his two constituents were causing unnecessary problems between him and me and assured him that I hadn't made a decision about their future. But the conversation went from bad to worse. I held my own throughout the meeting, but after I left the senator's office, Duke Short, from Senator Thurmond's office, called me.

"What the hell did you say to Domenici? He was angrier at you when you walked out than you walked in," he said laughingly.

I felt especially frustrated because I wasn't getting the kind of support from the Justice Department that was due to a presidential nominee in order to prepare for confirmation hearings. Traditionally, a nominee is prepped for Senate hearings by the department's legislative office they will be working in. In my case, no one from the department contacted me, nor did anyone return my calls until days before my confirmation hearings were to take place. My confirmation was playing out like a cheap Shakespearean drama—knives were coming my way from every direction. Yet, I managed to survive my Senate hearings led by contentious Democrats such as Senators Howard M. Metzenbaum of Ohio and Paul Simon of Illinois.

The threat of my nomination being held up by Democrats on an election year gave me nightmares. But at the end of my hearings, to the shock of all committee members including this nominee, Senator Thurmond produced a letter from the Staff Director of the Judiciary Committee on behalf of its Chairman, Joe Biden, stating that my nomination would be forwarded to the full committee for a vote on May 12, almost a year after I had met with Ed Meese and company. But the good news about the senate vote wouldn't last long. A few days after my confirmation hearings I received yet another shocker. It was Duke Short calling with the news that Senator Domenici had placed a hold on my nomination. I had expected the Democrats to make my life miserable, but I wasn't prepared to have a member of my own political party try to doom my nomination. That almost became a breaking point for me. I thought seriously of withdrawing my name, but Harley talked me out of it. He convinced me that if I did so, I would be acquiescing to my detractors and I would probably never be nominated by another president.

I placed a lot of stock in my getting confirmed, as did my husband, who gave up his military career to support my career. Harley's star was rising when he decided to step down and when after he did, *Time* Magazine September 3, 1990 issue featured him along with several other men who forfeited or stepped away from their own careers to support those of their wives.

Harley was one of the youngest Air Force generals to be promoted to three stars, but in March 1988, he retired. When we walked out of the Pentagon after his retirement ceremony, Harley's highly decorated uniform revealed his much-accomplished service to his country as a fighter pilot in Viet Nam, a B-52 pilot in the Strategic Air Command, and a war planner. Harley felt the Air Force was never going to tolerate the wife of a general officer exposed to such a high-ranking and visible political position. He also believed that I could do more good in government than he could by continuing in the Air Force. To him leading men and women in combat or leading them in preparation thereof was more important than being just another high-ranking flag officer. He had made a heroic decision and I was going to do everything in my power to see that he hadn't retired in vain, no matter what—I had to do everything to save my own political career.

I thought of making a last-minute cry for help to Senator Simpson who was by now not only a former neighbor but a friend and one I had asked to introduce me at my confirmation hearings. Traditionally, presidential nominees are introduced by senators from their designated home state, which in my case would have been Texas. It would have fallen on Senator Phil Gramm to introduce me; however, he wasn't especially one of my favorite senators and he, in turn, did me a favor by not showing interest in my nomination. That is why Senator Simpson along with the senators from Virginia, Paul Trible and John Warner where I was a resident, introduced me at my confirmation hearings.

My call to Senator Simpson about Senator Domenici's hold didn't have to be made because Duke Short, an aide to Senator Thurmond, offered to contact him in my stead. I nervously waited for the outcome and luckily, a day later, my secretary announced that Senator Domenici was on the telephone. "I've released your name," he announced sternly. Those four magical words brought the most peaceful feeling I had felt in a very long time. I held the phone pressed tightly against my ear to be sure I heard and understood every word the senator said. He went on to advise me that barring holds from any other senator, my name would be going up for a final vote before the full Senate. That day couldn't come quickly enough but sure enough it did. A few days later the Senate voted unanimously to confirm my nomination. What drama, what trauma, what nonsense, but then that's life in Washington politics-you take it or leave it!

My nomination would surely have been doomed if Senator Simpson had not called Domenici on my behalf.

A few days after I was confirmed, I met with Ed Meese to let him know that I wanted the deputy he hired out of CRS. He didn't hide his displeasure with my decision. But after I explained to him that I didn't think the man could ever be loyal to me given all that he had tried to do against my nomination, Meese seemed convinced. When it came time to get sworn in, the attorney general was busy fending off negative press reports, so the number three man in the department, Frank Keating, ended up with the task.

Ed Meese resigned a few months after I was sworn in, and Dick Thornburgh, the former governor of Pennsylvania, took his place. I didn't get to know Ed Meese. I experienced firsthand his lack of regard for my nomination, yet I think that was mostly because of his preoccupation with his own troubles. Twice he was investigated, and twice the investigations didn't find anything that warranted his case being sent to the grand jury. I felt sorry for the man. I don't disagree that he may have done some things that raised eyebrows or rubbed some the wrong way, but a person's character shouldn't be tried in the press day in and day out unless there is clear evidence that person has committed a crime. In my opinion, the press hounded Meese so much that he ended up resigning when he shouldn't have. As far as I am concerned, Ed Meese is a good and decent man and deserved better. But, here again Washington politics can be tough. It's not for the faint of heart and certainly not for the thin skinned.

When Thornburg arrived in the department, he gave me the support I needed to keep CRS on track to keep doing its mission. Thornburg reminded me of a cross between Elliot Richardson and Joseph Califano. His legal intellect and the compassion he showed for those less fortunate made me trust him and readily follow his lead. He expressed interest in having the department build better relations with minority groups, especially Hispanics, and he freely allowed me to pursue that goal. President George H.W. Bush's administration wasn't in the habit of attending many conventions representative of minority groups. But when an invitation from MALDEF, a legal defense fund to protect the rights of Hispanics in the United States, came for Thornburg to attend their conference in San Antonio, I encouraged him to go. Some staff in the White House opposed my recommendation, but Thornburg sided with me.

I understood why the White House didn't always respond to invitations from minority organizations that had liberal leanings. It was risky to put the president or a member of his cabinet in an atmosphere that could do more to yield negative publicity toward the individual and the administration than to establish goodwill with members of the organizations. But I was, and still am, of the belief that you have to begin to break ground with these groups even if they seem hostile. Thornburg had that vision and asked me and the other Hispanic high-ranking official in the department, Jimmy Gurule, to attend the MALDEF conference with him.

Jimmy and I flew with Thornburg and a couple of his staffers to San Antonio in a government airplane. When we landed, local law enforcement along with the federal security assigned to Thornburg escorted us into the city of San Antonio. The only other time I had been in a police-escorted caravan was when our senior class was escorted out of Houston during our senior trip. It was an exhilarating ride and I felt so important when our yellow school buses were breezed out of town by police motorcycles beeping their horns and flashing their lights to make way for us to head toward Taft in time to meet our school-imposed deadline. But this time, it wasn't Houston. I'd come a long way to find myself in a police escort with the attorney general of the United States, and as a member of his senior staff. It was a poignant moment for me to be back in my old stomping grounds, where years earlier I had been lucky to be assigned a desk at Kelly AFB.

When I saw the San Antonio Hemisphere tower rise up as our vehicle came cruising down Highway 281, I was overcome with emotion. My heart skipped as the bright city lights blinked along that stretch of Highway 281. As our party headed toward the riverfront, I recalled the days when I had stood on Flores Street waiting to catch the bus home from Durham College to Mary Street. I spied the many curious brown faces that stopped to stare at our party as we made our way out of the vehicles and into the hotel lobby. I stared at the largely Mexican-American crowd and waved at them. They were, after all, a part of me, and I felt very much a part of them.

The attorney general was the keynote speaker at the evening's event. Thornburg was a resounding success—the predominantly Democrat, Mexican-American audience gave him a standing ovation after his speech, and the leader of the group, whom I knew as a leading activist in the Democratic Party, gave Thornburg the traditional *abrazo* which is an expression of trust and respect.

A few months later, Thornburg resigned as attorney general to make a Senate run from his home state of Pennsylvania. Thornburg lost the election. I hadn't thought he'd lose; he had been popular as the state's governor. But that had been years earlier and the attitudes and viewpoints of voters can change at the drop of a hat. Besides, I thought those helping Thornburg with his campaign took off a bit too smug—acting as if Thornburg was a shoo in before he had even announced his candidacy.

Bill Barr, who served as Thornburg's deputy, was named by President George H.W. Bush to become the next attorney general. I worked for Bill only a few months before my term expired in April 1992. I found him to be aloof and disinterested in the activities of CRS. I'll admit the agency had its share of problems, but I felt strongly that the team of career civil servants I brought with me from other agencies helped me solve most of them. It was a different challenge every day trying to deal with staff issues, riots in Los Angeles, Haitians detained in Guantanamo, hate crimes on college campuses, etc. And to keep me even busier, I had to appear before Congress once a year to explain CRS's budget. The hearings could be contentious, especially if the Democrats decided to show their stuff.

During one of my hearings, Congresswoman Patricia Schroeder of Colorado went on and on about White House dinners and wanted to know if I was invited to them. Her high-pitched, nasal voice was more than I could stand. Never mind that the subject she raised had nothing to do with why I was testifying at the budget hearing. But sitting beside her was another congresswoman, also a Democrat. The pretty, short-haired woman was tough in her questioning, but she did it with style and grace. It's not by accident that Nancy Pelosi became Speaker of the House of Representatives. She's proven herself a true professional even if she and I don't much agree on how to fix the economic ills of America.

Barr, along with his deputy, George Terwilliger, kept their distance from me and CRS. I realized they had bigger fish to fry but I felt they could have been more supportive of me, especially since I was a member of the same administration as they were and had been very supportive of both of them. Yet, their idea of supporting me was to sic a high-level career civil servant on me, who, on top of everything else, was a Democrat. At first, the woman's calls were friendly; then she began screaming and chiding me for any little thing CRS did that bothered the main Justice power circle. I figured she was carrying the water for Barr and Terwilliger. Finally, after one of her tirades over the telephone, I called Terwilliger's secretary to meet with him. The secretary was even nastier than the high-level civil servant. I wondered if a nasty bug had bitten everyone over in main Justice, or if it was just those in Terwilliger's office. At any rate, I wasn't looking forward to meeting with Terwilliger. Our meeting started cordially, but when I confronted him about the woman's rudeness and overreaching in trying to supervise me, especially when she was a career civil servant, Terwilliger defended her by saying that as their special assistant she spoke for him and Barr.

"I have no problems with a special assistant calling me on your behalf. I have been a special assistant and I know what that job entails. But I won't put up with her nastiness and rudeness. Nor will I allow a career civil servant whom I outrank to supervise me. I have a few months left in my term; if you want me to resign beforehand, why don't you just say so." I said.

"No, you don't have to do that," he said anxiously.

The few months left in my four year term wasn't enough time to establish a long and trusting relationship with Terwilliger or Barr. They seemed to have their mind made up about me and CRS so why continue the conversation. Without either one of us saying as much as good-bye I got up and left. In the meantime, the high-level civil servant followed me out.

"I am the only friend you and CRS have in this department," she bellowed.

With friends like that who the hell needs enemies, I thought.

As timing would have it, a few weeks later, I was asked to serve on a departmental awards committee. Our function was to review the award nominations of career civil servants. To my surprise, Barr and Terwilliger's assistant was one of the nominees. Let me just say she wasn't one of the award recipients that year. I learned many valuable lessons while at Justice, but I especially learned not to burn bridges as the high-level civil servant had done with me—play nice with everyone who will allow it; you might run into them again when and where you least expect.

My four years at the CRS were filled with ups and downs, more downs than ups it seemed at the time. In government nothing is assured as safe and comfortable especially if you are a high ranking presidential appointee. But I didn't expect to be stereotyped in such a flagrant manner by colleagues and by others or ignored and dismissed by my own Republican colleagues; I got it from the top to the bottom on an almost daily basis. When we attended department meetings, I grew tired of being mistaken for the wife of one of my associate directors, who was Hispanic. Other times I was mistaken for my deputy's secretary, who was Jewish. One day, a member of a construction crew working in our suite of offices freely walked in and used my private bathroom while I was on the phone. When he walked out I heard him tell his fellow workers, "I just used the top guy's private restroom. His stupid secretary is in the room so if you want to go in there and use the bathroom, go ahead," he said. So there you have it, I waited so long to reach success in my public service career only to have some strange man take a piss in my private bathroom while I am on the telephone. Why did he do it? Because he stereotyped me. I was in such a state of shock that I didn't react until he had gone. I knew this, it would never happen again.

About the time my term appointment was due to expire, the '92 Bush/Quayle campaign called me for an interview. A woman by the name of Mimi interviewed me about a vacant position that she was eager to fill. As deputy of outreach, I would be responsible for identifying and working with special groups such as soccer moms, minority groups, and veterans groups to help re-elect President H.W. Bush. I was excited at the prospect of finally landing a job in a presidential campaign where I wasn't going to be spending all of my time standing in front of the copy machine. I had arrived! Or so I thought.

During my interview, Mimi seemed eager to have me on board as soon as possible. She explained that even though I'd be reporting to her, the "troika,"—three men that were at the head of the campaign, would want to meet me. But she explained in a lighthearted tone, "Don't worry, it will only be a pro forma interview. I've made up my mind about you." The troika Mimi spoke about consisted of Pete Teeley, Robert Moshbacher and Fred Malek, old friends of President Bush and the leaders of the 1992 GOP presidential election. I was aware of the men, but more through the media and political gossip than first-hand association.

The next day Mimi called and asked if I could visit the campaign headquarters again to meet with Fred Malek, who was the only troika member available to meet with me. When I walked into his office, Malek remained seated behind his desk. He read through my resume while resting his feet on top of the desk. He made a few comments about my work in HEW, but I didn't get a warm and fuzzy feeling from him. He avoided eye contact. I've learned over time that when a person does that, they are not comfortable with you, they are not telling the truth, or they simply don't like you. I think I scored all three that day.

The day before, Mimi told me something or other about going after upwardly mobile young people, soccer moms, and some other groups for their vote. I was preoccupied with the Rodney King riots in Los Angeles, worrying whether my staff was making inroads in preventing further rioting in the city. So much of what Mimi said had gone by me. And when she announced that the interview with the troika was only going to be pro forma, I paid even less attention. I figured I'd get up to speed on the function of the job when I reported to work, which I didn't think required a rocket scientist to do.

As the interview continued, Malek asked sarcastically, "How would you go about doing your job?"

"Well, that depends on what the campaign message is going to be, I answered.

"What do you mean?" Malek asked further.

"Well, what policy issue is the campaign going to concentrate on? Health insurance? The economy? Once the campaign theme is identified I'll be in a better position to figure what voters to target," I said.

The interview seemed to go downhill from there. That was not the answer Malek was looking for. I surmised from the look on his face that there was nothing I could say or do for that man to be impressed with me. When I left the room, he called Mimi back into his office. Mimi remained in Malek's office for a few minutes and when she came out, she had a harsh frown on her face.

"Why the hell didn't you tell him what I told you at the interview," she screamed.

With that kind of emotional outburst I knew she and I weren't going to do anything together that day or any other day. She was already yelling at me and I hadn't even had the chance to sit behind my desk. According to Mimi, Malek didn't tell her not to hire me; he only advised her to think carefully about the type of person she was going to put in such an important post. The deputy for outreach—important to what end? It seemed Malek didn't want to be the fall guy in case someone called in to complain about my not being hired, so he asked Mimi to seek opinions about me from others in the campaign.

Mary Matalin was one of two other people I met after Malek, but Mimi went into Mary's office before I did and what she might have told her doesn't take a fortune teller to figure. I felt the meeting was going to be a waste of time, since I didn't think there was a snowball's chance in hell that Mary would go against Fred Malek's doubts about my being able to be the deputy of outreach. During our meeting Mary sat in front of her computer staring at me like she was spooked, saying not much and offering very little. I was dead meat! That wasn't the first time I was turned down by the Grand Old Party, but this one hurt the most. And that hurt had to do with my inability to articulate the campaign's voter strategy back to them because I refused to believe what they wanted to hear made sense in re-electing President Bush. How can any campaign discuss what voters to target when it doesn't even know the campaign's theme? I came away feeling strongly that Malek and Mimi and others I met at the campaign weren't going to be effective in gaining voter support for Bush based on their attitudes and most importantly the way they were running the campaign. I was even more disappointed because I didn't have the opportunity to work for President H.W. Bush whom I truly liked and admired. Clearly he had one of the best resumes of anyone to ever run for President and should have been re-elected had it not been for the attitude of those running his campaign.

A few weeks after my meeting with Malek, my four-year term expired and I left CRS and public service, at least during President Clinton's eight-year term in office. I didn't hear again from the campaign. It took Malek and company a long time to fill the deputy for outreach position and when they did get around to doing it, they didn't hire an Hispanic. Malek's method of handling my candidacy for the job reminded me of Wholey's philosophy that "Not to decide is to decide!" But I became convinced that Malek and company did me a huge favor by not hiring me. I would have probably ended up being fired because I wouldn't have tolerated Malek's arrogance, nor was I going to put up with Mimi's hot temper which earned her the nickname, "screaming Mimi," from the campaign staff. And there was a problem that the candidate himself, George H.W. Bush, wasn't keeping up his end to get re-elected. I just couldn't figure out how that man let those high ratings he enjoyed early in his administration slip. His ratings just got lower as the election got closer, and then when Ross Perot threw his hat in the presidential ring, instead of trying to talk him out of running, Republican Party leaders abstained. They just never got around to running the numbers with Perot in the game. If they had, they would have realized that the Republican leadership was actually giving Bill Clinton the election.

After the defeat of President Bush, I began thinking of what to do next, which turned out to be writing this book while keeping my volunteer hand in politics. Much has passed in my life as a career civil servant and as a political/presidential appointee and there are many lessons learned that I hold dear. The words from my Kelly co-worker were prophetic indeed. I went into the government a GS-2, and came out a much higher grade than even she predicted. My career in the federal government spans four decades during which time I've been appointed to key high level positions by three different Republican presidents. I held a high level political post in President George W. Bush's administration from 2002 to 2009. Even though President Bush appointed me to a second five-year term to the Federal Service Impasses Panel, a new president can ask for any political appointees' resignation seconds after he takes office, which in my case President Obama did just that.

As I look back on my early life and my journey out of Taft, I am pleased with the way things worked out, regardless of how bad some events seemed at the time. Make no mistake, the bad was bad and I had little choice but to deal with it internally and fight every waking moment to not allow the bad to shape my outlook on this great opportunity of life that God gives to each of us.

Epilogue

I appreciate your having taken this journey with me. And I can only hope that you have enjoyed reading the story as much as I enjoyed telling it. I've always wanted to relate my journey through the early stages of my in the hope that it might be a form of inspiration to never give up or quit in the face of severe adversity.

Over the years, I've been inspired by many and knocked down by others, but in my quest to continue my journey and survive the challenges that I faced, I comforted myself with the caring and thoughtful words of others. One that comes to mind is Eleanor Roosevelt who once said, "No one can make you feel inferior without your consent." Her words have carried me through the cruel slights or degrading remarks made because of the color of my skin or my "foreign appearance," which still happens to me—can't tell you how often I'm asked, "What country are you from?" But life is about doing, not about sitting around feeling sorry for oneself.

In 2005 I returned to Taft to attend my 40th high school reunion. It turned out to be a joyous event, more so because the Mexican-Americans and the Anglos came closer together than at any other time since we first came together in elementary school. I had attended other reunions, but they were always the same; after a greeting here and there between us, the Anglos went to their side of the room, and we Mexican-Americans went to ours (the Black students have not attended any of our reunions). After many of these "separate reunions," I wasn't eager to attend the 40th one. But, I thought that after so many years, perhaps the Anglos had come to realize their past failings and understand the importance of being tolerant and of being equal. They did. In fact, I was curious to learn that one of my classmates, whose parents were two of the most prejudiced in Taft, has a son that married a Mexican-American woman. Who would have known? One Anglo after another hugged me as well as my other fellow Mexican-Americans and we hugged them back. In days earlier, the Anglos wouldn't have touched us if their lives depended on it and when some of them accidentally did touch us; they'd immediately wipe their hands on their clothing afterward.

Downtown Taft that once captivated me with the hustle and bustle of shoppers and car traffic is barely alive. In fact, if old man Taft could see what happened to his once prosperous land he'd turn over in his grave. The famous Green Hotel has been long gone along with the palatial *La Quinta*. Green Avenue is almost empty—many shops closed years ago with only a handful remaining open. It's no longer a novelty to see Mexican-Americans serve on the school board and city government; that's because they are almost 90 percent of the population. Yet, while the Mexican-Americans rule, there are tensions between certain factions within our community that could escalate and which has the potential to destroy the very town that so many of us struggled and fought to preserve.

The North Side which once belonged to the Anglos is now predominantly Mexican-American. But the South Side is now suffering from this new age of dominance. It has been left behind like a bad dream. Although, many homes on the South Side have been abandoned, some are being renovated and remodeled, making way for a new generation to improve the way it was when I was a child. Crime remains one of the major problems to be addressed. But at the same time new law enforcement efforts are taking place to make Taft a safe community. The once joyous West Pecan Street is more like a ghost town. There isn't a trace of the families that lived there when I was a child; some have died and others moved away to places like Pasadena, Corpus Christi and Houston. Many of the freshly painted houses with razor cut lawns and flowering gardens have been abandoned, replaced by dilapidated hovels that rattlesnakes and other animals now inhabit. Our home where *El doctor chiquito* (Dr. Pernod was no bigger than a minute earning him the Spanish nickname of little doctor) helped bring me into the world was destroyed years ago by hurricane winds. Amá's house, which sits at the corner of West Pecan and Peach Streets, waits for her return. But Amá passed away at the age of 95 in the winter of 2011. The house will just have to welcome some other family and together they will embrace a new life on the South Side, which I suspect will be far different from the one I experienced.

Mobile homes have been placed on empty lots because the tenants cannot afford to build a house. One particular mobile home, two streets over from West Pecan Street, caught my attention. A young man sat on a rumpled stuffed chair on the front porch drinking beer at 10 o'clock in the morning the day I arrived to conduct research for this book. One of the old timers told me that the same young man sits there day after day drinking beer. "His life is based on each day as it comes," the old man said in a matter of fact way.

It was sad, to say the least, to see the young man outside the trailer and so many other young people out of work because they either don't want to work or because they can't find a job. During my years on West Pecan Street every able bodied person worked. Amá may not have qualified for mother of year, but she taught me the importance of working not just to survive but to have a better life. Amá rose every day at 3:30 o'clock in the morning for her job as a short order cook. Never once did she complain about her work nor did she take one penny from the federal government to help support her family.

All things considered, either because of my personality or outlook, my life on West Pecan Street was actually a happy one for me. Early on, I learned to keep my eye on the ball, as Navy fighter pilots do when making night weather landings on a pitching deck. I focused on my imaginary ball as they focus on their high, low, left, right directory ball. Both of us for one reason, and that is to survive. It wasn't a comfortable feeling to have to look over my shoulder to make sure that a relative didn't follow me into my bedroom, or that a neighbor's friendly gesture wasn't a ruse to sexually molest me. Yet, I am thankful that West Pecan Street was a part of my life. I learned much from the good and bad things that happened on that street. When a person experiences discrimination at the level I did, you don't survive that by passing it off as a just another day in Taft. What I did was stay alert, fight back and I helped others do the same. The people and the happenings of West Pecan Street taught me the difficult challenges that come into our lives. They also, helped me to figure out how to overcome those challenges and to survive. The town's ways actually toughened me up and made me the person that I am today.

I've continued on the path of public service. Back in 1967 when I started working in the federal government, my salary was $3,800 a year. In 2009 my salary as a member of The Federal Services Impasses Panel in the Bush Administration was significantly higher. The place where I started my public service, Kelly AFB, was shut down a few years ago to save money. Yet, the federal government continues to grow by leaps and bounds creating more debt to the already "busting at the seams," federal budget. Millions of people across America depend on the federal government for their every day existence; if it's not their social security checks, it's their disability checks, or their welfare checks. It's been the Republican Party's philosophy that less government is better, but when I think about that theme, I realize it's far more complicated than that small answer. I don't want less government to mean less help for those who truly need it. I like a federal government that is lean but one that is able to function effectively.

I've had many different types of jobs and at different levels in the federal government. But in all those years, I have never seen the federal government bungle so gravely as it did during Hurricane Katrina and the lack of help for the wounded soldiers and veterans of the Iraqi conflict, so profoundly represented by ineptness at Walter Reed Military Hospital. Admittedly, the Obama Administration inherited this one and the question is, as they increase the size of our federal government will it function effectively and efficiently or continue to be bloated and bureaucratically callous.

While President George W. Bush sought to reassure our safety after 9/11 he wasn't in the long run, able to keep the public's trust in his leadership. His ratings were the lowest of any President in modern times when he left office. Interestingly, we seemed to forget his compassion toward African nations by spending millions to cure its population of AIDS. We seemed to forget that he more than any other President, appointed more women and minorities to high ranking positions traditionally held by Caucasian males. And while one may disagree with the action Bush's Administration took after 9/11 regarding terrorist suspects, the United States wasn't attacked anytime during the remainder of his years in office. There are things President Bush could have done different to win the hearts of Americans but rather than second guessing my boss, I leave it for history to judge his presidency.

As for the Republican Party, I will continue to stay with the party long after the balloons and streamers are gone. Currently the life of the party is alive but struggling to attract minorities and independents. To this day the Republican Party has not engaged in serious bridge building with minority segments of the population. That effort must begin if the party is to gain the political power necessary to implement their beliefs. While it is important to recognize that the base of the party is composed of people with conservative views, they alone cannot elect the next president of the United States. The changing diversity of this country is itself affecting the way America does business today and in the future. We cannot ignore this fact. Our country's well-being is at stake and being tolerant and inclusive are just two steps to keeping the party of Lincoln alive!

As for Hispanic Americans, the intolerance directed at my Spanish accent and color of my skin made me, for a period of time, ashamed of my ancestry. It took many personal experiences for me to admit who I was and appreciate where my ancestors came from in order for me to emerge proud of my heritage while never letting go of my Americanism. Hispanics/Latinos are the largest minority group, who, if we act as true Americans, could well dominate America's scene in every sense of the word.

Immigrants from Spanish speaking countries shouldn't be fearful of being mistreated and immediately deported. Yet, as immigrants become permanent residents and eventually citizens, they must remember that this country not only has laws to follow but traditions that keep this country strong and free. As long as their behavior stays within the rubric of the United States Constitution, no one will deny them their right to be a part of this great country of ours.

I started thinking about writing this book the day I left the CRS back in 1992. At first I didn't think there was much to say that might capture the interest of "reading" America and other countries. But within a few months after I began to write, and the more I wrote, the more I discovered that the story about my hometown and about my public service career, while not unique, did seem to create interest. It was like an octopus; it had several tentacles and in my case they reached across many segments of our society. My story, has many messages, but none is as important as the idea that to be even modestly successful, a person must meet life head on no matter how difficult or hopeless it seems. De Tocqueville said about life, "Remember that life is neither pain nor pleasure; it is serious business, to be entered upon with courage and in a spirit of self-sacrifice." We make our own lives as we wish although some of us have less to say about it than others. But in the end, we cannot let adversity stop us from fighting to live in a positive, uplifting way. We cannot afford to allow ourselves to give up on our dreams and our hopes when someone rejects or mistreats us. Life is what we make it. We get one shot at it and it is terribly wrong for us to abandon our dreams and our hopes in favor of the negatives from others.

In the final analysis I am thankful for the opportunities this great country has given me and will always do my part to preserve its traditions and support and defend America's freedom.

CPSIA information can be obtained
at www.ICGtesting.com
Printed in the USA
FFHW021759160719
53670314-59348FF